Essayism

THOMAS HARRISON

Essayism

Conrad
Musil &
Pirandello

The Johns Hopkins University Press   Baltimore & London

The Johns Hopkins University Press
701 West 40th Street
Baltimore, Maryland 21211-2190
The Johns Hopkins Press Ltd., London

∞ The paper used in this book meets the minimum requirements of
American National Standard for Information Sciences—Permanence
of Paper for Printed Library Materials, ANSI Z39.48-1984.

Library of Congress Cataloging-in-Publication Data

Harrison, Thomas J., 1955–
    Essayism : Conrad, Musil, and Pirandello / Thomas Harrison.
        p.   cm.
    Includes bibliographical references and index.
    ISBN 0-8018-4283-2 (alk. paper)
    1. Essay.   2. Conrad, Joseph, 1857–1924—Criticism and
interpretation.   3. Musil, Robert, 1880–1942—Criticism and
interpretation.   4. Pirandello, Luigi, 1867–1936—Criticism
and interpretation.   I. Title.
PN4500.H28   1992
    809.2—dc20   91-26510

Contents

Preface

In this book I have attempted to perform two tasks, one practical, the other ideal: a critical analysis of the literary-philosophical work of three writers of the twentieth century and the construction of a tentative groundwork for a theory of living. *Essayism* ultimately seeks to describe more than these writers' aesthetic and ontological positions—namely, a conscious bearing toward experience which those ontologies and aesthetics imply. This bearing is concerned above all with the logic of action, with reasons for living in one way or another, with the possibility of *enhancing* those reasons.

Moving from ontology to ethics by way of aesthetics, the six main chapters of this book are designed to be readable independently as well as in sequence. The relations between Conrad, Musil, and Pirandello emerge by analogy rather than direct comparison, as do the relations between the intentions of this book and those friends in dialogue with whom those same intentions have taken shape, including Allen Mandelbaum, Lillian Feder, Burton Pike, Luigi Ballerini, Thomas Sheehan, Gianni Vattimo, Elfie Karner Raymond, Giorgio Agamben, Mary Ann Caws, and, most recently, Nanette Barrutia. As always, my most attentive reader has been my brother Robert Harrison. I would also like to thank all those with whom I had the fortune to study at the Graduate Center of the City University of New York, Sarah Lawrence College, and the Overseas School of Rome, as well as my colleagues at the University of Utah, Louisiana State University, and the University of Pennsylvania.

Essayism

Introduction

If Ulrich, the protagonist of Robert Musil's novel *Der Mann ohne Eigenschaften* (1930–43; *The Man without Qualities*), had been asked what aim he had in mind with his ceaseless investigations of natural science and mathematico-logical problems, "he would have answered that there was only one question really worth thinking about, and that was the question of right living."[1] While neither Ulrich nor his author provides a definitive answer to the question, it remains the overriding concern of their investigations, existential in the one case, literary in the other. *The Man without Qualities,* Musil remarks to an interviewer in 1926, "aims to provide materials for . . . a new morality."[2] The same could be said of many works of Joseph Conrad and Luigi Pirandello, with more justification, in fact, than of almost any fiction in Musil's time. Not that André Gide, D. H. Lawrence, and others were unconcerned with morality. Nor even that Pirandello and Conrad would necessarily have agreed with Musil's characterization of the fictional enterprise. In fact, both of them have usually been read in terms quite different from those that Musil proposes, namely, as analysts of grim and rather hopeless conditions in which morality itself remains all but impossible to fix. And yet it is their diagnosis of these very conditions, in which "prior values are deposed and new values not yet posited," that Conrad and Pirandello share with Musil.[3] Despite their differences, *Lord Jim* (1900) and *Il fu Mattia Pascal* (1904; *The Late Mattia Pascal*), *Heart of Darkness* (1902) and *Uno, nessuno e centomila* (1926; *One, None, and a Hundred Thousand*) find their central concern in that search for a perfect accord between thinking, feeling, and acting in which right living can be said to consist.

If Conrad, Musil, and Pirandello do not quite succeed in discovering a solution to such an accord (perhaps also because in a postpositivist era it can no longer be reached), they nonetheless formulate a solution for living *in the absence* of this accord. This solution to the absence of a solution is the topic of the present study. Taking my cue from Musil, I call it essayism.

"It was," Musil writes of his protagonist,

approximately in the way that an essay, in the sequence of its paragraphs, takes a thing from many sides without comprehending it wholly—for a thing wholly comprehended instantly loses its bulk and melts down into a concept—that he believed he could best survey and handle the world and his life. (*GW* 1 : 250; *MWQ* 1 : 297 [62])

Ordinarily we think of an essay as an informal analysis of a topic in writing. Implicitly, the topic is greater in scope than its short and self-limiting treatment. Moreover, the essay usually presents its point of view as only that—one stance among possible others, advancing no universal or exhaustive claims. The object is one thing, its theoretical treatment another. In fact, it is probably this very difference between a thing in itself and a "thing as viewed" that Ulrich's essay strives to remunerate, offering not a single perspective on an issue but a number of them. Like Montaigne, who compiled a variety of interpretive tools, articles of knowledge, and conflicting opinions into the body of his *Essais*, Ulrich aims to take a thing from as many sides as possible. The essay allows for these flexible perspectives, freely pursuing whatever diction, rhetoric, or supporting evidence its argument appears to require (whether factual or fictitious, exemplifying or analogical, ironic or earnest). In fact, to judge by its master practitioners from Montaigne through Roland Barthes, we might say that the essay possesses no definitive mode of procedure. What, if anything, the essayistic styles of the last four hundred years have shared is precisely a rejection of fixed, established, and authoritative literary method. And this may be why theoreticians of the essay have agreed that this open, self-seeking form—more digressive than systematic, more interrogative than declarative, more descriptive than explanatory—tends to be antigeneric.[4] The essay rejects a fixed perspective and lens.

And yet an essay is not only a literary genre. One of its strongest connotations is preserved in the variant *assay,* as in assaying one's strength or assaying an ore to determine its metal. An essay sizes up a situation, examining and testing its characteristics. It is, in fact, this activity of "weighing" or "measuring" that was originally denoted by the Renaissance figure of the assayer (or the Italian *saggiatore*). Related to this meaning of weighing is the one offered by the French *essayer:* to attempt, to try, to put to trial or to the test. An essay is an act undertaken in deliberate uncertainty, an experimental endeavor and project. Admitting that the achievement of its goal is far from likely, the essay suggests a "tragic and incessant combat for a satisfaction that is almost beyond reach."[5] It is the form of an absolute striving, accompanied by a recognition of its merely relative means. And this is why Georg Lukács speaks of the genre as a poetics of longing. The essayist can never be more than a precursor, he writes, "and it seems highly questionable whether, left entirely to himself [or judged solely on the merits of his proleptic act] he could lay claim to any value or validity."[6]

To these three meanings of intellectual method, phenomenal test, and interminable project, Musil adds another:

The translation of the word "essay" as "attempt," which is the generally accepted one, only approximately gives the most important allusion to the literary model. For an essay is not the provisional or

incidental expression of a conviction that might on a more favour-
able occasion be elevated to the status of truth (of that kind are only
the articles and treatises, referred to as "chips from their work-
shop," with which learned persons favour us); an essay is the
unique and unalterable form that a person's inner life assumes in a
decisive thought. (*GW* 1 : 253; *MWQ* 1 : 301 [62])

The key word in this passage is *decisive,* which in the German
original suggests an action distended over a present in progress. As a participle, *Entscheidend* means literally "deciding,"
engaged in the process of deciding. Musil's passage draws a
contrast between a "conviction" (*Überzeugung*), which could
be promoted to the status of a truth, and a "decisive thought."
Where does the difference lie? A conviction is the form of a
decision already taken; an essay is rather the shape of the
"inner life" in the act of *reaching* a decision. As explained by
various analyses in *The Man without Qualities,* this inner life is
not constituted by subjective certainty but, rather, by an encounter between subject and object, or between an intuitive
possibility and the constraints of the language in which it is
expressed. Not only does the essay give shape to a process
preceding conviction, and perhaps deferring it forever. More
important, it records the hermeneutical situation in which
such decisions arise. For this reason the essay ultimately requires novelistic form, which can portray the living conditions in which thought is tangled.

Before addressing this development of the essay into a
novel, we should recognize a philosophical issue that underlies the aesthetic decision. Why was it that Ulrich considered
the essay the most appropriate way to approach thought and
experience? Because that is how he perceived the world itself
to operate. Essayism, a paradigm for both thinking and acting, is a response to an ontology in which experience appears
already to transpire in the manner of an essay. Generally diffused in the time in which Musil, Conrad, and Pirandello
were writing, this ontology of the essay supplies the ground
for an ethical and cognitive methodology.

The ontology of the essay was already in the making by the time the German idealists conceived of being as realization, or temporal and spatial self-actualization. For Schelling, Hegel, and others, every existent thing was at once an effected and an effecting thing. Being, a process of self-realization, amounted to the history of the forms in which it produced itself. Hegel viewed this history as unfolding the principles of World Spirit in a logical narrative. While his model of rational historical progression found decisive elaboration in political theory, it was still another scheme that proved to inspire artists and metaphysicians at the end of the nineteenth and the beginning of the twentieth centuries: Schopenhauer's more turbid vision of the principle of realization as blind, egoistic, and pointless desire. Hegel's epic narrative turned into a tragic drama of insatiable craving. For Schopenhauer the motor drive of history was not spirit at all but will, and will meant ceaseless striving, holding its subjects captive to an insuperably essayistic condition, tempted and attempting in endless process. Whatever the ultimate goal of this drive, it could not be historically realized. In this incessant and futile striving, the philosophy of realization gave way to a philosophy of *non*realization. Reality, in the metaphysical sense of a unitary and stable condition of being, remained unachievable. As long as the craving of willful activity entailed ceaseless overcoming of all definitive accomplishment, it militated against its own will to realization. And this condition, for Schopenhauer, constituted life's objection to itself.

A partial solution to the philosophy of nonrealization came with Nietzsche, offering also a turn to a properly ethical essayism. While agreeing with Schopenhauer's basic perception of experience as self-trying, Nietzsche reversed the judgment his predecessor had placed on it. Such experience offered a fruitful rather than futile condition. The aim of willful strife was not the accomplishment of being but the adventures of becoming, not survival but power. And power meant the enhancement of present conditions. Will was not eternally frustrated but boundlessly productive, not incapable of achieving its goal but on the way, not empty but pregnant with future. A universe of absurd and irrational conflict now appeared as a vast laboratory of experimentation.

How can we account for Nietzsche's and Schopenhauer's different evaluations of the same condition? Schopenhauer judged historical becoming by the yardstick of an eternal and unchanging standard. Clearly, if the object of historical effectuation is the permanence of Platonic being, then no right living can be achieved except by a retreat from action. For Nietzsche, on the other hand, unity, permanence, and rational purpose were not "reality principles" at all; they were ideality ones, in contrast to which historical occurrence could only be found wanting. What, then, does one do with the question of ethical justification, which seems always to rely on the counter of some ideal? Now the justification for historical occurrence no longer consists in how well it approximates an ideal but in how well it produces one. Actual experience becomes the exclusive ground for every ideal (including unity, permanence, and those others it fails to fulfill). In the context of becoming, the value of history can now be measured by the amount of idealism it succeeds in fostering, or by the resolution with which it shapes and reshapes the conditions for existential possibility. Theoretically speaking, "what should be" already depends on a prior sense of "what could be." The actual is not justified by its agreement with a predetermined potential but by its self-disagreement, or the degree to which it continues to reassess such potential.

We can already spy an emerging ethos in this Nietzschean revision of the philosophy of realization. To live in accordance with the transformative nature of history is to act as a furtherer of concrete potential, to operate in the manner of an experiment. Nietzsche calls a person who lives in this way a *Versucher*. The word *Versucher*, literally "tempter" or "attempter," comes from *Versuch:* an attempt, a trial, a test, an act of research or experimentation. A *Versucher* is a searcher and researcher, tempted by the goal of determining the "whither" and "for what" of humanity.[7] An analogous figure is Musil's "possibilitarian" (*Möglichkeitsmensch*), who tends not to act out a given situation's explicit scenarios but rather to seek its inherent possibilities, the "valences" of its constitutive elements, the solutions these elements might be found to yield. A possibilitarian is less interested in realized than virtual forms of a historical network, its as yet undetermined potential. With Ulrich in *The Man without Qualities*, as earlier with the protagonist of *Die Verwirrungen des Zöglings Törless* (1906; *The Perplexities of the Pupil Törless*), we have an image of "an unfinished, trying and tried person" (*die Darstellung eines Unfertigen, Versuchenden and Versuchten*).[8] Another type of possibilitarian can be found in the protagonist of Conrad's *Lord Jim*, who is striving to determine "what could be" his own ideal. In fact, the greater part of Conrad's characters are driven by precisely this compulsion to attempt achievements beyond their reach, whether in the form of heroic action or, in the case of his narrators, of theoretical understanding. In Pirandello possibilitarianism assumes the features of a recurring and insuperable destiny, namely, the struggle of characters to realize their innermost potential beyond the quotidian forms in which their lives are trapped. In all three novelists character is portrayed as an open existential project within a world of relatively closed actuality.

The idealism at work in these characters and narratives is not of the abstract sort that Lukács criticizes in the modern novel, defending subjective ideals against the objectively necessary conditions of actual history. As all three novelists make equally clear, the very question of possibility is first raised by these characters' concrete situations. "It is actuality [*Wirklichkeit*] that awakens possibilities," Musil writes, "and nothing could be more wrong than to deny this" (*GW* 1 : 17; *MWQ* 1 : 13 [4]). It is actuality itself that first puts these characters to the test, compelling them to strive to transmute their habitual modes of understanding and action. Human destiny consists in a struggle between an imaginative agent and a virtually intractable historical condition. To live is not only to essay the possible; it is already, and primarily, to *be* essayed. Wrenched away from apparently stable present conditions toward amorphous realms of future achievement, the characters of Conrad, Musil, and Pirandello testify to the trials of actively developing experience. In the language of traditional philosophy they are subjected to a contest between freedom and determinism, subject and object, value and fact, feeling and thought, which can never be fully resolved. None of these novelists privilege the ideal or romantic element in the conflict. If they have any vision of self-realization, it lies not in their characters' unflagging commitment to an ideal but rather in these characters' acquiescence in an insuperable struggle. Pirandello makes the most of the fateful facticity in which these characters are caught, Conrad of the ensuing battle, and Musil of its ultimate goal, namely, that accord between thinking, feeling, and acting mentioned earlier.

To understand this essayistic, or trying, destiny more clearly, let us return for a moment to the paradoxical transformation of the philosophy of realization into a philosophy of nonrealization. As it appears in Nietzsche, an ontology of ceaseless becoming is also an ontology of utopia. Utopia, however, is a self-ironizing notion. It labels both an aspiration toward an unrealized condition and also the unrealizability of the same object of aspiration. With Nietzsche reality becomes utopian in both of these senses, incessantly striving to transform and overcome its "real" condition. Every apparent realization of experience is already predicated on a derealization, or destruction, of some prior state of affairs. Each operative form must first be derealized for a different realization to come to pass (itself derealized in turn in a perpetual and restless cycle). Following Pirandello, the existential correlative of such a process could be described as follows:

People have a superfluity within them which continuously and uselessly torments them, never letting them be satisfied with any condition, and always leaving them uncertain of their destiny. An inexplicable superfluity, which, in order to vent itself, creates a fictitious world in nature . . . and yet one with which they themselves neither know how to, nor can, be content [*non sanno e non possono mai contentarsi*], so that without pause they restlessly and longingly alter and realter it.[9]

The issue is not, in Lukácsian terms, the theoretical "mistake" entailed by the construction of this superfluous and formalized world; it is, rather, the ineluctability of the mistake, for it is one and the same superfluity that causes both the marking and the overcoming of historical boundaries, both the doing and the undoing of experience. Superfluity is of the very nature of existence.

When this self-critical superfluity of experience becomes conscious, two consequences follow. First, a person feels compelled to question all empirical configurations and reality principles (such values or ideologies as an inherited political system, monogamy, a work ethic, and so on). Resulting from an interaction between intention and accident, every reality principle offers only one possible theorization of the world, a formal sedimentation of circumstances that might just as well have turned out differently. When this consciousness arises, the mind develops a hermeneutics of suspicion toward not only all formalizations of experience but also the very principles of formalization (the codes of morality, the habits of lifestyle, the rules of reason). What then becomes suspect are theorizations of the world themselves. The perception of the essayistic evolution of the world leads to a search for alternatives to these uncogent world theses. The first consequence represents the critical dimension of essayistic practice (the active assayal of historical conditions or theorizations, whether on the part of a character or a lucid, philosophical narrator) and the second its utopian one (the quest for alternative and more flexible forms of organization). Inseparable though they be, the first type of essayism is the subject of Part 1 of this book, the second is the subject of Part 2.

In its critical moment essayism finds its context amid a host of investigations into the formal constitution of experience contemporaneous with the work of Conrad, Musil, and Pirandello: Mach's research into the physical indeterminacy underlying and belying all laws of mechanics, Husserl's reduction of phenomena to intentional acts of consciousness, the rigidification of vital flux in *Lebensphilosophie*, Wittgenstein's understanding of language as a form of life, and the principle of "psychophysical isomorphism" in Gestalt psychology (or the identity of mental and empirical structure). Presenting life as a struggle within and against the prefigurations of experience passed down by history, Conrad, Musil, and Pirandello become outspoken critics of precisely "those possibilities of existence which 'circulate' in the 'average' public way of interpreting Dasein today."[10] Heidegger's "average" possibilities of existence are analogous to the paradigms in the normative grammar of Husserl's "natural attitude"—that spontaneously realistic theory of the world by which we operate, endowed with its own logic of thought and feeling. In this initial and critical moment Conrad, Musil, and Pirandello are bent on dismantling the theses of this natural attitude. Here their affiliations reach beyond phenomenological research to that decidedly militant stance toward everyday conceptualizations of the real which is so visible in futurism, surrealism, and other aspects of the avant-garde at the beginning of the century. Here, at the midpoint between the "will to a system" of the early nineteenth century and the "philosophy of difference" of the late twentieth, art attempts to rally to the defense of everything excluded or repressed by systematic interpretations of experience (particularity, contingency, and whim; multiplicity, simultaneity, and contradiction; epiphanic, unconscious, and associative patterns of meaning formation). Art suddenly sees its task as the very opposite of that Hegelian-Lukácsian one of unifying disparate life forces into a synthetic and normative image. Rather, it devotes itself to the very destructuration of norms.

Essayistically practiced, this destructuration is more than iconoclasm, more than an attack on norms from some separate and secure vantage, and more than a leap of imaginative faith. It is instead an *immanent* critique of those very same norms and structures, a measuring of their logic by the same criteria of unity and coherence they already espouse. Conrad, Musil, and Pirandello perform this critique not only by means of dramatic irony but also by theoretical analysis, or that obsessive speculation that pervades their work.

An example of this destructuring operation lies in the *umorismo* effected by Pirandello's art. Humor, Pirandello explains, is a mischievous procedure, exposing the duplicity and contradiction underlying every synthetic and harmonious rule. Deliberately "decomposed, interrupted, [and] interspersed with continuous digressions," humorous texts vigorously oppose the construction of systems.[11] They divulge their meanings by contrast rather than syllogistic analogy. While an epic or dramatic artist tends to combine "disparate and opposing elements" into the unity of a character, a humorist does the opposite: "he *decomposes* that character into his elements." The humorist "knows no heroes"; "he knows what legend is and how it is formed, what history is and how it is formed: all of them compositions, more or less ideal, and perhaps most ideal when they pretend most to be real: compositions which he amuses himself to decompose." The humorist *begins* with current, coherent visions and takes them apart. "He sees the world, if not exactly nude, in shirt-sleeves, so to speak; the king in shirt-sleeves," divested, along with his soldiers, "of those hateful informs of theirs" (*U* 166; *H* 143).

Conrad also finds his central topics in such heroes, idealists, and self-righteous characters (Jim, Kurtz, and Marlow). Revealing "the convention that lurks in all truth and . . . the essential sincerity of falsehood," his narratives tend to hinge on an uncanny dramatic rupture upsetting the stable and cogent orders on which these lives are based.[12] Seemingly self-evident occurrences begin to elicit the unraveling operations of an analytic consciousness, a thinking and rethinking of an internal motivation that fails to be addressed by a reigning logic. As in Pirandello, the result is a profound distrust of the "objective" and "epic" organization of experience in a narrative mind, endowed with its own strategies of explanation and adages of wisdom.

As for Musil, both *The Man without Qualities* and the earlier *Törless* recount nothing less than the story of a consciousness questioning the most widespread conventions of interpretation, offsetting them with satirical and discursive critique, on the one hand, and instances of dramatic anomaly, on the other (the torturing of a student in the earlier novel, for example, and Moosbrugger's vicious murder in the later).

It is not long before this hermeneutics of suspicion turns inward, toward the objectifications defining the active subject. This subject, or person, comes to appear as a conglomeration of largely unchosen qualities, lacking inherent coherence. Are these qualities really one's own or just the outcome of some mechanical coordination? To try to get at the essence of this subject is like attempting to determine the contents of an iron box by tapping it with a hammer (*LJ* 35). The effects of this type of suspicion on a living character, dramatically figured in the fictions of Conrad and Pirandello, are most explicitly described in *The Man without Qualities*. With the intellectual living of Ulrich there arises a "pathos of distance" toward the historical present. Experience loses all immediate purpose, producing the sensation of a "missing soul" in each of one's acts. One's habitual means of conduct are suspended. Normal occurrences elicit abnormal responses. As the configuration of experience becomes questionable, so does the logic of one's innermost convictions and feelings. To see how these suspicions can lead to an ethical program, we must again turn to Nietzsche. We others "who thirst after reason," he writes, "are determined to scrutinize our experiences as severely as a scientific experiment—hour after hour, day after day. We ourselves wish to be our experiments and guinea pigs."[13] It is as precisely such living experiments that Conrad, Musil, and Pirandello portray their seafarers, their men without qualities, and their characters in search of an author.

Experimentation inaugurates the second, utopian moment of essayism. This is the immanent historical idealism, or possibilitarianism, which is prepared for by essayistic destructuration. The issue is now how to restructure the means of theoretical and existential operation. Needless to say, it cannot be done by replacing one reality principle with another (whether the "dynamo of the future" or the "language of the unconscious"). All new ideologies will only petrify the possible once more. Aiming not to actualize the possible but to possibilize the actual, essayism is faced with the task of relinquishing the very impulse to impose an ideal on the real. Only then can a realistic restructuration of experience take place. In fact, it will not be a restructuration at all but, rather, a discovery of the possibilities inherent in the structures already available. What is called for by the utopian phase of essayism are essentially more flexible, more imaginative, more functional, and, yes, more pragmatic organizations of experience than the ones ordinarily passed on from generation to generation.

At this moment experience begins to reveal its own richness and multiplicity. The monological lyric of unappeasable longing, or Lukács's abstract idealism, gives way to a drama peopled by countless players, all vying for justice. In the place of a single, and now fallen, reality principle there arise unlimited numbers, each open at any point to revision. Inasmuch as one cannot reject the possibility that it *"may include infinite interpretations,"* the world becomes infinite all over again.[14] And only now can conscious experience start to realize itself in the manner of an essay, its progressions interrupted by digressions, its identifications by differentiations, its unities, equilibria, and relations inviting additional review. In Ulrich's decision to survey and handle his life in the manner of an essay lies an intuition that the indeterminacy of every object of vision can actually be recompensated by multiplicitous interpretation. A pluralistic perspective does more justice to phenomena than any single point of view, regardless of how encompassing this view presumes to be. Resisting the temptation of the very logic underlying every reality principle—namely, that correspondence between "image" and "significance" on which meaning appears to rely—an essay gathers into a single composition "many things that, according to common opinion, are mutually incompatible." If, as Musil continues, the essay resists "objective synthesis," it does not do so out of indecisiveness, or "indeterminacy" (*Unbestimmtheit*), but rather out of "overdetermination" (*Überbestimmtheit*).[15] The essay is a utopian attempt to develop the possibilities of form to a virtually infinite degree. In this second, constructive moment, the emphasis in the essay's "hermeneutics of suspicion" shifts from the word *suspicion* to *hermeneutics*, for this overdetermination of symbolic significance can be produced only by researching the formative possibilities already inherent in language. Essayistic evolutions of experience are not articulated by entirely new forms but only by new relations among the forms that are given. Instead of choosing a definitive image for an ideal and unitary significance, like classical art, the essay proceeds by investigating the contexts from which such an image or significance was first abstracted. Instead of a theory of a phenomenon, it offers a "theorization," an exegesis of the linguistic horizon from which that phenomenon receives its meanings. No doubt, this exegesis is what Lukács had in mind when he claimed that the essay never offered a pure and original artistic form. The subject of an essay is, rather, something that "has already been given form, or at least something that has already been there at some time in the past; hence it is part of the nature of the essay that it does not create new things from an empty nothingness but only orders those which were once alive."[16] Instead of advancing new forms, the essay rethinks the ones we have.

If Lukács distinguishes the essay from artistic creation (occurring *ex nihilo?*), Theodor Adorno elucidates its difference from science and philosophy. While science and philosophy try to abstract their concepts from the idioms in which they are concretized, the essay begins its construction precisely by investigating such contextualized concepts and prestructured meanings; "it wants to help language, in its relation to concepts, to grasp these concepts reflectively."[17] To grasp these concepts reflectively means to test their valences, to submit them to other frames of reference, to discover their potentials for combination—in short, to rethink their hermeneutical capacities.

Lacking the naiveté to propose a "natural" or "immediate" embodiment of a significance in an image, the essay reaches out "for what lies behind the image," attempting to shape experiences that "cannot be expressed by any gesture." Which experiences does Lukács have in mind? "From all that has been said you will know what experiences I mean. . . . I mean intellectuality, conceptuality as sensed experience, as immediate reality, as spontaneous principle of existence; the worldview in its undisguised purity as an event of the soul, as the motive force of life." Conceptuality as a "spontaneous principle" of human existence means the very mediation of reality by form. If the object of the essay cannot be represented by classical art, it is because this object— namely, intellectuality, the interpretive process at large, the nature of conceptuality, the implicit structure of any worldview—underlies the very possibility of formal expression. If, as Lukács claims, poetry makes destiny appear as form, then the essay makes form appear as destiny, as the very "destiny-creating principle." Seeking "the soul-content indirectly and unconsciously concealed within forms themselves," the essayist reveals the destiny inherent in forms.[18]

Of course, this does not mean that the essayist is not an artist. Conrad, Musil, and Pirandello are as capable of giving form to destiny as anyone else; they simply do so in a less exclusively iconic, less historically mimetic way than most writers of fiction, taking as the "primary substance" of their representations not empirical occurrences so much as their formative patterns. And this substance requires a frequent disunity of event and significance in their narratives, as though, in the uneasy and shifting relation between these two elements that classical artists are wont to equate, the essayists sought alternatives to equational logic. The humorist is admittedly a critic, says Pirandello, but always "an imaginative critic" (*U* 141; *H* 119). Musil stresses the same thing. The superprecision, or overdetermination, pursued by the essay is not a pedantic but an "imaginative" precision (*phantastische Genauigkeit*) (*GW* 1:247; *MWQ* 1:294 [62]), a creative discovery of new rational relations. Only through imaginative precision can "constantly new solutions, connections, constellations, [and] variables" be found in the world.[19] Tying all this back to Lukács, we might conclude that, where "form appears, even in its abstract conceptuality, as something surely and concretely real," "the end-point of poetry can become a starting-point and a beginning."[20]

With the constructivity of this project in mind, let us return to Pirandello's aesthetic of humor. Though humor is predicated on a perception of contradiction, it necessitates a step beyond that perception. It is not synonymous with a poetics of rupture or a critique of surface incongruence. To call up the famous example, we see an elderly matron dressed like a teenager, and we laugh. We have perceived an incongruity. The matron has contaminated one norm with another. She has disrupted the expectations of our perceptual logic, the tenets of our familiar world thesis. At this point of laughter we still occupy the domain of critical, dismantling essayism; in fact, merely the domain of the comical, not that of the humorous. For the situation to become humorous we must perceive *a logic* in the apparent contradiction. It may be that the woman is trying to please her husband, whose love she feels slipping away toward younger women. Now muted by sadness, our laughter gives way to a *feeling* of the contradiction we previously perceived. But what has really caused this feeling? A reflection has followed the initial perception. The recognition of an inconsistency has evoked an activity of interpretation (quite different from that recurrence to a norm informing comic perception). Restlessly suspended among contradictory images, the spirit becomes "obstinately determined to find or establish the most astonishing relationships between these images" (*U* 141; *H* 119). The condition of perplexity inspired by the perception of contradiction stimulates an effort to detect ties among contrasting forms. In the very experience of a disjunction between image and meaning lie the seeds for a no longer adequational logic, an occasion for connecting variables that preserves both their difference and their uneasy union. In the absence of formally coherent intuitions, interpretation explores the still unexamined relations of things.

How does this connectivity inform Conrad's, Musil's, and

Pirandello's novels and plays? In fact, if the three authors are essayists, as I claim, why do they write fiction at all? Even here connections undermine generic differences. Conrad's, Musil's, and Pirandello's fictions engage in essayistic procedure on a larger scale than a literary essay allows. Governed not merely by that conflict between an objective narrative event and its conceptual interpretation which readers like Benedetto Croce and Lukács identify as artistic failure but also by an active pursuit of discursive multiplicity, the hermeneutical investigations of Conrad, Musil, and Pirandello aim to recombine the forms they investigate into a higher type of unity than that permitted by the traditional genres of the essay or the realistic novel. In what, asks Croce, does Pirandello's work consist? In "some artistic bursts, suffocated or disfigured by a fitful and inconclusive philosophizing. Neither clear-cut art nor philosophy, then: impeded by an orginary vice from unfolding according to one or the other."[21] The same could be said of the other two writers. But this tension between a form and its conceptualization marks the very beginning of the essayistic endeavor. It is in the service of essayistic production that the fictions of these three authors move from an image to its conceptual context and then back again, measuring historical occurrence by understanding and understanding by occurrence; relativizing the object through subjective vision; establishing discursive analogies; showing the real story to be the story of *interpreting* the story. The governing principle in each case is hermeneutical irresolution, intuited to be the only means toward the achievement of a "final" and "complete" interpretation.

Thus, it is the very logic of essayistic form which requires the more expansive genre of what Hermann Broch called the "gnosiological novel," one focusing its investigations on the very possibilities of knowledge.[22] The essayism of Conrad, Musil, and Pirandello requires the forms of historical life, delineated in fiction, as the ultimate subject on which to exercise its theorizations. What is decisive in their work is not action in itself but the possibilities it harbors. In themselves the dramatic events of these fictions seem "insignificant." *Lord*

Jim revolves entirely around an incident "as completely devoid of importance as the flooding of an antheap"; and yet this incident also suggests a truth "momentous enough to affect mankind's conception of itself" (*LJ* 57). It calls for the divulgatory efforts of conceptual, analogical, and symbolic thinking. And, if the historical occurrences of these fictions find the fluidity of their significance in theory, this theory, in turn, needs the context of an intractable historical fate. While the essayistic project is subjective and open, its topic is objective and closed. The arena of the essay lies between these two, between the definite and the indefinite, the fact and the idea, in an intellectually destined clash.

Part One

The As Yet
Undetermined
Relations of
Things

1

Joseph Conrad

The Perception
of Unreality

"It's extraordinary," reflects Marlow, as he narrates *Lord Jim*,

how we go through life with eyes half shut, with dull ears, with dormant thoughts. Perhaps it's just as well; and it may be that it is this very dullness that makes life to the incalculable majority so supportable and so welcome. Nevertheless, there can be but few of us who had never known one of these rare moments of awakening when we see, hear, understand ever so much—everything—in a flash—before we fall back again into our agreeable somnolence. (*LJ* 87)

This passage hints at both a figure and a force by which Conrad's early and best fiction is organized: an opposition between somnolence and awakening, blindness and insight, darkness and light, which serves the interest of heightened awareness. Marlow's experience alludes to a strategy of enlightenment by which a character is suddenly jolted out of slumber into an awakening. Typically, the agent of change is a dramatic crisis, a rupture of a coherent and comfortable set of existential conditions in which the character is proceeding with knowledge, self-assurance, and apparent mastery of the situation. *Lord Jim* offers the tale of a young mate on a ship that collides with a submerged derelict in the still of the night. The moment reveals the real weight of Jim's heroic code, for, destined though he was—or thought he was—"to shine in the midst of dangers and storms," Jim deserts the ship. In *The Nigger of the "Narcissus,"* written three years earlier, in 1897, the sailors undergo an analogous challenge to their fortitude and substance. It comes in the form of a consumptive and decadent sailor by the name of James Wait, abetted by a resentful subversive called Donkin. Together they nearly incite their comrades to mutiny. In *The Secret Sharer* (1912) a nocturnal stowaway tests a captain's command of his ship and his commitment to legal justice. Will he break the law by harboring this murderer and endanger his ship to see the man off, or will he betray his double and thus himself by proxy? His somnolence is broken. So is that of the steadfast Marlow in the wilderness of the Congo in *Heart of Darkness*. Witnessing the "merciless logic" of Kurtz's lawless life, he wants to condemn but cannot.

These works seem to follow, as if by prescription, the Aristotelian formula for tragedy. A sudden turn of events or reversal of fortune (peripeteia) occasions a recognition or realization (anagnorisis) on the part of the witnessing character. The truth, as Marlow has it, "can be wrung out of us only by some cruel, little, awful catastrophe." What was it that compelled every dockside hand to attend the inquiry of Jim's desertion? "Whether they knew it or not, the interest that drew them there was purely psychological—the expectation of some essential disclosure as to the strength, the power, the horror, of human emotions" (*LJ* 197, 35). What is it that Marlow experiences in *Heart of Darkness?* As incisive as specific interpretations may be, Marlow could not be vaguer, more symbolic, and more metaphysical in describing what he found in the Congo.[1] Pressed for words, he resorts to abstractions. It was an "inner truth," a "terrible frankness," "truth stripped of its cloak of time," something "monstrous and free," a "dream" more real than everything he had previously known.[2] All further specification is just a matter of detail. What is the symbolic significance of the "Nigger" of the *Narcissus?* Of Brierly's suicide? Of the ubiquitous doubles that people these elusive fictions? Everything is far from clear. When we reflect on the inordinate commitment of the captain to the stranger in *The Secret Sharer,* we conclude, with Michael P. Jones, that the captain must simply be mad.[3] And yet the structure of these stories suggests that in every case some truth comes to light, a truth as moral as it is metaphysical.

To appreciate the strength of this enlightenment figure, we should note that it is operative not only on the level of the fictional drama, or in the interaction between circumstance and character, but on two other levels as well. It appears in the illumination of an empirical "fact" through a literary work and in the enlightenment of a reader through the aesthetic experience. Let us begin with the second of these levels.

In the final paragraph of Conrad's most programmatic statement of aesthetics, the original preface to *The Nigger of the "Narcissus,"* he writes that his artistic goal is to duplicate for his reader the visionary experience we have observed in Marlow:

To arrest, for the space of a breath, the hands busy about the work of the earth, and compel men entranced by the sight of distant goals to glance for a moment at the surrounding vision of form and colour . . . such is the aim, difficult and evanescent, and reserved only for a very few to achieve. . . . And when it is accomplished—behold!— all the truth of life is there: a moment of vision, a sigh, a smile—and the return to an eternal rest.[4]

A sudden awakening, a vision, then a fall into indefinite somnolence and rest. Laborers have been momentarily transformed into readers. Neither an experience nor a vision, the agent of transformation is in this case a work of art. Disrupting the mechanical entrancement of workers to chores, it forces them to read their world in exactly the way that an intuitive moment makes Marlow understand "ever so much— everything—in a flash."

The figure of enlightenment can also be traced in the relation of the literary work to its empirical material. As Conrad recounts it in the author's note to his 1915 collection of stories, *Within the Tides,* the formal cause of his fiction is a "conscientious rendering of truth in thought and fact." As an artist, Conrad has always operated according to the principle of a "scrupulous fidelity to the truth of [his] own sensations."[5] To be sure, both claims leave the question of the actual relation of this truth to thoughts, facts, and sensations unanswered. Are sensations essentially equivalent to truth (supporting a reading of Conrad as literary impressionist) or, rather, a vehicle for truth's transmission?[6] While the question cannot be immediately resolved, the evidence suggests that truth is ultimately different from the sensations and thoughts and facts. It is something that just might shine through them. Art may thus be defined as

a single-minded attempt to render the highest kind of justice to the visible universe, by bringing to light the truth, manifold and one, underlying its every aspect. It is an attempt to find in its forms, in its colours, in its light, in its shadows, in the aspects of matter and in the facts of life what of each is fundamental, what is enduring and essential—their one illuminating and convincing quality—the very truth of their existence. The artist, then, like the thinker or the scientist, seeks the truth and makes his appeal. (*NN* xi)

The truth at which Conrad's writing aims is not immediately visible in the universe's forms and colors. It is, rather, those forms' one illuminating quality, which requires the revelation of art and causes, in turn, an illumination of the dramatis personae and the reader.

Given the predominance of this enlightenment figure, it is not surprising that critics have attempted to describe the contents of such revelatory moments. What is the light that comes to oppose Conradian darkness and all rudely interrupted sleep? What objective characteristics of the world or the self do his dramatic crises reveal? What metaphysical or moral facts correspond to this "truth" at which his fiction aims? These questions arise quite naturally.[7] In fact, in the most radical reading, Conrad's cruel and revelatory catastrophes break life into two antithetical orders, one a "false" or superstructural consciousness, the second a "base," a ground, or a revealed ideal. It is this second order that would appear in Marlow's journey in *Heart of Darkness*, in the destinies of Jim and Leggatt (of *The Secret Sharer*), and in the perilous context to which weathered seamen commit themselves.

Nor is it surprising that most interpretations of Conrad have fallen, schematically speaking, into positive and negative readings of this base reality. The positive reading finds definable contents gleaming at the bottom of the awakening (usually in the form of luminous values and moral principles, or the "few simple notions" that Conrad defends throughout his work). The positive approach sees the Conradian awakenings as constituting new evidence of old moral directives, defended against the mechanics of motivation which the crisis has exposed as somniferous. On the whole the superstructural world would be marked by lies of self-interest, the base by inalienable truths.[8] The negative reading, on the other hand, identifies the ultimate object of the Conradian revelation as a nihilistic vision, the coming into light of a paradoxical and metaphysical darkness. Negative interpretations of the Conradian "message" arise in reaction to the distinct difficulty of even recognizing the object of the awakening in question.[9]

While much rings true in both the negative and the positive readings, both risk being misled by an image contained in the enlightenment picture itself: The awakening A seems to effect a transition between states of knowledge 1 and 2. However, to seek to determine the precise nature of this 2 is to overlook the dialectical function of the awakening, or the relation to 1 in which it consists. Otherwise put, the awakening involves an action of A on 1 and not necessarily the advent of 2. Instead, this 2 is the desideratum of both Conrad's activity as an artist and his fictional dilemmas. This quest for 2, which Conrad calls truth, is the "formal cause" of Conrad's essayistic art, its motivating drive, as it were. Inherent in the "enduring" and "essential" dimensions of the perceptible world, this truth is the intended discovery of his art, not its inevitable achievement.

Returning to the Preface of *The Nigger of the "Narcissus,"* we find that art is described as an attempt to "render justice" to the visible universe, an attempt to find in the universe's forms and colors the very truth of their existence. Like the thinker and the scientist, the artist seeks the truth and "makes his appeal." This appeal constitutes his only "sincerity." If he "be deserving," his appeal might be answered. Art is an inherently essayistic endeavor, a project justified by its very ambition and procedure. The truth lies beyond the signs of its presence. It can at best be approximated.

Onto this deferral of the accomplishment of the artist's investigation we must add the suspicion that truth may actually have little to do with the empirical phenomena that the artwork represents—not only because truth underlies the world's forms and colors, as though hidden from view, but especially because it is only through artistic form that this truth seems to take on a face. When attempting to explain what a character, an author, or a reader understands "in a flash," Conrad embraces the same type of abstractions as Marlow. The truth of his tales—neither a fact nor a value, neither a directive nor a precept of knowledge—consists only in that which strikes the artist as "enduring," "fundamental," "essential." The essential is what is essential: The awakening remains describable only tautologically, in terms of itself. What is true in a fragment that is snatched from the rush of time is something the subjectivity of the author finds "convincing." While an incident "as completely devoid of importance as the flooding of an ant-heap" (namely, the desertion of the *Patna* by Jim) seemed to contain a truth "momentous enough to affect mankind's conception of itself" (*LJ* 57), the incident becomes luminous only on the condition that it be displayed "in the light of a sincere mood." At bottom the aim of the Conradian novelist is a modest one. Suspicious of the "debasing touch of insincerity," he endeavors to create "for himself a world, great or little, in which he can honestly believe." Believable primarily only to the artist, this persuasive world is destined to remain "individual and a little mysterious." The "metaphysical project" of the writer is only a rhetorical effort "to make unfamiliar things credible." [10]

The Conradian illuminations are thus characterized by the most curious blend of predicates: empirically observable and subjectively projected, historically insignificant and philosophically momentous, "theoretical" in the two senses, not always compatible, of the visible and the mental. While the goal of the awakening is truth, this truth is not given either inside or outside the objective contents of a literary work. It must be essayed and belabored. Perhaps it will be recognized in the attempt to achieve it, like a world in which one can believe, or the credibility of things unfamiliar. The artist has no real grasp of the condition of knowledge, or realization 2. In fact, it may even be that the aesthetics of visibility is informed by no vision at all, as Conrad confesses in a letter to Norman Douglas: "There's neither inspiration nor hope in my work. It's mere hard labour for life." In the meantime the essay must be groping: "I have often suffered in connection with my work from a sense of unreality, from intellectual doubt of the ground I stood upon." [11]

We must begin with this sense of unreality, this doubt of the ground or disruption of realization 1, as the only foundation of Conrad's attempted theoretical transcendence. Our investigation must start with what is most obvious about the awakening as Conrad presents it, namely, that it is not an awakening *to* but an awakening *from.* It is "eventual," tentative, and perhaps even inconclusive. Otherwise put, we must view Conrad as searching and researching the truth from a standpoint of obstructed visibility and slumber, from a position of untruth, marked by foundations that are none. Only by essaying the solidity of the "matter" and the "facts" of an unreal slumber can he properly seek the real and the enduring. Ironically, then, Conrad's tales of adventure thematize not the sea that seems to be their subject but the ground providing shelter.[12]

Within this essayistic framework, a positive reading indicates Conrad's wished-for determination of the real, a negative one its preliminary and necessary indetermination. If a new determination of the real proves to hold between the two, it may have to preserve indeterminacy within it. Negativity would then constitute the possibilizing condition of a positive essay. Let us then begin with this doubt of the ground, recognizing the awakening to function primarily as a transformation of the otherwise real into unreality.

The slumber disrupted by Conradian crises is simultaneously epistemological, metaphysical, and moral. At moments of dramatic crisis everything the Conradian character is, or thinks he is, is called into question. The unexpected occurrence challenges not only the protagonist's fidelity to a standard but above all the intellectual foundations of the standard. The stowaway in *The Secret Sharer* questions not the captain's conception of duty so much as the sense of self on which that duty is based. So does the grounded *Patna*, an emergency testing the limits of self-discipline even more than the "guilt" that the court of law tries to assess. At these moments of dramatic reversal the very ground on which Conrad's characters stand is taken out from under them; no new one is supplied. The protagonist is suspended in a world defying its own logic.

Conrad is concerned with exposing the ubiquitous inevitability of this vulnerability. It is the "commonest sort of fortitude" that prevents us from "becoming criminals in a legal sense," Marlow remarks. While communally enforced restraint serves only a compensatory function, it is from a deeper than criminal weakness that no one is safe;

from weakness unknown, but perhaps suspected, as in some parts of the world you suspect a deadly snake in every bush—from weakness that may lie hidden, watched or unwatched, prayed against or manfully scorned, repressed or maybe ignored more than half a lifetime. . . . And there are things—they look small enough sometimes too—by which some of us are totally and completely undone. (*LJ* 26–27)

What is the nature of this "us" undone by small enough things? According to "An Outpost of Progress" (1896), it is made of the characters, the capacities, the emotions, and the principles defining persons as what they are. If there is something revelatory about people, as Alfred Adler suggested, it is not the personal "style of life" they construct on the basis of the most common sort of fortitude but their performance under adverse conditions.[13] What is exposed at such moments of stress is the fragility of power, its nature as a strategic defense. In the related terms of Otto Rank, the "will" lauded by philosophers as the very source of power is originally a counterwill, coming into existence as a reactionary "No!" to the imposing "Thou shalt!" of an outside force.[14] In keeping with these post-Nietzschean suspicions, Conrad dramatizes the total and complete undoing that a chink in one's defense can provoke.

Let us look closely at an instance in point. "An Outpost of Progress" unfolds as follows. Two white men have been left unassisted to manage a trading station in the wilderness of Africa. Closely united at the beginning of their lonely sojourn ("ascending arm in arm the slope of the bank"), Kayerts and Carlier become increasingly uneasy and hostile toward each other in a growing sense of defenselessness.[15] As rations grow scarce and with no sign of supplies on the way, they argue, threatening to kill each other over a cube of sugar. A chase ensues; a shot rings out: Kayerts has killed Carlier. The very next day Kayerts hangs himself.

If there is a moral to this story it comes early on, in the form of a narrative reflection on the origins and limitations of human power. Conrad had begun his tale by stressing that Kayerts and Carlier are specimens of no-more-than-average humanity: two "perfectly insignificant and incapable individuals, whose existence is only rendered possible through the high organization of civilized crowds" (*OP* 128). Society had always taken them under its care, "forbidding them all independent thought, all initiative, all departure from routine," to the point where they "could only live on condition of being machines" (*OP* 131). The narrator ponders these insignificant individuals and generalizes his observation to humanity at large:

Few men realize that their life, the very essence of their character, their capabilities and their audacities, are only the expression of their belief in the safety of their surroundings. The courage, the composure, the confidence; the emotions and principles; every great and every insignificant thought belongs not to the individual but to the crowd: to the crowd that believes blindly in the irresistible force of its institutions and of its morals, in the power of its police and of its opinion. (*OP* 129)

The tale of the barbaric reversion of Kayerts and Carlier can thus be read as a negative image, commenting less on individuals removed from their settings than on those still in them. The belief in safety and inborn strength is the essential prerequisite for the appearance of human substance: "the composure, the confidence; the emotions and principles"; the very forms of judgment; every achievement and external feature, including one's character. In turn, the belief in safety is contingent upon the support of a crowd, a collection of persons all acting as one. It is the crowd that generates the morals, the creeds, and the abilities of the individuals composing it. And yet, if belief in safety is the "master-belief" underlying all others, the relation is as circular as that of Musil's debtor-objects: One's belief in safety is sustained only by belief in the police and socially enforced restraint.[16] The slumber is aggressively guarded. "An Outpost of Progress" shows that, when Musil's "institutions for the maintenance of public safety" are removed, the stitching of consciousness threatens to come undone.

Such undoing has analogues in a great number of Conrad's works: in Arsat's abandonment of his brother ("The Lagoon" [1898]), in Almayer's folly, in Jim's exile and death, and in Kurtz's return to barbarism. When things go well, the stubborn resistance of human agents or a type of "disdainful mercy" of fortune steps in to stop the crises from enacting a mortal catastrophe (*NN* 90). What are some of the modes of this subjective resistance? Single-minded intention, commitment to ethical principles, fidelity to one's "innermost self"—these are some dimensions of the armor that aim at protection.

The two Marlows recounting the tales of *Lord Jim* and *Heart of Darkness* repeatedly invoke such subjective resistance to encroaching threats. Throughout each narrative, Marlow undergoes experiences that stun him with the "irremediable horror" of a scene:

It had the power to drive me out of my conception of existence, out of that shelter each of us makes for himself to creep under in moments of danger, as a tortoise withdraws within its shell. For a moment I had a view of a world that seemed to wear a vast and dismal aspect of disorder, while, in truth, thanks to our unwearied efforts, it is as sunny an arrangement of small conveniences as the mind of man can conceive. But still—it was only a moment: I went back into my shell directly. One *must*—don't you know?—though I seemed to have lost all my words in the chaos of dark thoughts I had contemplated for a second or two beyond the pale. These came back, too, very soon, for words also belong to the sheltering conception of light and order which is our refuge. (*LJ* 190)

Here is an awakening in which Marlow confronts a potential catastrophe: a collapse of the very "conception of existence" sustaining his everyday life. His retrospective analysis focuses on the metaphysically constitutive power of subjectivity. By means of pragmatic and theoretical restraints, structures of consciousness convert a vast and dismal disorder into a "sunny arrangement of conveniences." As in "An Outpost of Progress," the conveniences act primarily as a refuge from danger. The theoretical scaffolding of this shelter is language, metonymy to the language of reason. It is to the "sheltering conception of light and order" that Marlow returns "directly," like a tortoise to its shell.

Is this masking of the true nature of things endemic to consciousness, like a veil of Maya, or does Marlow lack the courage for a truth that can actually be seen? It seems to be Marlow. Driven though it be out of its own conception of existence, his imagination seems actually able to catch a glimpse of what is behind the veil ("I had a view of a world

. . .")`. It is simply *he* who fails to follow the vision through, maintaining that a return to shelter is indispensable. This passage is symbolic of a whole series of strategies for shirking "the vision" which a crisis essays.

Marlow, a restless seaman in *Heart of Darkness,* is used to clearing out of town for any part of the world at a day's notice. This time he is tempted by a "snake": the mighty and winding river of the Congo. Not long after assuming charge of his boat he discovers that the land represented by "the biggest—the most blank" part of the map is in fact much vaster, more dismal, and more unrestrained than he had ever imagined. "We are accustomed," he tells his audience, "to look upon the shackled form of a conquered monster, but there—there you could look at a thing monstrous and free" (*HD* 11, 37). Again let us not ask what this thing monstrous and free is in itself; let us examine the ways in which it is shackled.

Throughout the narrative Marlow suggests that the most effective way to conquer the monster is to avoid confronting it, to consign it to oblivion. Although he has voluntarily sought out the very "center of the earth," Marlow is frequently unwilling to confront the atrocities before him. One scene has him turning a bend in the river to be struck by a terrifying uproar of savages on the shore. This uncanny and overwhelming experience appears to harbor metaphysical proportions. Marlow does his best to understand it:

What was there after all? Joy, fear, sorrow, devotion, valour, rage— who can tell?—but truth—truth stripped of its cloak of time. Let the fool gape and shudder—the man knows, and can look on without a wink. But he must at least be as much of a man as these on the shore. He must meet that truth with his own true stuff—with his own inborn strength. . . . An appeal to me in this fiendish row—is there? Very well; I hear; I admit. (*HD* 38)

At this point Marlow seems prepared to meet this truth, to admit it and look on without a wink. But as one of his listeners interrupts his narrative with a cynical remark, we understand that he did not fulfill his promise:

Who's that grunting? You wonder I didn't go ashore for a howl and a dance? Well no—I didn't. Fine sentiments, you say? Fine sentiments be hanged! I had no time. I had to mess about with white-lead and strips of woollen blanket helping to put bandages on those leaky steam-pipes—I tell you. I had to watch the steering and circumvent those snags, and get the tin-pot along by hook or by crook. There was surface-truth enough in these things to save a wiser man. (*HD* 38)

Marlow is undoubtedly earnest about his duty to pilot the ship. Steering a perilous route through the insidiously shallow river, he in fact did not have an opportunity to go ashore for a howl. There is, however, deliberate bathos built into this description of Marlow putting bandages on steam pipes while such an uncanny scene is occurring on shore. In this fiendish row lies an appeal to Marlow which he hears but is unable to answer without risking his functional balance. His need to steer the boat and his "lack of time" (as he falls in with the regular progress of his machine, unable to linger in a moment) counteract his willingness to respond to the siren call. In the "surface-truth" of these physical chores lies a wisdom that shields him from a truth that is deeper.

"What saves us is efficiency—the devotion to efficiency," Marlow muses, as he distinguishes between the ethic of his bourgeois contemporaries and that of Roman warriors set in a once barbarous England. The Romans were unable to mollify the effects of the darkness through distractive labor or an imperialist ideology (*HD* 9−10). Well-defined labor, on the other hand, guarantees the exclusion of every thought that does not further the project at hand. In *Lord Jim* work is also portrayed as a means of distraction. When Marlow is reflecting on how to help Jim live down the shame of having deserted his ship, one of the obvious solutions is to put him to work on a nearly deserted island. "To bury him," Marlow thinks, "would have been such an easy kindness!"

It would have been so much in accordance with the wisdom of life, which consists in putting out of sight all the reminders of our folly, of our weakness, of our mortality; all that makes against our efficiency. (*LJ* 106)

Here, as in the previous citation, "wisdom" is ironically linked to an enforced oblivion deliberately screening human mortality. In passages such as these Conrad shows more than a Victorian anxiety about the debilitating effects of the *vis contemplativa;* he challenges the fear underlying its opposite.[17]

Similarly, the dreamlike world of the jungle raises the suspicion that it is really Marlow's self-chosen activity that is a "noisy dream," focusing his mind on the task at hand and immuring him to his uncanny surroundings. "I did not see it any more," he says of the sinister horizon,

I had no time. I had to keep guessing at the channel; I had to discern, mostly by inspiration, the signs of hidden banks; . . . I had to keep a look-out for the signs of dead wood we could cut up in the night for next day's steaming. When you have to attend to things of that sort, to the mere incidents of the surface, the reality—the reality I tell you—fades. The inner truth is hidden—luckily, luckily. (*HD* 34, 36)

Marlow is grateful to these "mere incidents of the surface," for they block out their larger context.

Work is just one of the protective strategies at a person's disposal. After claiming that the only way to respond to "the appeal of truth" is by meeting it with one's "own true stuff," Marlow makes an important addition: "Principles won't do. Acquisitions, clothes, pretty rags—rags that would fly off at the first good shake" (*HD* 38). Theories, morals, ideals, and convictions also embody the surface truth, the factitious and consoling shelter. When challenged, they fail; when loudly proclaimed, they are only idling. Principles importune us like beggars, depriving us of our power to deliberate on the spot. This is why Marlow is so taken by the figure of Jim. Standing on behalf of all those people "whose very existence is based upon honest faith, and upon the instinct of courage," Jim seems to be one of those fellows capable of resisting the "solicitation of ideas." "Hang ideas!" Marlow exclaims. "They are tramps, vagabonds, knocking at the back-door of your mind, each taking a little of your substance" (*LJ* 27). Principles and ideas do not express one's own true stuff. They mislead and diminish it. As Conrad's writing progresses over the years, so does his mistrust of consciousness. Measured by the monstrous irrationality of fortune, he writes in *Nostromo* (1904), skepticism and irony can only be luxurious "affectations."[18] The political ideals of the anarchists in *The Secret Agent* (1907) are secretly personal impulses "disguised into creeds."[19] Consciousness translates experience into terms reassuring the agent of conscious control.

Although Jim appears immune to the solicitation of ideas, time and again he is seduced by precisely that—an idea. The heroic profession of sailing announces itself to him as a function of "a course of light holiday literature." In fact, on board his first ship Jim is more distracted from his surroundings than Marlow from the events in the Congo jungle. Not work but a personal dream immerses him entirely in a world of his own, making him forget his reality and replay in his mind the sea life of romantic literature: "He saw himself saving people from sinking ships, cutting away masts in a hurricane, swimming through a surf with a line . . . always an example of devotion to duty, and as unflinching as a hero in a book" (*LJ* 4, 5). Even his apparent immunity to the solicitation of ideas is prompted by an idea.

How far does this seduction of the idea extend? To the understanding of oneself and the world at large. The challenge posed to Jim by a real emergency at sea is the same as the one attending the captain's first command in *The Secret Sharer.* "I wondered," the captain reflects, "how far I should turn out faithful to that ideal conception of one's own personality every man sets up for himself secretly."[20] Twice Jim has the opportunity to vindicate his ideal conception, or ego ideal; twice he fails, first by missing a heroic opportunity, and then by behaving like a coward.[21] Henceforth he is destined to a strange combination of evasion and confrontation, fleeing every place that harbors a memory of his ignoble desertion while seeking new occasions to make good his failings.

As Marlow comments, "no man ever understands quite his own artful dodges to flee from the grim shadow of self-knowledge" (*LJ* 49). Beneath this sentence lie two possible readings of Jim's ideal conception of his personality. Either it is just such "an artful dodge" or is an image of his truest and innermost possibility. Both readings are plausible; in fact, it is the duplicity of readings that interests Conrad. Even so, it is the second interpretation that requires more attention than it has received, particularly concerning the question of whether or not Jim actually succeeds in living up to his ideal.

In martyring himself as lord of the region of Patusan, Jim seems to succeed in his heroic aspiration, giving up his life for the sake of an ideal. Can we finally say that Jim has proved true to himself, atoning for his moral and intellectual failings? Marlow tends to think so. Jim "had at last mastered his fate" (*LJ* 197). And yet this mastery of a fate that was ideally his occurs only at the expense of his historical one. We remember how the circumstances of Jim's downfall develop. He has become the de facto ruler of the Far Eastern land of Patusan when Gentleman Brown and his fourteen pirates descend upon the village with ravenous intentions. The natives besiege these white men and wait for Jim to decide the intruders' fate. When Jim returns, he resists the natives' desire to disarm the pirates, accepting instead the Europeans' promise that they will return whence they came without fighting. He sets them free. The spitefulness of Gentleman Brown is such, however, that, as he sails down the river, he massacres a band of men (which includes the prince of Patusan) who had stood peacefully aside for the passing. To atone for the carnage he has provoked, Jim delivers himself to Doramin, the ruler, to be shot.

Lord Jim is not merely the story of a man struggling to live up to his own ideal but also of an ideal destroying its bearer. It is not a matter of a would-be hero who reveals his true stripes but of a man of the greatest potential who is destroyed by his voluntary assumption of responsibility. When he goes to Doramin to be shot, Jim abandons a living woman "to celebrate his pitiless wedding" with "a shadowy ideal of conduct" (*LJ* 253). *The Secret Sharer*'s "ideal conception of the personality" is here a shadowy ideal, and the reason is clear: to be faithful to his ideal Jim must negate his historical being. Jim takes the project of "self-overcoming" to the extremity of martyrdom. To be true to oneself in the mode of a martyr involves as much deception, false consciousness, and bad faith as any other form of self-discipline, indeed even more.[22] A new hint of that "flavor of mortality" accompanying every lie in *Heart of Darkness* arises here. In addition, it becomes evident that the only difference between Jim and the cynics with whom he is contrasted (Brown and, by extension, Donkin and Wait) is one of degree. Each operates under the sway of an idea.[23]

Lord Jim is a tale of the delusion of self-consciousness at large. For Jim was "one of us." "It was solemn, and a little ridiculous, too, as they always are, those struggles of an individual trying to save from the fire his idea of what his moral identity should be, this precious notion of a convention, only one of the rules of the game, nothing more" (*LJ* 50). The hamartia of Jim is a risk inherent to becoming what one is: the attempt to reify what amounts to a mere image. Unsuffered though his own ideal may be, the logistics governing its formation is endemic to all forms of self-consciousness, as Musil's man without qualities realizes in his resistance to adopting an identity. It is the mistake of looking to the rulebook for strategies of playing, of applying to conditional experience the measure of unconditional standards, which will call for uncritical obedience and complete submission.

What is more, the "exalted egoism" of a Jim is produced not by self-determination at all but by anonymous processes of self-objectification, images contained in "the eye of others" (*LJ* 253, 90). Why else would Jim flee every site where his breach is recalled? It is this system of interpersonal recognition, this *regard de l'autre* underlying the code of honor, that makes Jim experience such shame.[24] Relying on precisely such recognition, Jim is unable to abandon the haven of Patusan, for it would mean forfeiting that notice from which his identity derives, a notice that acts as his only reliable standard of definition. "Leave! Why! . . . It would have been—it would have been harder than dying. . . . I must feel—every day, every time I open my eyes—that I am trusted"; "I must stick to their belief in me to feel safe" (*LJ* 151, 203). Belief is conveyed by the other, whether through the agency of a book, as when Jim first took to sea, or through the norms of a group.

What Jim is trying to save from the fire, then, is not his moral identity but his idea of what this identity *should be,* a difference as great as the one between fact and value. His self-image is an ideological illusion, a dream of the sort people fall into the minute they are born (*LJ* 130).[25] Thus to accuse Jim of failing to conform to his own self-image, as readers have done, is to beg the issue, for it implies that there is a possible alternative. In Conrad's work the self-image to which one aspires is always hatched in the dark; in Nietzsche's words, it is a fiction without which life would not be possible.

"When once the truth is grasped that one's own personality is only a ridiculous and aimless masquerade of something hopelessly unknown," Conrad writes in 1896, the year that he began *The Nigger of the "Narcissus,"* "the attainment of serenity is not very far off."[26] It is a serenity that Conrad's own fiction fails to attain, as its characters and narrators endeavor to penetrate this very same masquerade. Those who attended Jim's trial desired to understand the hopelessly unknown bases of human motivation, expecting some disclosure as to "the strength, the power, the horror, of human emotions. "Naturally," Marlow adds, "nothing of the kind could be disclosed," not even to Jim himself (*LJ* 35).

What is it that drives Jim to abandon the *Patna?* Fear? Cowardice? Egoism? The instinct for self-preservation? "I wanted to know," claims Marlow, "and to this day I don't know, I can only guess" (*LJ* 48). While courage is the sine qua non of the seaman's trade, one always finds something else beneath it. "One is always afraid. One may talk, but. . . ." The French lieutenant is reflecting on how Jim could have abandoned his ship:

He put down the glass awkwardly. . . . "The fear, the fear—look you—it is always there. . . ." He touched his breast near a brass button. . . . "Yes! yes! One talks, one talks; this is all very fine; but at the end of the reckoning one is no cleverer than the next man—and no more brave. Brave! This is always to be seen. . . . I have known brave men—famous ones! *Allez!* . . ." He drank carelessly. . . . "Brave—you conceive—in the Service—one has got to be—the trade demands it. . . . *Eh bien!* Each one of them . . . if he were an honest man—*bien entendu*—would confess that there is a point . . . when you let go everything (*vous lachez tout*). And you have got to live with that truth—do you see? Given a certain combination of circumstances, fear is sure to come. . . . Man is born a coward. . . . But habit—habit—necessity—do you see?—the eye of others— *voilà.* One puts up with it." (*LJ* 89–90)

Jim has simply come to such a point where *vous lachez tout.* The force of habit, the demands of the trade, the eye of others—these regulative supports have abandoned him under the pressure of a menacing moment. He has been stripped of the prerequisites of willful action.[27] If this is true, then the French lieutenant who took charge of the *Patna* after its officers fled is not the foil for Jim that he seems to be. The lieutenant, we remember, succeeded where Jim failed, staying on board the *Patna* for thirty hours under the peril of a collapsing bulwark. If he did, however, it was only under the force of a command and the demands of the trade. He was not "taken unawares." In truth, Jim was not afraid, at least not of any specific threat; "he was afraid of the emergency" (*LJ* 59, 54). Caught unprepared, he was unable to call on an idea to rule his action.

When one idea falters, another takes up the slack. Part of the motivation of Jim's desertion consisted of, if not an idea, at least that "contagion of example" to which he had seemed immune. What leads Jim to jump from the *Patna* is nothing less than the persuasive image of officers scrambling for their lives, an ironic inversion of the rhetoric that took him to sea to begin with. "He wanted me to know," Marlow reports, that

he had kept his distance; that there was nothing in common between him and these men. . . . Nothing whatever. It is more than probable he thought himself cut off from them by a space that could not be traversed, by an obstacle that could not be overcome, by a chasm without bottom. (*LJ* 64)

At the very moment when he has the opportunity to prove his autonomy, however, Jim succumbs to the rule of others. What occurs is a contaminating penetration of identity. The officers have manned the lifeboat and call up the *Patna:* "Jump, George! Jump! Oh, jump! . . . Geo-o-o-orge! Oh, jump!" (*LJ* 68). Jim jumps. But he has mistaken his person, for George is another mate, still on board the *Patna* but dead. If Jim's jump is an unconscious attempt to undo this death, it is also a collapse of ego control. His final fall in Patusan occurs in the very same way, brought about by the seduction of rhetoric and its corollary effect of sympathetic identification. When he pardons Gentleman Brown, he is also pardoning himself by proxy.

In Conrad's work there is no psychological autonomy to speak of, no internal ideology to which a character might appeal for the groundwork of action, not even in the unflinching Singleton in *The Nigger of the "Narcissus,"* whose law is the sea. The circumstances with which Conrad's characters are confronted are so imposing that they put the characters in a condition of perpetual response. And there is always a hidden link in the chain of "subjective integrity," a link that constitutes the very process of self-mediation. When Jim was attempting to justify his behavior on board the *Patna,* for example, Marlow reports, he "was not speaking to me, he was only speaking before me, in a dispute with an invisible personality, an antagonistic and inseparable partner of his existence—another possessor of his soul." Although Jim appeared "as genuine as a new sovereign," this other possessor of his soul represented an "infernal alloy in his metal." It was that "familiar devil" lurking in the breast of every person (*LJ* 57, 28, 21), impinging on one's autonomy and binding one indissolubly to characters ostensibly one's opposite—Marlow to Jim, Jim to Brown, Brierly to Jim, Marlow to Kurtz, the captain to Leggatt, the two officers to each other in "The Duel" (1908)—all of them thrust into intimate battle.

This syndrome of the familiar devil is the phenomenon of the double: the reflection of the self in an objective image that initially appears different from oneself but turns out to be an unverifiable face of the subject itself (as alluded to in the name of the boat *Narcissus*).[28] The phenomenon of the double entails not only the conscious/unconscious dynamics within a single person but also the imponderable mechanics of psychic complicity, underlying Conrad's principle of human solidarity as surely as it does the very menace to that principle. Every identification with the other threatens to break down that "blessed stiffness before the outward and inward terrors" which constitutes fidelity to a "few simple notions." The "contagion of example" is the price to pay for a susceptibility to influence from which Conrad's characters are all but unable to free themselves.

Marlow's own devil reveals characteristics of the devil in general. It lets him in for "the kind of thing that by devious, unexpected, truly diabolical ways causes [him] to run up against men with soft spots, with hard spots . . . and loosens their tongues at the sight of [him] for their infernal confidences" (*LJ* 21). And this tendency is what allows him to construct a tale, in the same way that Jim needs to voice his dispute before a witness. The hermeneutical ties between self and self are the basis for the story. Conrad's narrative "monologues" are really dialogues, mediated by numberless listeners and speakers who, in the end, cannot understand themselves on their own. The tales are correlatives of a mutual rather than autonomous experience of self, a situation in which no person can assert an identity except through the presence of another, and often not even then. Swimming away from his ship into voluntary exile, even Leggatt in *The Secret Sharer* is unable to forgo this extrinsic bond. Stopping to rest on a ladder of a ship, he encounters his sharer: "When I saw a man's head looking over . . . I—I liked it. . . . I don't know—I wanted to be seen, to talk with somebody, before I went on" (*SS* 111). The captain too needs to confront this double before he can steer his ship. The examples are numerous, as in *Heart of Darkness,* where Marlow and Kurtz rupture each other's self-enclosure, and (as in *Lord Jim*) Marlow begins to understand himself only in the relation between himself as active agent (or character) and reflective interpreter of this agency (or narrator). For our present purposes it is sufficient to recognize that the contagion of example and mimetic persuasion is ineluctable. The "identities" of Conradian characters mutually determine each other.

When one adds to these facts Conrad's keen attunement to the delusiveness of consciousness, the very notion of knowing oneself begins to look exceedingly naive. By standing trial Jim *does* face up to what he is, but this "facing up" leaves him faceless. He does undergo an essential disclosure after all, but it is a disclosure of the nondisclosure of his inner principle: its obscurity, its contradictions, and its built-in lies.

The paradoxical nature of self-knowledge receives its subtlest portrayal in the story of a character consistently read as one who had always failed to face up to who he is: *Lord Jim's* Captain Brierly. Big Brierly seems to possess that very heroism and instinct of courage to which Jim aspires. Accordingly, his participation on the committee investigating Jim's desertion is marked by "contemptuous boredom." Brierly was not bored, however; "he was exasperated." All the while he was holding silent inquiry into his own case, and the verdict came up as "unmitigated guilt" (*LJ* 43, 36). Within barely a week he committed suicide.

The reason for Brierly's suicide may not be the one that seems most plausible—a recognition that his heroism is only a surface lie and that beneath it he is as weak as Jim. For, unlike Jim, Brierly has had no occasion to *know* himself as a coward. Far from seeing a face beneath his mask, Brierly awakens to exactly the opposite: the mask of self-delusion. He sees his illusions precisely as unsupported but ineradicable articles of faith. Thus the only logic for Brierly's suicide is that it furnishes an escape from the lie of living. Had Brierly succeeded in knowing himself, he would have had the option of accepting his new self-image and adjusting his action accordingly, perhaps in the manner of Svidrigailov, the "happy" nihilist of *Crime and Punishment.*[29] Brierly did not have this option (aside from the fact that his pride would not have allowed it), for he would have remained unable to know whether this new self-image were true; any truer, that is, than the one he gave up. Brierly knew only that he needed to believe in order to live and that this belief had been permanently shattered. The final irony about Brierly is thus not that even in his moment of truth he is gripped by illusion but that he knows it. On that fateful day he committed "his reality and his sham together" to the keeping of the sea (*LJ* 42). Self-worth is a lie without which Brierly is unwilling to live, unable even "to will." And man, as Nietzsche knew, would rather will nothingness than not will at all.[30]

Principles are acquisitions; ideas are beggars; autonomy is delusion; knowledge is a rhetorical pretense. Kurtz's substance in *Heart of Darkness* is inversely proportionate to his intellectual power. He hid in "the magnificent folds of eloquence the barren darkness of his heart" (67).[31] The same magniloquence marks the loafers, anarchists, revolutionaries, and nihilists that people Conrad's later works, especially *The Secret Agent* and *Under Western Eyes* (1911). Their self-certainty grows with their theoretical sophistication, as if inextricably bound to their faith in consciousness, making them the opposite of Singleton, the silent and "unthinking" helmsman of the *Narcissus.*[32] And yet, if Conrad is often in the position of Dostoevski, siding with Alyosha but giving the more convincing role to Ivan, he also insists on submitting even the most persuasive ideas to the test of action.

If ideas and opinions are untrue to experience, facts at least speak for themselves. Or so it seems. Concrete situations expose precisely the hollowness of mental delusion. In the face of experience all rationalizations begin to founder; theories and opinions dissolve like mist. Yet even here Conrad twists the screw. Surprising though it be, a fiction that posits action as a test of intention also relegates the order of factual occurrence to the realm of mere surface appearance. Why else would Conrad's narratives test the logic of chronological order as well as cause and effect, measuring "self-evident" data not only by objective standards but also subjective ones? When Jim tries to explain to the court what happened to make him jump, Marlow underscores the futility of this very attempt at enlightenment: "They wanted facts. Facts! They demanded facts from him [the very repetition conveying contempt], as if facts could explain anything." The facts those men were so eager to know "had been visible, tangible, open to the senses," but they came equipped with no exegetical key. To expect them to reveal their secret was like hoping to discover what lay in an iron box by tapping it with a hammer (*LJ* 18, 35). The positivistic garnering of information suppresses the only fact that is important: that the facts are no more than interpretations. As Pirandello writes, a fact is like "a bag that cannot be held empty. The examining judge will realize this if . . . he tries to have it held without first filling it with all those reasons that certainly determined it, and which he may not even imagine."[33] The same hermeneutical problem surfaces in Törless's inability, in Musil's novel, to explain to his professors why he assisted in torturing a schoolmate: The facts of the matter only hide something that has no language of its own—the matter itself. Accompanying the facts about Jim's desertion was "something invisible, a directing spirit of perdition that dwelt within, like a malevolent soul in a detestable body" (*LJ* 19).

Jim can no more explain why he abandoned his ship than can the mate in *The Secret Sharer* explain why he has murdered a mutinous sailor. "You don't see me coming back to explain such things to an old fellow in a wig and twelve respectable tradesmen, do you? What can they know whether I am guilty or not—or of *what* I am guilty, either?" (*SS* 131). The schematic language of the law is unable to assess anomalous behavior, a difficulty encountered also during the trial of Moosbrugger in *The Man without Qualities*. Normative principles and rational ties, incontrovertible facts and sound ideas—any and all keys of analysis are here confounded. Between Conrad's eccentric personalities and the patrons of institutional exegesis there can be no discourse. Indeed, Jim's and Leggatt's decisions to flee Europe amount to a vote of no confidence in the collective mind of these "respectable tradesmen" (if not in the mind itself, a gesture occasionally directed by Marlow toward his audience).[34] A four-page letter to Jim from his unknowing father in which the "old chap" conveys information about a favorite dog and a pony ("which all you boys used to ride") must go unanswered. What could Jim have to say to "all these placid, colourless forms of men and women peopling that quiet corner of the world as free of danger or strife as a tomb, and breathing equably the air of undisturbed rectitude"? After the bewildering event of his desertion, Jim has begun to inhabit "the other side of the earth" (*LJ* 208, 207).

We have been describing the ruling metaphors of a familiar and somniferous world structured by a combination of factors: *restraint,* as in the shackling of anomalous forces; *protection,* as through a deliberate pacification of one's surroundings; *pragmatic application,* as in the focusing of attention on labor; and *ideology,* in the broadest sense of principles and methods of understanding. It is becoming increasingly clear that those Marlovian moments of awakening in which "we see, hear, understand ever so much . . . in a flash" do not entail a revealed alternative to conceptions of everyday existence but merely a wide-eyed vision of their artificiality. What one understands at those revelatory moments is that within all security lurks insecurity, within all harmony discord, within all reason some mad desire. "I was made," Marlow admits in *Lord Jim,* "to look at the convention that lurks in all truth and on the essential sincerity of falsehood" (*LJ* 57). Jim's resolve slackens the minute it should harden; the lieutenant's strength masks weakness; the safety of the tradesmen hides danger; habits guard against chance; work deflects engagement; beliefs show a lack of conviction. Compassion and charity add up to egoism and pride. As Marlow ventures into the core of the world in *Heart of Darkness,* his impressions conform to the same paradoxical pattern. The notion of the "primal" becomes a lie. Kurtz is a "sham," Marlow's waking hours a nightmare. Everywhere lurks the principle of duplicity, as in *The Secret Sharer*, where the morality of Leggatt has a murderous effect. "It was clear," reflects the captain, as he considers the case of the "criminal" who has boarded his ship, "the same strung-up force which had given twenty-four men a chance . . . for their lives, had, in a sort of recoil, crushed a mutinous unworthy existence" (*SS* 124–25). It is by the same principle that, in both *Lord Jim* and *Heart of Darkness*, Marlow's irreducible doubt can be said to constitute knowledge and Kurtz's immorality a "moral victory" (*HD* 70).

Marlow says that, in their conversation about Jim, he and Stein had approached "nearer to absolute Truth, which, like Beauty itself, floats elusive, obscure, half-submerged, in the silent still waters of mystery" (*LJ* 132). As Nietzsche warns, the road to this Truth can kill. Indeed, it kills a good number of Conrad's characters. How else can we account for the transformation of Kurtz from idealist to immoralist? His soul "had looked within itself," Marlow reports, "and, by Heavens I tell you, it had gone mad" (*HD* 65). After killing Carlier, Kayerts experiences a similar moment "of complete knowledge":

He had plumbed in one short afternoon the depths of . . . despair and now found repose in the conviction that life had no more secrets for him. . . . His old thoughts, convictions, likes and dislikes . . . appeared in their true light at last. . . . He had been all his life, till that moment, a believer in a lot of nonsense like the rest of mankind—who are fools; but now he thought! He knew! (*OP* 166–67)

Like Kurtz, Kayerts also judges "the horror!" and takes his life. Conrad's suicides refuse the lie of all unequivocal truths. When Decoud, in *Nostromo*, finds himself stranded on an island, the result is as fatal as the wilderness on Kayerts. Solitude "from mere outward conditions of existence," the narrator comments, "takes possession of the mind and drives forth the thought into the exile of utter unbelief" (*N* 556).

Or, in the words of *Under Western Eyes:* "No human being could bear a steady view of moral solitude without going mad."[35] Madness, solitude, suicide, and "utter unbelief"— these mark the effects of a reality that is none, a region in which the "mere outward conditions of existence" threaten to vanish altogether. Indeed, "to Jim's successes there were no externals" (*LJ* 138).

This process of derealization is caused not by a characterological flaw in a protagonist but rather by the disturbance and implosion of those structures—ideas, values, facts, judgments, and laws; delusions of mastery, autonomy, courage, and safety—that define the truth of the everyday. As consciousness is faced with nonidentity, it loses its bearings. The "doubt of the ground" produces a vision of unreality, immersing Conradian characters in a utopian region "blocked out by the classification of the world,"[36] whether they are able to find their way back from it, like Marlow, or remain marooned, like Jim. With the implosion of superstructures even the base disappears. Kurtz "had kicked himself loose of the earth," says Marlow, "and I before him did not know whether I stood on the ground or floated in the air." He had stepped "over the threshold of the invisible" [*HD* 65, 69]. Leggatt, too, has been "driven off the face of the earth." Jim has gone out "and shut the door after him." Once he reached Patusan, it would be "as though he had never existed." There he would have "nothing but the soles of his two feet to stand upon, and he would first have to find his ground at that" (*LJ* 142). With all its defense of a community bound by a single code of ethics, even *The Nigger of the "Narcissus"* alludes to this utopian overreaching of boundaries, for the sailors of Singleton's generation exist "beyond the pale of life" (*NN* 25).[37]

Conrad's narratives explore this critical condition on the fringes of normalcy. Their interest lies not in social readjustment so much as its opposite: situations of extremity, enormity, and anomaly. Moreover, these experiences of extremity do not constitute merely negative or barren ruptures. Applied to Singleton, beyond the pale of life means also "within sight of eternity" (*NN* 25). When Marlow's last listener receives the packet wrapping up the final facts about Jim, he is automatically reminded of "horizons as boundless as hope . . . in the hot quest of the Ever-undiscovered Country over the hill, across the stream, beyond the wave." As one who approaches "with slow feet and alert eyes the glimpse of an undiscovered country," the man "read on deliberately." To read deliberately is to adjust to the probability that here those conceptions of "light and order" habitually sustained by words and judgment might be defied. Among Singleton and the "everlasting children of the mysterious sea" speech is nearly impossible, explanation definitively so. "I affirm nothing," Marlow says in "summary" of his tale of Jim. That "white figure in the stillness of coast and sea" was destined to remain "always mute, dark—under a cloud," at the "heart of a vast enigma." And this is why Marlow is interested in the voluntary martyrdom of the last episode of Jim's life. He wonders whether it did not offer Jim "that supreme opportunity, that last and satisfying test for which I had always suspected him to be waiting, before he could frame a message to the impeccable world" (*LJ* 204–6, 208).

You remember that when I was leaving him for the last time he had asked whether I would be going home soon, and suddenly cried after me, "Tell them! . . ." I had waited—curious I'll own, and hopeful, too—only to hear him shout, "No—nothing." That was all then—and there will be nothing more; there will be no message, unless such as each of us can interpret for himself from the language of facts, that are so often more enigmatic than the craftiest arrangement of words. (*LJ* 206)

No message shall be conveyed, either through the voice of Jim or the agency of Marlow or the judgment of the listeners. The significance of Jim's dilemma did not lie in a moral; it resided in "a subtle and momentous quarrel as to the true essence of life, and did not want a judge"; it was a quarrel that "made discussion vain and comment impossible." And as for that supreme opportunity, that final utterance "which through all our stammerings is . . . our only and abiding intention," Marlow can only stress that "the last word . . . shall never be said . . . the last word of our love, of our desire, faith, remorse, submission, revolt" (*LJ* 57, 205, 137–38). Or does Conrad actually succeed in having this last word by not having it—by expressing, in other words, these final conditions about which comment is impossible, conditions such as love, acquiescence, and revolt, all of them nourished by an unyielding commitment and insuperable tension? If there is anything final about these conditions, it is that they embody the yearning for an absolute unity of self and ground, an absolute motivation, a condition of unconditional belief and commitment—that is, the very desiderata that the absence of truth makes all but impossible. If the Conradian fictions offer a last word at all, it is one that hearkens to the intrinsic doubt of this irreducible tension, the doubt of all "sovereign power" ordinarily enthroned in a fixed standard of conduct.

Far from using situations to rationalize principles, then, Conrad represents situations to which rationalization is unequal. Far from vindicating a value, a law, or a moral code, his fictions indicate regions beyond their borders. What we are left with is the inherent strife of desire, faith, submission, and remorse toward the indeterminacy of the conditions from which they arise. And this is a situation of critical indecision, or of an essayistic resistance to resting in any "final solution." Marlow's statement to the effect that he was being made "to comprehend the Inconceivable" must thus be read as an allegory for the need for interminable comprehension (*LJ* 57). *Comprehend* does not mean to furnish a reason but "to gather together," as in a complex hermeneutics of multiple narrations, reports within reports, facts interspersed with judgments, disrupted chronological sequences, numerous subjectivities contaminating each other.

When we recognize that Conrad has no intention to philosophize, judge, or moralize in the ordinary sense of the terms, and that the cases informing his fiction elude the conceptions by which experience is habitually ordered, only then can we understand why Conrad describes the writer's task as he does in the Preface to *The Nigger of the "Narcissus."*

Only then does it become clear why he clings to the word *truth* rather than abandoning it altogether.

According to the Preface to *The Nigger of the "Narcissus,"* aesthetic illumination is produced as follows: The artist rescues a fragment from the remorseless rush of time, freeing it from those familiar and somniferous contexts to which it is ordinarily submitted, and displays it "unquestioningly" in the light of a sincere mood. To free the fragment from a careless context requires a critical operation, an assaying of the "alloys" with which it is mixed. *Unquestioningly* means "without evaluation," without imposing further categories of judgment upon the thing. The task rather is merely to hold up the fragment and "disclose its inspiring secret: the stress and the passion within the core of each convincing moment." This procedure is what distinguishes the artist's pursuit of truth from that of the philosopher or scientist. The philosopher delves into ideas, the scientist into facts, the artist, by implication, into things themselves. What such an artist aims to achieve is neither the "clear logic of a triumphant conclusion" nor "the unveiling of one of those heartless secrets which are called the Laws of Nature" (*NN* xiv–vi); it is that which is most fundamental and convincing in the visible universe: the "stress and passion" of individual moments. As perplexing as this formulation may be, it accounts for both the material and the form of Conrad's work.

Regarding the material, Conrad's clarification about the nature of artistic truth makes it clear that, at least at this stage of his career, his fiction will have no place for the merely incidental, the humorous, or the light (the subjects of comedy, satire, or entertainment). On the contrary, it will be drawn to what is heavy, decisive, and crucial. Drama and tension will be the measure of these moments' claims to artistic attention, even if they embody an "immoral" event like the desertion of a ship or the headhunting of Kurtz. Morality will at most be the *stage* for an ethical drama, understood as a situation of radical tension and indecision.

How will Conrad speak about these metamoral occurrences? We have a clue in his distinction between the respective rhetorics of art, philosophy, and science. Geared toward "the attainment of our ambitions" and "the glorification of our precious aims" (*NN* xi), science and philosophy serve pragmatic and moral ends. Both speak "authoritatively to our common sense" and "intelligence." Now it is already clear that the Conradian artist is interested neither in furthering these ambitions nor in contributing to the storehouse of common sense. His artistic project, on the contrary, is to salvage the essence of particulars from these general rounds of pragmatic ends. The artist will focus not on the potential uses, meanings, and purposes of the moments he selects but on their intrinsic stress and passion, their significance as events in themselves. This, if anything, is their inherent "truth," which does not lend itself to general statements.

The Kantian resonance of these statements is not incidental, even if, in the same preface, Conrad distances himself from the notion of the aesthetic as an end in itself.[38] Conrad's manifesto suggests that the truth of moments is not given its due by the instrumentalized languages of conceptual reason. When the moment is classified as an instance in a theoretical order or a means in a practical scheme, it ceases to be an occasion of autonomous value. The implication of this autonomous and transcendent particularity is important: However much Conrad strives to illuminate the essential truth of his subject—or, rather, precisely *insofar* as he strives for this goal—the subject calls out for treatment that is neither philosophical nor scientific, neither pure nor practical, but aesthetic. It calls out to be displayed as an "aesthetic idea."

An aesthetic idea, writes Kant, is "that representation of the imagination which induces much thought, yet without the possibility of any definite thought whatever, i.e., *concept*, being adequate to it, and which language, consequently, can never get quite on level terms with or render completely intelligible." Aesthetic truth induces thought without any definite thought corresponding to it. It aims at a "universal" remaining beyond its reach. If there is a truth in the aesthetic idea, it thus lies in its form rather than its content. Aesthetic truth, we might say, is conveyed by the perceptible form of an ungeneralizable particular that appears convincing, persuasive, or credible in itself. To be persuasive this formed perception cannot be motivated by any consideration other than its faithful representation of the credibility of the phenomenon in question. In fact, if Kant calls these imaginative representations "ideas" (*Vorstellungen*) rather than images, it is because they "strain after something lying out beyond the confines of experience, and so seek to approximate to a presentation of rational concepts (i.e., intellectual ideas), thus giving to these concepts the semblance of an objective reality."[39]

An imaginative representation aims to communicate more than the perceptible form of an immediate moment (the "color, light, and facts of life"). Indeed, the final goal of the artistic representation is something essential and fundamental about the phenomenon in question. But such a representation of the essential can only be essayed. And the most successful essay will be an aesthetic one, again for a reason articulated by Kant. An imaginative representation not only strains after something lying out beyond the confines of experience; it also offers a fuller representation of this idea than any concrete example: "The poet essays the task of interpreting to sense . . . rational ideas . . . [or] things to which examples occur in experience, e.g., death, envy, and all vices, as also love, fame, and the like, transgressing the limits of experience he attempts with the aide of . . . imagination . . . to body them forth to sense with a completeness of which nature affords no parallel."[40] The writer gives concrete embodiment to ideas only partially represented in rational exposition, on the one hand, and phenomenal history, on the other—ideas such as those about which no final statement is possible: faith, submission, love, revolt.

What, then, do we make of the stress and passion that is expressed by the Conradian representations? Without risking a pathetic fallacy, we cannot really say that stress inheres in an objective particular. There must first be a subject to whom the particular relates. Stress and passion record the *effect* of the moment on a sentient agent. As though to justify this fact, Conrad stresses that the sine qua non of artistic revelation is the disposition with which artistic labor is undertaken. The rescued fragment must be displayed in the light of a sincere mood, against the backdrop of the "stammerings of conscience" (in the context, that is, of the subject's not knowing how to respond to the event in question). This is the logic that makes what is "enduring and essential" in the visible world synonymous with what the artist finds convincing and believable. Unlike the objective truth of those laws, dicta, and facts discovered by the scientist and philosopher, the truth of the artist is intimately bound to this subjective element: "Confronted by the same enigmatical spectacle [as the philosopher and scientist, i.e., the visible universe] the artist descends within himself, and in that lonely region of stress and strife, if he be deserving and fortunate, he finds the terms of his appeal" (*NN* xi–xii).

Initially it appeared that the artist chose to represent certain historical phenomena rather than others on account of their intrinsic stress and passion. Now, however, it appears that this stress and passion are not qualities of things but of the artist's own soul. This paradox can be resolved by the consideration that the truth of the aesthetic idea is a function of none other than *perceptible* form, a function, that is, of the effect of the thing on a viewer, in this case the artist, who, phenomenologically speaking, "intends" that thing in a particular way and displays the intention to others. This intended reality is the aesthetic idea, fusing image and concept, thing and thought in a representation. Like the stress and the strife, the truth in question is a "third" condition, neither the objective essence of the phenomenon in question nor a merely subjective interpretation, but, rather, a unique and revelatory mediation.

The special truth of "illuminated fragments," or aesthetic ideas, is doubly revelatory, and this revelation, in turn, is doubly subversive. In themselves, historical experiences of stress and passion are especially revelatory of a sentient agent, in a way, for example, that contentment, peace, and serenity are not. At such moments the subject is divided, riven by strife, at odds with itself, revealing itself as other than a coherent and simple self-unity. Stress and passion constitute a critical revelation, as in a tragic catastrophe. As far as artistic material goes, Conrad chooses to illuminate already illuminating moments (however critical, essayistic, or "negative" the illumination they offer). What is more, once they are turned into aesthetic representations, these momentary fragments become illuminating not only in an intransitive sense (that is, convincing in themselves); they also become illuminating in a transitive sense (illuminating something beyond themselves). This subtle addition is captured in the ambiguous grammar of Conrad's statement: The artist's task is "to hold up unquestioningly . . . the rescued fragment before all eyes. . . . It is to . . . reveal the substance of its truth— disclose its inspiring secret: the stress and passion within the core of *each* convincing moment" (italics added). An aesthetically highlighted phase of life (that is, the fragment made even more disclosive than it already is) reveals the passion evoked not only by itself but by *each* convincing moment. These epiphanic events reveal more than they actually embody; their disclosure is double, immanent as well as transcendent.

The truth they disclose is also doubly subversive. What is subverted here is the habitual criterion of truth as a correspondence between language and thing (*adaequatio verba ad rem*), the conception, for example, of philosophy and science. The truthfulness of Conrad's stressful phases of life depends precisely on the fact that they escape, disrupt, or worry moral and intellectual orders, in short, the discursive codes in which we ordinarily seek to articulate the truth. In Conrad's fragments, to speak with Adorno, "the claim of the particular to truth is taken literally to the point where there is evidence of its untruth"—to the point, that is, where literal languages of explanation fail to apply.[41] The subversion goes even further. These stressful phases of life do not merely *transcend* all theoretical and practical orders of truth, in a type of aesthetic autonomy; they actively militate against them. The stress of these fragments decisively negates the very conception of truth as single, unequivocal, rational, harmonious, and noncontradictory. While Conrad and his narrators are motivated by a traditional enlightenment quest, the fragments they discover actively expose the limitations of the languages in which truth is ordinarily housed. What is at stake in this fiction of unknowing is precisely the dissolution of these habitual modes of understanding. The "untruth" of disruptive and unassimilable phases of life points to another type of truth in the light of which its conventional idioms appear untrue.

Truth thus breaks into two, if not three, dialectically related moments. On the one hand, we have the "truth" articulated in conceptual, superstructural languages (the classifications of facts, ideas, strategies, motivations, and values) and dismantled by Conrad's subversive fiction. On the other, we have Truth as a label for the essential and fundamental, but conceptually voiceless, infrastructural nature of experience, to which thought fails to do justice and which Conrad belabors to bring to light in moments aesthetically presented. Truth in the third and final sense (with neither quotes nor a capital T), the truth of the aesthetic idea, lies in the journey from the first of these conceptions toward the second. Like the dramatic experience of the awakening, the artwork traces a dynamic move from the essaying of "truth" in a negative mode to an essaying of Truth in a positive one, embodied in the aesthetic endeavor of the essay. This chapter has analyzed the first type of essayal in the service of the second. What remains to be seen is the contour of the third—the ethico-intellectual project in which the journey occurs.

2

Robert Musil

The Suspension
of the World

*In history we no longer follow the course of a spirit immanent in
the events of the world, but the curves of statistical diagrams.*
—Italo Calvino, "Cybernetics and Ghosts"

If one takes seriously arguments such as those of Ernst Mach,
Nietzsche, and other philosophers around the turn of the
century concerning the epistemological illegitimacy of all interpretations, then reality in the broadest, metaphysical sense
comes to lose its definition. In place of the recognized artificiality of ideological constructs there arises a "new infinity of
the natural," confronting a person, in Musil's words, with
"the burden of gazing into the midst of the as yet undetermined relationships of things." [1] This burden is the very start-
ing point of Musil's fiction, vividly dramatized in his first
novel, of 1906, *The Perplexities of the Pupil Törless*. The perplexed gaze of *Törless* is the dramatic correlative of a loss of
theoretical method, experienced by philosophers of the time
as the most pressing task of the intellect. [2]

At bottom, the confusions experienced by this pupil in the
course of his adventures at boarding school stem from a critical sounding, or philosophical essayal, of those symbolic lan-

guages that the "normal" social world, through its plenipo-
tentiary, the academic institution, is trying to teach him. On
one level his questions concern the actual content conveyed
by the intellectual disciplines. History, logic, mathematics,
and physics—even the moral codes and adult common sense
Törless resolves to accept at the end of the novel—do not
draw a convincing picture of what "is the case" in the world.
Neither, by consequence, do they furnish directives for action. On this level *Törless* reflects Musil's reaction to the various positivisms, phenomenologies, and transcendentalisms
he was studying in the course of obtaining his doctorate in
philosophy, as if he had already decided that the only question worthy of an intellectual was the simple question of
"right living" (*GW* 1:255, *MWO* 1:303 [62]). And yet this
final and only real issue depends upon all the others.³ Neither
Törless nor the man without qualities of the later novel will
be able to respond to this issue without first determining the
status of knowledge. Törless demands that values be based on
facts, or on precisely what the traditional sciences are unable
to grasp.

On another and deeper level, however, the pupil's confusions arise from a suspicion concerning the very form of the
symbolic disciplines, as if that were the ultimate cause of the
inadequacy of their contents. Törless's real confusions do not
concern the applications or rules of the academic sciences so
much as the legitimacy of their interpretive claims. Do these
disciplines explain experience, or do they merely schematize
its causes and effects, in laws and forces, in measurable quan-
tities and mechanical operations? And how do these disciplines legitimize their methods? "When someone is trying to
teach us mathematics," Wittgenstein remarks, as if voicing the
frustrations of the pupil, that person never begins "by assuring
us that he *knows* that a + b = b + a."⁴ It is thus the failure of
language in all its forms which disturbs Törless—not the fact
that what a certain language says may be "false" but that saying itself has not assumed a proper voice (*GW* 6:65; *YT* 86).
Within the various symbolic languages he seeks the referent:
the objective world about which they speak.

If Törless concerns himself with symbolism at all, it is only because he wants to decipher the world invariably invoked but never encapsulated by the explanations one is offered. There is nothing "mystical" in his or his author's concern; it is a desire for the same objective knowledge at which science itself aims. "If mathematics torments me," Törless explains to Beineberg, his mystical friend, "it's because I'm looking for something quite different behind it from you—what I'm after isn't anything supernatural at all, it's precisely the natural that I'm looking for" (GW 6 : 83; YT 112). But "the natural"—its subtle infinity—is precisely what has gotten lost, inextricably buried in the accounts of philosophy, science, mathematics, and logic. Part of the problem lies in the fact that the theoretical disciplines have not adequately theorized their own methods, furnishing no convincing criterion for what counts as valid data of study. For, if one agrees with Mach that experience is a sum total of sensations (as Törless's author generally does), then dreams, feelings, and the motions of "innerness" are equally, if not more, objective elements of this experience than the abstract processes and laws into which the academic disciplines have translated it. In his attempt to find a way within this forest of voiceless and symbolically transmuted sensations,

Törless was assailed by a sort of madness that made him experience things, processes, people, all as something equivocal. As something that by some ingenious operation had been fettered to a harmless explanatory word, and as something entirely strange, which might break loose from its fetters at any moment now.

True: there is a simple, natural explanation for everything, and Törless knew it too; but to his dismayed astonishment it seemed only to tear off an outer husk, without getting anywhere near laying bare what was within. (GW 6 : 64; YT 85)

Törless's ultimate confusion stems from a suspicion that the intellectual mediation of the real only envelops the real in silence, no interpretation ever penetrating beyond the surface of experience and no inscription proffering its potential meaning.

His suspicion is therefore double, and carries over to Musil's later novel, *The Man without Qualities:* that the processes of the world are irreducibly ambiguous, while the codes that transcribe them are not. What begins to take shape in these reflections is a meditation on the cognitive validity of ontology, a sense that both the subject and the object of all cognitive acts may actually be functions of a third and more primary process. Unlike his author, Törless could not have known anything about this primary process and only alludes to it as a still inarticulate problem. In the speculations of Mach, the philosopher on whom Musil wrote his dissertation, however, this primary process assumes the dignity of the "third and most important problem of science": the mobile relation of "psychophysics," or "the law of the connexion of sensations and presentations."[5] Like other thinkers at the beginning of the century, Törless is bewildered by the discovery of the inherent "perspectivism" of the understanding, by a budding intuition that things themselves are inextricable from the codes in which they are articulated. For "the real thing, the problem itself," still firmly lodged in Törless at the end of the novel, is

this shifting mental [*seelische*] perspective upon distance and closeness. . . . This incomprehensible relationship [*Zusammenhang*] that according to our shifts of standpoint gives happenings and objects sudden values that are quite incommensurable with each other, strange to each other. (*GW* 6 : 139; *YT* 188)

By the second page of the novel Musil alerts us to the potentially paralyzing consequences of this hermeneutical confusion. The young Törless gazes at life "only as through a veil." He experiences the outer world as "only a shadowy, unmeaning string of events, indifferent stations on his way, like the markings of the hours on a clock-face." This bewilderment, or *Verwirrung,* extends even to the adolescent's own relation to himself, to that subjective core he is so intent on grasping throughout his experimental experience:

Between events and himself, indeed between his own feelings and some inmost self that craved understanding of them there always remained a dividing-line [*eine Sheidelinie*], which receded before his desire, like a horizon, the closer he tried to come to it. Indeed, the more accurately he circumscribed his feelings with thoughts, and the more familiar they became to him, the stranger and more incomprehensible did they seem to become, in equal measure. Throughout his experience Törless searched for a "bridge, some connexion, some means of comparison, between himself and the wordless thing confronting his spirit" (*GW* 6 : 8, 25, 65; *YT* 12, 34–35, 87).

Musil does not succeed in resolving this bewildering problem in the years following *Törless;* he accepts it as given. What does change, however, in the twenty-four years separating *The Man without Qualities* from *Törless* is an attitude, from visible and earnest distress to ironic pleasure in intellectual entanglement. It is this shift that allows for the generic conception of *The Man without Qualities,* a tale no longer of a naked psyche struggling with a voiceless world but of a sophisticated society's self-discussions; not of an individual "trying to lip-read words from the twisted mouth of someone who's paralyzed and simply not being able to do it" but of the unending conversations of a vociferous and articulate community (*GW* 6 : 89; *YT* 119). Representation is still in crisis; however, the entire culture has now recognized it as "a mysterious disease of the times." That phrase is the title of a chapter in the later novel which refers to the epoch of Törless, from 1895 to 1906, as one still imbued with hope and glimmers of genius, and suggests the difference between *Törless* and *The Man without Qualities.* By August 1913, when the action of *The Man without Qualities* unfolds, what had gotten lost is a "prognostic," an "illusion":

Like what happens when a magnet lets the iron filings go and they tumble together again. . . . Ideas that had once been of lean account grew fat. Persons who had previously not been taken altogether seriously now acquired fame. What had been harsh mellowed down, what had been separated re-united. . . . Sharp borderlines everywhere became blurred . . . the good was adulterated with a little too much of the bad, the truth with error, and the meaning with a little too much of the spirit of accommodation (*GW* 1:57–58; *MWQ* 1:62 [16]).

Törless's personal bewilderment has assumed cultural proportions and institutional form. To discover a method for right living, the mature Törless of the later novel must begin by sorting through some of these differences and adulterations, this "good" and "bad." And to do this means first to dismantle the ideological apparatus in which the two conditions have become confused.

The first two parts of the colossal and unfinished *The Man without Qualities* are framed as a dramatic, allegorical encounter between a highly trained intellectual, Ulrich, the man without qualities, and the prewar culture, represented by the flaccid, idealistic ruling class of an empire in extremis. The reason these sophisticated liberals of the Austro-Hungarian Empire have decided to pool their mental resources is in order to plan a jubilee for the seventieth anniversary of their emperor's reign. And yet, without anyone conceiving of it in quite these terms, the reign of Emperor Franz Joseph has come accompanied by a virtually insuperable burden, the burden of an archaic and disorganized bureaucratic tradition, superimposed on mutually incompatible subcultures soon to declare their animosity in the outbreak of World War I. The centralized government of this "Emperor of Peace," as the jubilee has decided to call him, represents "merely a world that had not been cleared away," a fossilization of custom, perspective, and law. And yet, by adopting the progressive thinking of the bourgeoisie, this ruling stratum fully intends to persist in its domination of the political and intellectual world. The crowning task of the committee charged with staging the celebration is to discover a "new idea" to guide the age, one that will also show Austria "the way back to its own true nature" (*GW* 1:86–88; *MWQ* 1:97–100 [20, 21]). The ironic relation between conservatism and revolution goes even deeper than this, however, for the revolution has a reactionary origin. The Austrians have decided to celebrate 1918 only after having received wind that the German Reich is preparing to celebrate its own merely thirty-year reign in the very same year. Like its own bureaucracy, then, the Austrian campaign is "collateral" to an original fact; it is the "Collateral Campaign" (*Parallelaktion*), the "inexistent center of the novel."[6]

The Collateral Campaign, a net ensnaring the minds of the various characters of this novel, epitomizes the confusion of Vienna and all of Europe at the beginning of the century concerning its own political, moral, and metaphysical foundations. Only the man without qualities and the novel's narrator are concerned with epistemology, the science underlying all others. As a result, both those directly enlisted in the campaign ("the spirit's stewards on earth") and the sundry characters along its fringes (Clarisse, Walter, Meingast, Hans Sepp) end up seeking, each in inadequate ways, a new interpretation by which to sum up the world, a universal morality to replace or update the programs of the past. The imminent need is for a revaluation of values. An even more pressing need, but recognized as such only by Ulrich and the narrator, is a revaluation of the very means of evaluation. "At that time," writes the narrator, glancing askance at the impending war, "there were hundreds of . . . unanswered questions, all of the greatest importance. They were in the air; they were burning underfoot. The time was on the move. . . . But one simply didn't know what it was moving towards. Nor could anyone quite distinguish between what was above and what below, between what was moving forwards and what backwards" (*GW* 1:100, 13; *MWO* 1:114, 8 [24, 2]). The echo of Nietzsche's famous description of the disorientation of the world upon the death of God ("Wither are we moving? . . . Backward, sideward, forward, in all directions? Is there still any up or down?") is not incidental, for, like Nietzsche, Musil attempts to chart the vagrancy of this world unhinged from its "sun"—a sun, one begins to suspect, it never really had.[7]

One of Musil's most striking metaphors for the campaign's efforts to fetter the world to a harmless explanatory word is that of a "dot" with which people equip themselves to stare at in secret. All who submit a proposal to Ulrich, the honorary secretary of the Collateral Campaign, are unequivocally committed to a precise interpretation of the world. They have kept their eyes glued their whole lives long on

a secret dot [*Punkt*] that everyone else refuses to see, although it is so obviously the very dot from which originate all the calamities of a world that will not recognize its saviour. Such fixed points, where the person's center of gravity coincides with the world's center of gravity [providing, in mystical terms, a union of *Seelesgrund* and *Gottesgrund*], may be for instance a spittoon that can be shut with a simple catch . . . or the introduction of Öhl's shorthand system . . . or conversion to a natural mode of living, which would call a halt to the way the world is running to waste, as well as offer a metapsychical theory of the movements of celestial bodies, a plan for simplifying public administration, and a reform of sexual life. (*GW* 1:140; *MWQ* 1:162–63 [ch. 37])

The dots are metaphors for ideological reduction. As one moves up the scale from these anonymous quacks to the illustrious executive members of the campaign, the points of view become larger, more encompassing, and more spongy. Less preposterous perhaps than those outlined above, the proposals entertained by the intellectual elite of Vienna are no less facile. Count Leinsdorf envisions world harmony in the union of capital and culture (*Besitz und Bildung*); General Stumm thinks what is needed is to put some military order back into the civilian mind; Arnheim has a personal stake in the *Interresenfusion Seele-Geschäft* (the fusion of interests of soul and business); Meingast proposes a return to the creative power of will; Clarisse seeks reason in madness; Diotima, the hostess of the group's soirees, follows a more practical route, perusing the card catalog of the library before resolving on the idea of developing more workable relations of Eros than she has thus far enjoyed. Some of these are moral programs, others philosophical ones; all of them aim at formulaic control.

Chapter 108 of *The Man without Qualities* reveals the weak point of not only these formulas for world harmony but all systematizations of existence. They include some "irrational, incalculable remainder" (*irrationalen unberechenbaren Rest*) as an ultimate factor in their explanations. Religions conceive of this *Rest* as the inscrutability of God; Meingast calls it will, General Stumm understands it as honor, discipline, and "Service Regulations Part III." In the intuitive system of Bonadea's nymphomania it is called "the heart," which tempts her to commit sexual indiscretions. Although even the ingenuous Bonadea had a system, however, Austro-Hungarian politics possessed none (*GW* 2:522; *MWQ* 2:270 [109]). The terminal disease of "Kakania" (Musil's dysphemism for the *kaiserlich-königlich* empire), of which the above-mentioned thinkers are symptoms rather than cures, is its lack of an encompassing system.

The ability to invoke a system to justify one's behavior is called possessing a worldview, a Weltanschauung. And this ability, Musil adds, is something that modern citizens have lost (*GW* 2:520; *MWQ* 2:268 [108]). No doubt the loss is partly due to the fact that positivists, physicists, psychologists, and philosophers had already exposed the hidden omissions, or *Reste,* of inclusive explanations of the world.[8] Nor can there be any doubt that Musil contributes a greater share to the theoretical critiques of systems than any other novelist of the century. And no less important than his perception of ideological failure are his analyses of its consequences.

A world that no longer submits to a Weltanschauung comes finally to be experienced as a series of "remainders." The collapsing structures reveal themselves to be reliant on a plethora of first principles upon which nothing can be rationally built. If to General Stumm the intellectuals of his age seemed never to be content, it is on account of this very realization: because "their thoughts never came to rest, and beheld that eternally wandering remainder in all things, which never comes into order" (*GW* 2:519; *MWQ* 2:267 [108]). Two of these intellectuals, the protagonist and the narrator of *The Man without Qualities,* hold out indefinitely, contesting the speculations of their contemporaries precisely in the measure to which they offer facile formulations of this wandering residue, compressing the world into a dot or propounding Weltanschauungen in an age that no longer allows for them.

At this point in his investigation of systematic understanding Musil moves from a metaphor of a remainder, or residue, to a metaphor of clothing. In the same way that the systematic articulation of the residue in all things seems to impart shape to the nature of reality, so the choice of one's clothes lends personality to one's character. Admittedly, in the harmonious aesthetic experience of a well-clad body, one tends to overlook the difference between the domains so coupled. On the other hand, clothes, "if lifted out of the fluidity of the present and regarded, in their monstrous existence on a human figure, as forms *per se,* are strange tubes and excrescences, worthy of the company of a shaft through the nose or a ring extended through the lip." The remainder of this enchanting communion of signifier and signified—the final and unacknowledged factor in every explanation, is the arbitrariness of the linkage itself. It occurs no differently, Musil remarks, when a tangle of lines on a piece of paper emits some sublime meaning. The disclosive power of these figures is no less uncanny than if a halo were suddenly to pop up behind a man's head as he was putting a sandwich on his plate at a tea party. And yet "such a power of making the invisible, and even, indeed, the nonexistent, visible is what a well-made dress or coat demonstrates every day!" (*GW* 2 : 526; *MWQ* 2 : 274–75 [109]).[9]

This metaphorical exchange between form and content transcribes a strange hermeneutical circle. Based though it be on an arbitrary leap of the imagination, or on an enabling tertium quid, the disclosive effect of clothing is anything but imaginary. Clothes reveal something about us after all, for the simple reason that we chose them to begin with, pre-investing them with special significance. Clothes are "debtor-objects" (*Schuldnerdinge*): By extending them credit, we get reimbursed at an exorbitant rate of interest. "In fact," and here Musil draws a deduction on the basis of his metaphor, "there *are* only debtor-objects. This quality that clothes have is also possessed by convictions, prejudices, theories, hopes,

---

belief in anything, thoughts, indeed, even thoughtlessness possesses it, insofar as it is only by virtue of itself that it is penetrated with a sense of its own rightness" (*GW* 2 : 526; *MWQ* 2 : 275 [109]). Judgments have as convoluted a relation to the issue they address as clothes to the person who wears them. Garments of mind, as of body, are not significant in themselves but only as the consequence of some prior belief.[10]

This circular system of faith and preinvestment pervades "belief in anything." "*Credo ut intelligam,*" Musil writes a few pages after his passage on debtor-objects, is the condition for the very possibility of knowledge. Before I am able to understand, I must believe. Only through a prior decision to believe do I begin to benefit from the signifying power of the symbolic language. Conviction does not result from reflection; it enables that reflection to take direction. The belief "that in some point of knowledge one possesses absolute truth," as Nietzsche noted, is the conviction that originates the very notion of truth. "Such a belief presumes, then, that absolute truths exist; likewise, that the perfect methods for arriving at them have been found; finally, that every man who has convictions makes use of these perfect methods." Or to paraphrase the determination of the best logicians: the "first stage of logic is judgment, whose essence consists . . . in belief."[11] Every origin prefigures its end, and each investment establishes a line of credit.

As in many other passages of *The Man without Qualities,* here Musil gives figurative expression to arguments discursively unfolded by the philosophers of his time. But, as usual, his metaphorical flashes illuminate more than immediately appears. The larger ramification of consciousness is functional practice. Like Heidegger, Musil understands "preunderstanding" as a requirement of action at large. "In love as in commerce, in science as in the long jump, one has to have faith before one can win and reach one's aim." A person does not usually recognize, for example,

that he must believe he is something more in order to be capable of being what he is; he must somehow have the sense of that something more above him and around him, and yet at times [as with a Weltanschauung] he may be suddenly deprived of it. Then he lacks something imaginary. (*GW* 2:528–29; *MWQ* 2:277–78 [109])

This extension of an epistemological suspicion to the domains of practical action underscores the dependence of even the most spontaneous ethics on quasireligious, quasi-aesthetic operations. To give this principle a more modern formulation is to say, with Althusser, that "there is no practice except by and in an ideology." [12] Not only to understand, but even to act, one must jump from an *Abgrund* to unfounded principles.

An example of the anxiety this situation can provoke in a person who demands coherence between life and thought can be found on Törless's obsession with the unreal reality of mathematical operations. The fact that rational calculations can be successfully made on the basis of imaginary numbers (such as i, the square root of -1) exposes the uncanny function of those remainders accompanying cognitive endeavors and the data they yield. Törless carries his perplexity straight to his math teacher, who tries to dispel the student's questions by invoking Kant's *Critique of Pure Reason,* a work, he says, that "treats of the grounds determining our actions" (*die Bestimmungsstücke unseres Handelns*) and furnishes "those mental necessities [*Denknotwendigkeiten*] . . . which . . . determine everything although they themselves cannot be understood immediately." But, after reading Kant, Törless is all the more sure: "There's nobody who knows where the first mesh is that keeps all the rest in place" (*GW* 6:77, 82; *YT* 103, 110).

Thus it would seem that a hermeneutical analysis of belief leads in one of two directions, either to a circle of broken connections or to an originary and primordial silence. For life to be possible this silence must be filled at all costs, even the cost of error. And this is precisely what happens. The filling is accomplished by a primal delusion (*Verblendung*) called understanding. Only by means of this *Verblendung*, writes Musil, do we manage "to live alongside the most uncanny things and remain perfectly calm about it because we recognize those frozen grimaces of the universe as a table or chair,

---

Musil: The Suspension of the World

a shout or an outstretched arm, a speed or a roast chicken." This reduction of the universe into the solid and pragmatic constituents of a stable worldview amounts to a "vivisection" that Musil retraces in thought.[13] If we ordinarily succeed in living between one open abyss of sky (*Himmelsabgrund*) above our heads and one slightly camouflaged abyss of sky beneath our feet, it is only thanks to the fact "that in between them we treat a stratum of forms [*Schichte von Gebilden*] as the things of the world." When one takes stock of this conscious stratification of the surroundings, one concludes that it is

> an extremely artificial state of mind that enables man to walk upright between the circling constellations and permits him, in the midst of the almost infinite unknownness of the world around him, to place his hand with dignity between the second and third buttons of his coat.

And, in order to achieve this state of mind,

> not only does every person need his own artifices [*Kunstgriffe*] . . . but these personal systems of artifice are . . . artfully built into the institutions for the maintenance of society's and the community's moral and intellectual equilibrium [*Gleichgewichtsvorkehrungen der Gesellschaft und Gesamtheit*]. (*GW* 2:526−27; *MWQ* 2:275−76 [109])

Metaphysically speaking, the "infinity of the natural" has always been the horizon for life; but through a series of perceptual reductions it has been compressed into a Weltanschauung, or relegated to the status of the worldview's unknowable remainder. Whatever the system devised, it offers a fictitious economy, built of the hypothetical "entities" imagined by the codification.

There is undoubtedly something arbitrary about this stratum of forms constitutive of an interpreted world. Whether they be an oven, a smile, a political choice (or Heidegger's *Vor-* and *Zuhandene*), they segment the real into partial unities. Psychologically, they are the qualities (the *Eigenschaften*) defining a person's character; philosophically, they are the synthetic results of inductive and deductive reasoning; morally, they are the concepts of "duty," "responsibility," and "freedom." One wonders whether such concepts take shape purely by chance or on the basis of some historical apriority? In Musil's time the issue at stake was called the phenomenological constitution of the world: the appearance of experience as always already shaped for human purposes. The question of the actual logistics of this constituted appearance is then open to discussion. Two voices in this debate bear particular relevance for Musil: Ernst Mach and Edmund Husserl.[14]

Experience in itself, writes Mach in the *Analysis of Sensations* (1886), is an indeterminate fluctuation of sensations without any laws of its own, without substances, identities, causes, or repetitions. "Nature exists only once, it knows no repetition of the same cases." Logical order and scientific patterns are merely read into this nature as the mind translates it into concept, that is, through a simplification, schematization, and idealization of facts. Physical necessity does not exist, Mach affirms; "there exists only logical necessity," which is in turn a psychological necessity, or requirement of thought.[15] The result is that the random flux of experience is structured as a stratum of forms, causes, effects, and regularities which goes by the name of reality (or actuality, *Wirklichkeit*), which, needless to say, is structured differently in different communities of mind. What goes by the name of reality is "in great measure *conventional* and *accidental*," and in no way an accurate reflection of the way things are.[16]

Husserl, a staunch critic of Mach on a number of scores, shares Mach's belief that the world is symbolically shaped by consciousness. Before the world can be experienced at all it must have already submitted to a "transformation." The ordinary or traditional course of human experience "compels our reason to pass beyond intuitively given things . . . and place at their basis a 'physical truth.'" And yet this course of experiences and the "physical truth" that it comes to posit "might also have been differently ordered." If, for instance, an experimental formation or scientific principle had never been articulated, "the physical world might have been other than it is with systems of law other than those actually prevailing." In general one can conclude that "the whole *spatio-temporal world . . . is . . . mere intentional Being,*" or "reality" as the mind happens to intend it. History and nature do not consist in a hard order of fact, as the "natural attitude" has it; their appearance is constituted by consciousness. Objective reality, or the "being which for us is first," is therefore "in itself second." With regard to its own essence, reality "lacks independence." It "is not in itself something absolute . . . it has no 'absolute essence' whatsoever." Once one grants the mental constitution of experience, then "'the real world,' as it is called, the correlate of our factual experience . . . presents itself as *a special case of various possible worlds and non-worlds.*"[17]

Even so, the phenomenal world is not merely a fabrication of consciousness, as though one pole of the psycho-physical relation were doing all the work. There is "another" Mach in addition to the first one (and in addition to this Husserl), who recognizes that sensations are not always indeterminate and fluctuant but sometimes perceived from the start in clusters. As in the experience of a melody, these relationships, organizations, and connections are given in the perceptions of sensations themselves, not added to the sensations by thought. Immediate experience can occur in a phenomenology of patterns, partial unities, or *Gestalten.*[18]

At the end of his dissertation Musil notes that there is "a conflict in Mach's own views" according to which experience is defined as pure indeterminacy, on the one hand, and, on the other, as intrinsically patterned. Musil remarks that, while the logical ordering of reality by means of science is undoubtedly fictional in procedure, the procedure is not entirely arbitrary or independent of "objective facts." It is experience itself that offers blatant regularities; science merely attempts to furnish theoretical correlates of such perceptions. "This regularity which first induces us to deduce a necessity is thus found in facts," writes Musil. "And naturally it cannot be eliminated from facts by means of idealization; on the contrary . . . it is at the basis of every step accomplished by such idealization; idealization is motivated in facts." The necessity Mach calls purely logical is therefore "not necessity proper; on the contrary, it is necessity only if to begin with there exists that other necessity which resides in facts, even if we never completely grasp its real structure with the means at our disposal" (*B* 124, 122–23; *MT* 80, 79, 80).

There is thus another, not merely mental, necessity also at work in the formation of reality in patterns, regularities, and repetitions. It is a necessity which might best be understood in the context of a metaphysics characteristic of this entire European epoch: vitalism, or *Lebensphilosophie.*

According to the general lines of this philosophy of life which bridges the period between Nietzsche and Henri Bergson, the idealization of facts is a symptom of life itself as a self-formative process. Experience is self-production and "will to form," a thrust toward expansion and growth which actualizes itself in appearances and values. This self-formation is also a type of self-representation, an activity of "fictionalization." As life becomes and articulates itself, perspectives, positions, and productions overcome their predecessors, literally making the real unreal and the unreal real. In this framework consciousness is only *one* of the operators of fictionalization, partaking of a process already inherent to experience. It simply happens to be the easiest place to see this perspectival production of the world occurring.

It is this self-productive process of life which causes the institution of functional, pragmatic relationships between a plurality of possibilities, actions, elements, and structures mutually determining each other. Practice gives birth to its own regulations. "It is not thought," remarks Musil in one of his essays, "but merely the need for practical orientation which compels the formation of stereotypes [*Formelhaftigkeit*], in fact, the stereotypes of concepts no more than those of gestures and sensory impressions, which after a couple of repetitions become as numb as the representational processes tied to words."[19] In the same reading character is at once a fictitious and historical unity: "a tendency to repetition one has acquired involuntarily" (*GW* 1 : 252; *MWQ* 1 : 299 [62]). History has its own necessity independent of mind; it simply happens to be an "unlawful necessity" (*ungesetzliche Notwendigkeit*), or a contingent mechanicity endowed with merely practical motivation.[20]

The Man without Qualities invokes this metaphysics of patterns, structures, and unities as often as it does a metaphysics of fluctuation, indeterminacy, and irrationality. What seems always to happen in experience, for instance, is that "every play of forces tends . . . towards an average value and an average condition, a compromise and a state of inertia." It is as if, alongside its thrust toward self-transformation, experience has an equal tendency to perdure in whatever state it happens to have achieved. The forms and values in which life has been actualized thus frustrate its own will to form. What then grows susceptible to one's mistrust, thinks the man without qualities, "is the cut-and-dried way that life is divided up and the ready-made forms it assumes, the ever-recurring sameness of it [*das Seinesgleichen*], the pre-formations passed down by generation after generation, the ready-made language not only of the tongue but also of the sensations and feelings" (*GW* 1 : 251, 129; *MWQ* 1 : 298, 149–50 [62, 34]). As form gets the better of content, the condition of becoming fossilizes into that of being. The creative mobility of experience congeals into an image of itself, a self-representation or approximation. And this petrification of a state of affairs composes the reality on which a community bases its reality principles. Indeed, "its likeness occurs" or "the like of it happens" is the title of Part 2 of *The Man without Qualities* (*Seinesgleichen geschieht*), the five hundred pages housing the bulk of the novel's narrative events, those fictional but all too actual "occurrences" of human experience.[21] History evolves as a manifestation of its own self-appearance, as random congealments of the real into mere self-likenesses.

The implications of this practically motivated necessity are many. Regardless of one's creative efforts and original leaps, in the course of time "one's ordinary and non-personal ideas intensify quite of their own accord and the extraordinary ones fade . . . with all the certainty of a mechanical process." Whether what attempts to take shape is a thing, a lifestyle, or even an intuition, its self-codification belies its more extensive potential. Sometimes, for example, one may seem to have an entirely personal mental experience. The minute one articulates it, however, it "no longer has the form of the thought [*des Gedankens*] in which it was experienced, but already that of the thing thought [*des Gedachten*]," and, unfortunately, this form is "a non-personal one, for the thought is then extroverted and adjusted for communication to the world." When we pride ourselves on having discovered the solution to a problem through a flash of inspiration, we claim responsibility for an act that occurs no less mechanically than that of a dog trying to get through a narrow door with a stick in its mouth: "it goes on turning its head left and right until the stick slips through." [22] Likewise, the clue to every human personality resides in an "impersonal element," in "certain simple and fundamental patterns of behaviour, an ego-building instinct, like the nest-building instinct of birds, by which the ego is constructed of many materials according to a few methods." Indeed, for all the apparent differences among a thousand human beings, once you analyze them "all you're left with is two dozen qualities, forms of development, constructive principles [*Ablaufarten, Aufbauformen*], and so on, which is all they consist of" (*GW* 1 : 112, 252, 66; *MWQ* 1 : 129, 299, 72 [28, 62, 17]).

This selfsame pattern of forms and likenesses penetrates even the recesses of one's subjectivity. The most unique and personal experiences become data fed "on to the stage, into books, into the reports of scientific institutions and expeditions, into communities based on religious or other convictions." That is, they return to the subject in a theorized, stereotyped, and "formulized" form that is no longer the original one. It is no surprise that such formulations as narcissism, paranoia, and the Oedipus complex then structure the experiences of others. Even one's innermost passions are modeled on preexistent models. "One loves because there is love, and in the way that love has always been; one is proud as an Indian, a Spaniard, a virgin, or a lion; indeed, in ninety out of a hundred cases even murder is committed only because it is considered tragic and magnificent" (*GW* 1:150, 2:365; *MWQ* 1:174, 2:73 [39, 84]).

Whatever the cause of this stereotypical and lawless necessity that goes by the name of history—whether logical, practical, or a paradoxical law of vitalistic becoming—the question inevitably arises, for Ulrich, as it did earlier for Törless, whether what one is experiencing in those preformations is really "*my* truth": "The goals, the voices, the reality, the seduction of it all, luring and leading one on," thinks Ulrich, "all that one follows and plunges into—is it the real reality or does one still get no more than a breath of the real, a breath hovering intangibly on the surface of the reality one is offered?" (*GW* 1:129; *MWQ* 1:149 [34]). As one's "own" truth begins to appear derivative, subjectivity loses its authenticity.

If a young man is intellectually alive, reflects Ulrich, he is continually sending out ideas in all directions. "But only what produces resonance in his environment will radiate back to him and condense, whereas all the other messages are scattered in space and lost." One cannot help experiencing, he continues, a "disquieting feeling of 'everything I think I am reaching is reaching me,' a gnawing surmise that in this world the untrue, careless, and personally most unimportant utterances will echo more strongly than one's own inmost, most real ones" (*GW* 1:116, 129; *MWQ* 1:134, 149 [29, 34]). Two questions immediately arise: Does this functional process of impersonal structures afford any opportunity at all for individual expression? Or is the personal, subjective domain structured just as mechanically as the setting in which it operates? Perhaps, that is, the two are imprisoned in what the biologist Johannes von Uexküll called a functional circle (*Funktionskreis*) of receptor and effector systems (*Merknetz* and *Wirknetz*), the former prestructuring an organism's receptivity to outward stimuli and the latter its possible reactions.[23] Musil tends to lean in the second direction, conceiving of modern history as an arena of "qualities without a man, of experiences without anyone to experience them," a situation that effects a "dissolution of the anthropocentric attitude" (*GW* 1 : 150; *MWQ* 1 : 174–75 [39]).[24]

This structuralization of vital flux might be bearable if it did not enforce a normalization of the elements composing it. Necessary as history may be, all too often it manifests an unnecessary absence of originality, a conventionalism repressing its own potential. The regularities are excessive, the conformity unimaginative. Instead of realizing the "fullness of life's possibilities," culture propagates models that have long since lost their motivation. One might conceive of the organized articulation of life in two separate moments. In its productive moment this articulation is actual spiritual formation, or culture in the sense of *Bildung*, by which symbols and relationships are actively produced and function as instructive, formative principles. In a subsequent and negative moment these principles degenerate into formulas, outliving themselves in a backward glance, reducing themselves to rules of thumb, tokens of what may once have been meaningfully "the case." Culture (*Kultur*) degenerates into civilization (*Zivilization*).[25] The historical epoch depicted in *The Man without Qualities* is a world of the latter, a world already formulized, in which once vital forms now reproduce themselves in their own self-likenesses, copies of copies, duplicated and transmitted as equivalent to what they represent. At this moment of sterility history is derived from its own derivations, leaving Diotima disturbed by the fact that the cultural continuity of "problems affecting one's own humanity so closely as . . . the noble simplicity of Greece, or the meaning of the prophets, resolved themselves . . . into an immense variety of doubts and possibilities," or into that "affliction from which modern man is well known to suffer and which is called civilisation. It is a frustrating state of affairs, full of soap, wireless waves, the arrogant symbolic language of mathematical and chemical formulae, economics, experimental research and mankind's inability to live in simple but sublime community" (*GW* 1 : 102–3; *MWQ* 1 : 117 [24]). In the era of civilization what was once understood as the unitary unfolding of "History" has lost its cogency.[26] It has dissolved into a pluralistic inconsistency of localized practices and discourses, codes and structures, mutually incommensurable principles of development.

Through this formulization of the world, things, feelings, and people lose their "essences" and ontological status. Reality turns into a context of assignments and references, a system of relations volatilizing and simulating the being of the world.[27] Entities become variables in encompassing formulas, signifiers in normative linguistic systems. The real world of the twentieth century is not composed of Wilhelm Dilthey's "lived experience" but merely its derived and reflected forms. The probability of learning something unusual from a newspaper, as Ulrich reflects, "is far greater than that of experiencing it; in other words, it is in the realm of the abstract that the more important things happen in these times, and it is the unimportant that happens in real life." Thus what may have once been viewed as a solid and authentic basis for the production of meaning—whether a value, a personality, an intention, a body of knowledge, a faith, a desire, a feeling, or a decisive historical event—has turned into an element in a self-referential system. Even something as material and tangible as water begins to lose its historical self-evidence. Long ago it was believed to be "akin to air." Then "water-sprites, elves, mermaids and nymphs were invented. Temples and oracles were founded on its banks and shores":

And there now was water, a colourless liquid, blue only in dense layers, odourless and tasteless . . . , although physiologically it also included bacteria, vegetable matter, air, iron, calcium sulphate and calcium bicarbonate, and this archetype of all liquids was, physically speaking, fundamentally not a liquid at all but, according to circumstances, a solid body, a liquid or gas. Ultimately the whole thing dissolved into systems of formulae that were all somehow connected with each other, and in the whole wide world there were only a few dozen people who thought alike about even as simple a thing as water.

Of those who bothered to think about water only a few dozen agreed; the rest proceeded to talk about it "in languages that were at home somewhere between today and several thousands of years ago" (*GW* 1:69, 112–13; *MWQ* 1:76, 129:30 [18, 28]).

The formulization of the world produces both an automatism of perception and a proliferation of forms devoid of their once self-evident function.[28] Realities give way to Husserl's "unities of meaning," virtual significances, secondary elements of an uncertain primary process. The formulas encapsulating such unities are no longer sustained by "spiritual motivation"; they originate that motivation by chance and suggestion. In fact, the very notions of motivation—of governing intention, personal experience, and even a "subject"—now appear as naivetés, fictions that were credible only when thought was oblivious of its own mechanics.

To put it in the terms Musil wields so ironically (namely, those appropriate to the "skim-romanticism and yearning for God that the machine-age had for a time squirted out"), by the second decade of the century it had come to seem that spirit (*Geist*) lacked spirit. For, in post-Kantian usage, spirit means both the motivation of historical becoming and also its "phenomenology," its formal result. However ironic the context in which he places the project, Musil, like many of his contemporaries, was concerned with recuperating spirit at the "first" and deeper level—not as the arbitrary sum of its formal expressions but as the formative process itself, the self-configuring whole. At this deeper level *Geist* is a word for that all-pervading *pneuma*, or breath, diffused throughout the universe and holding all contraries together in tension, the "sympathy of the Whole" of the ancient Stoics. *Geist*, writes Musil, "mixes things up, unravels them, and forms new combinations." It was in deference to this *Geist* that the man without qualities lived so undecidedly. "Undoubtedly— he said to himself—what banished him to an aloof and anonymous form of existence was nothing but the compulsion to that loosing and binding of the world that is known

by a word one does not like to encounter alone: spirit,"
Arnheim, his arch-antagonist, is willing to admit this much
about his young colleague: "the man had reserves of as
yet unexhausted soul." For in the course of time, Arnheim
goes on to explain, "every human being . . . dissolves his
soul in intelligence, morality, and lofty ideas . . . and in this
his best-beloved enemy the process had not been completed"
(*GW* 1 : 103, 153, 2 : 548; *MWQ* 1 : 118, 178–79, 2 : 112 [25,
40, 112]).

How can one define this soul, or spirit, that eludes its own
forms of expression? Certainly not positively, as Ulrich's contemporaries attempt to do. Rather, it is the illusion of something still missing from the lawless relations. Negatively put,
the soul "is simply what curls up and hides when there is any
mention of algebraic series" (*GW* 1 : 103; *MWQ* 1 : 118 [25]).
It is related to what Törless senses as the ambiguity underlying and belying all clear and distinct ideas. Why, after all, do
things appear odd to him which seem perfectly ordinary
to others? What is it about them that makes them seem
strange? "Something about them that I don't know about,"
Törless concludes. "But that's just it! Where on earth do I get
this 'something' [*Etwas*] from? I feel its existence; it affects
me; just as if it were trying to speak" (*GW* 6 : 89; *YT* 119). In
his intuition that everything "is fluctuating, a part of a whole,
of innumerable wholes that presumably belong to a super-
whole [*Überganze*], which, however, he doesn't know the
slightest thing about," Ulrich senses the same thing as Törless,
though less as an inlying essence than as an encompassing
relation. While his contemporaries are content to abbreviate
the universe into partial schemas, formulas, and systems
cum remainder, Ulrich seeks that order of the whole which
transcends every secondary distinction. "He wants as it were
the wood and the others the trees" (*GW* 1 : 65, 17; *MWQ*
1 : 71, 13 [17, 4]).

The *Etwas* that Ulrich seeks is the entirety of *Geist*, which
is missing in each of its manifestations. In Husserl's terms,
Ulrich is intent on "making the world absolute in a *philosophical* sense" (which "is wholly foreign to the way in which

we naturally look out upon the world").[29] He is searching for a "magic formula, a lever that one might be able to get a hold of, the real spirit of the spirit [*den eigentlichen Geist des Geistes*], the missing, perhaps very small, bit that would close the broken circle." But the circle cannot be closed. Nor can the essence of things, which they never had, be discovered. All that can be done is to recuperate the possibility of forming new empirical combinations: the constructive first moment of *Geist*. With his reserves of as yet unexhausted soul, Ulrich "was the expression of nothing but this dissolved condition [*dieses aufgelöste Wesen*] that all phenomena are in nowadays," an expression, that is, of the fallen moment of this *Geist* (*GW* 1 : 155, 65; *MWQ* 1 : 181, 72 [40, 17]). His task will be that of bringing about the other.

If spirit, or soul, is dissolved in intelligence and ideas, Arnheim's remark makes it clear that the soul is equally lost in moral conventions. In the last completed chapter of *The Man without Qualities* which Musil himself saw to press, Ulrich draws a firm distinction between the ordinary conception of morality—the catalog of mores that regulate human behavior—and the source of these regulations, or morality proper. Morality was for Ulrich "neither conformism [*Botmässigkeit*] nor the sum of acquired knowledge, but living out the infinite fullness of life's possibilities" (*GW* 3 : 1028; *MWQ* 3 : 431 [38]).[30] In these figures of spirit, soul, morality, and sometimes will in *The Man without Qualities,* we observe the slow emergence of tentative gestalt for the real. But it is a reality that can be manifested only in a tentative and self-constructive fashion. The *Etwas* Törless senses at the bottom of things is akin to a "moral energy" (*moralische Kraft*), a "spiritual force" (*seelische Kraft*) (*GW* 6 : 25; *YT* 34). "Morality is imagination," the narrator declares in the later work, and this is something that history has not come close to deploying. While the methodologies of reason, science, and technological organization have progressed at a staggering pace, the imagination that applies such methods has remained "fixed and closed." Alongside the selective systematization of selfsame forms and qualities there stands "a mound of broken shards, which are feelings, ideas, and life's potentialities, heaped up in strata just as they came into existence—always no more than side-issues—and subsequently were discarded" (GW 3 : 1028; MWQ 3 : 431 [38]).

We can now understand why Törless views the outer world only as through a veil, as an indifferent, shadowy, unmeaning string of events. Three steps have been involved: the world has been dissociated from consciousness; it has dissolved into formulas beyond which nothing substantial is visible; and this realization has instilled a moral confusion. Recognizing what Husserl calls "the detachability in principle of the whole natural world from the domain of consciousness,"[31] Törless has witnessed the "failure of that power of association which generally causes our life to be faultlessly reflected in our understanding, as though life and understanding ran parallel to each other and at equal speed" (GW 6 : 64; YT 85). What exists "already *realiter*" for Törless is only one among many possible determinations within "the undetermined . . . marginal field of [his] factual experience at the time being." Confronting the purely "hypothetical construction of practical life," Törless considers this construction infinitely relativized by its spectrum of potential significances, by "this shifting but ever-present horizon through which the world-thesis receives its essential meaning."[32] Things have become indistinguishable from the codes in which they are articulated, without the help of an interpretive key. The question "What for?" arises and goes unanswered.

The fragmented and unpersuasive world thesis has a comparable effect on the man without qualities. The book, we remember, opens with Ulrich's plan to take a year's leave from life. Feeling like "a traveller sitting down on a bench for eternity," he decides there is no reason to do anything until he has discovered an appropriate way of using his abilities. The first picture of the man without qualities shows him attempting to apply some objective measure to this unreal actuality. Standing at the window trying to calculate the energy consumed by people "doing nothing at all," Ulrich shrugs his shoulders and thinks, "It doesn't matter what one does. . . . In a tangle of forces like this it doesn't make a scrap of difference." He turns from the window "like a man who has learned renunciation, almost indeed like a sick man who shrinks from any intensity of contact." His epistemological research has produced its moral effects. And yet the burden of gazing into the still undetermined relations of things marks only the beginning of Ulrich's ethical project. Striding past the punching ball that hung in his dressing room, the man without qualities "gave it a blow far swifter and harder than is usual in moods of resignation or states of weakness" (*GW* 1:19, 47, 13; *MWQ* 1:16, 49, 8 [5, 13, 2]).

We supply Ulrich's thoughts and feelings as they develop throughout the book. His life has "run out of the sense of necessity as a lamp runs out of oil," leaving him with nothing to fall back on but the "resistance of a primal instinct against this world petrified into millions of tons of stone, against this rigid lunar landscape of feeling into which one had been set down with no will of one's own." This "unlawful necessity" bears witness to a world from which "God withdrew his credit." Nowhere can one discover "any sufficient reason for everything's having come about as it has. It might just as well have turned out differently" (*GW* 2:593, 1:130, 2:259, 1:131; MWQ 2:361, 1:150, 2:278, 1:151 [116, 34, 109, 34]). Historical actuality was ruled by the "Principle of Insufficient Reason," like the haphazard organization of a "a bad play." The same roles, complications, and plots always kept arising. The motivating concepts of actions were only "metaphors that [had] been left to congeal." Ulrich can therefore see no motive "to attach more importance to what is than to what is not" (*GW* 2:364, 574, 1:16; *MWQ* 2:73, 337, 1:12 [84, 114, 4]). The only thing to do, he decides, is to abolish reality entirely.

God, Ulrich thinks, "is far from meaning the world literally; it is an image, an analogy, a turn of phrase [*ein Bild, eine Analogie, eine Redewendung*], which he must make use of for some reason or other, and it is of course always inadequate; we must not take him at his word, we ourselves must work

---

out the sum that he sets us."[33] In fact, only when taken literally does the figurative process of life degenerate into a petrified mass of formulas, correlates of an inflexible reality principle. And that is precisely when one should think of abolishing it. One must abolish the real and "regain possession of unreality [*sich wieder der Unwirklichkeit bemächtigen*]." To regain possession of unreality would mean to erase all the congealed metaphors and "upholstery of fatty tissue that . . . makes reality look round and plump" (*GW* 2 : 357, 575, 573; *MWQ* 2 : 65, 338, 336 [83, 114]). It would mean recalculating the sum of unreal and unspirited reality principles in accordance with the selective principle of artist and reader, who leave out of the story everything they have no use for. The task, however approached (and mysticism is admittedly one, though not the most disciplined, solution), becomes that of "transforming the world's haphazard state of consciousness into a single will." At that point one would act as though in a dream or fantasy, not letting one's emotions succumb to the "medial condition" of reality but developing them instead "to their full passionate intensity." Rather than the history of the world, one would live the history of ideas, "in the manner of art," like a character in a book (*GW* 1 : 251, 2 : 573, 367, 573; *MWQ* 1 : 298, 2 : 336, 77, 336 [62, 114, 84, 114]).

All these are metaphors for metaphor itself, for experience as a figurative process, in which repossessing oneself of unreality means nothing less than restoring the "primal condition of life" (*GW* 2 : 574; *MWQ* 2 : 337 [114]). It is easy to see that this restoration envisions art as the real task of life, art "as life's *metaphysical* activity."[34] One should stress, however, that this vision implies neither an aestheticist negation of nor a subjective flight from the objective order of things.[35] For it is the objective order itself that contains this "nonsensical yearning for unreality [*Unwirklichkeit*]" as the motivating principle of its constitution (in which, one might add, the subject is never anything more than a single formation). It is this yearning for unreality which "actualizes" the real in an exclusionary forest of symbolic forms, as though showing that incorrigible tendency toward abstraction that Musil's contemporary Wilhelm Worringer derives from humanity's "spiritual space-phobia [*geistige Raumscheu*]."[36] Even the person most compulsively committed to reality has an entirely figurative relationship to concrete experience. In truth, "reality is something that the worthy practical realist [*Wirklichkeitmensch*] does not ever wholly love and take seriously":

As a child he crawls under the table, when his parents are not at home, by this brilliantly simple trick making their living-room into a place of adventure; as a growing boy he hankers after a watch of his own; as the young man with the gold watch he longs for the woman to go with it; as a mature man with watch and wife he hankers after a prominent position; and when he has successfully attained the fulfillment of this little circle of wishes and is calmly swinging to and fro in it like a pendulum, it nevertheless seems that his store of unsatisfied dreams has not diminished by one jot, for when he wants to rise above the rut of every day he will resort to a simile [*Gleichnis*]. Obviously because snow is at times disagreeable to him, he compares it to women's glimmering breasts, and as soon as his wife's breasts begin to bore him, he compares them to glimmering snow. . . . He is capable of turning everything into anything—snow into skin, skin into blossoms, blossoms into sugar, sugar into powder, and powder back into little drifts of snow—for all that matters to him, apparently, is to make things into what they are not. (*GW* 1 : 138; *MWQ* 1 : 160–61 [37])

Musil is doing more than underscoring the irony that the most deluded dreamer of all is the practical realist, gazing at a dot that shifts and recedes with every present horizon. He is making a metaphysical assertion, to the effect that "even ordinary life is of a Utopian nature." This answers Ulrich's question of "why all figurative [*uneigentlichen*] and (in the higher sense of the word) untrue utterances were so uncannily favoured by the world." No sooner are the structures of reality erected than they are resisted by the force of a dream. And the stronger the dream, the less willing is the dreamer to give it life. Is there anyone, Ulrich asks, "who would not be at a loss if whatever he had been passionately demanding all his life long were suddenly to happen? If for instance the Kingdom of God were suddenly to burst on the Catholics or the Utopian State on the Socialists? . . . One gets used to demanding and isn't ready at a minute's notice for the realisation of it" (*GW* 2 : 363, 1 : 148, 288; *MWQ* 2 : 72, 1 : 172, 342 [84, 39, 69]). Regaining possession of unreality would simply mean taking this utopian compulsion to its practical conclusion, rectifying the fact that the development of reality "is at least one hundred years behind [that of] thought" (*LWW* 339). Like the Collateral Campaign, life should be made to provide "an opportunity . . . for giving practical reality to the things one believed greatest and most important." It should bring "ideas into the domains of power," rather than banishing them to the realm of dream (*GW* 1 : 93, 109; *MWQ* 1 : 106, 125 [22, 26]).

What Musil has in mind with the appropriation of unreality involves not idealistically negating the objective order but liberating the idealization of facts; not turning "life into art" but turning art into life; not imposing arbitrary form on things but allowing their forms to develop less arbitrarily than usual.[37] If anything, Musil agrees with Lenin's and Lukács' critiques of the implicit idealism and subjectivism of Machian empiriocriticism on which he was nourished.[38] Beneath Ulrich's fantasy of reinventing reality lies essentially the same conception of the twofold responsibility of art by which Lukács presumed to call writers like Musil to task: to depict the "dynamic infinity" and "intensive inexhaustibility" of objective particulars; and to reorganize these particulars in a new extensive order.[39] Far from "abstracting reality out of existence," as Lukács claims, Musil is interested in rediscovering reality's intensive and extensive dynamic. What he asks of both art and life is that they formulate an "actual idealism" at equal remove from naturalistic acceptance and subjectivist wish. Naturalism, he writes in his essay on Spengler, had offered "reality without spirit, expressionism spirit without reality: both of them non-spirit [*Ungeist*]" (*GW*

8 : 1059; *PS* 149). Or, in the words of a discarded preface to *Nachlaβ zu Lebzeiten,* poetry should "describe not what is, but what should be; or what could be as a partial solution to what should be" (*GW* 7 : 970).

And thus Musil transcends the mimetic aesthetics of orthodox Marxism in the same utopian direction as Theodor Adorno. Allowing for the "moment of unreality and nonexistence" in art, Adorno stresses that such a moment "is not independent of the existent, as though it were posited or invented by some arbitrary will." Aiming to undo "the conceptualization foisted on the real world," art must necessarily "slough off a repressive, external-empirical mode of experiencing the world." To achieve a synthesis of not this order but its *membra disiecta* (scattered members), art must dialectically negate the ruling metaphors of a historical existence and give voice to what they exclude. And, though it is impossible to bring it to any final fruition, such a synthesis represents nothing but a higher and more sophisticated operation of *Geist,* a development of the same "principle whereby spirit has dominated the world."[40]

If there is anything inadequate about the way this spirit has ruled the world, it lies not merely in the fact that spirit has shown insufficient motivation but also that it has consistently settled for a univocal, narrative order, a linear chronology, a slow conceptual progress, a one-way schema of agents and actions, and causes and effects (the order that critics like Lukács then ask artists to mime, demanding that they display the "stable" determinations of things in the greatest possible "purity, clarity, and typicality").[41] No doubt, the narrator of *The Man without Qualities* reflects, there are people who still experience the world in terms of these personal narratives, "saying 'we were at So-and-So's yesterday' or 'we'll do this or that today'" (*GW* 1 : 150; *MWQ* 1 : 175 [39]), but the schema is too limiting, unduly exclusive, and mechanically selective. Musil sees the need to replace this paradigm of personal, logical, and diachronic order—which is not the way things occur at all—with another based on more flexible and multiple functional relations. To grasp both the intensive and extensive determinations of things, one must suspend both "narrative order" and the world it has produced in deference to essayistic order. Essayistic order alone can allow for a constructive determination of potential.

3

Luigi Pirandello

The Mechanical
Phantasmagoria

In 1921, seventeen years after *The Late Mattia Pascal* was first published, Pirandello addressed a criticism of his readers that the story was not realistic. Critics were dissatisfied with the novel, Pirandello explains in his appendix to the third edition, because of the unpredictability of its main events, the improbability of the story line, and that most grievous of sins, the absence of moral teaching. The criticism was mainly based on the aesthetics of *verismo* (verism), which Pirandello himself had followed in the early stages of his career, in which the novelist was expected to offer an impersonal representation of the objective forms of everyday living.[1] Causes and effects were to be tied in a chain of logical necessity, and the narrative order that ensued was to be readily detectable to the eye of a positivist (a style Pirandello parodies in *One, None and a Hundred Thousand*).[2] The narrative order espoused by *verismo* found analogous support in the work of Lukács, undiscovered though it was at that time in Italy, which asked that an artwork express not only the typical and normative nature of particular phenomena but also the essential "determinants" of this particularity (namely, its material and social history).

Measured by such criteria, the plot of *The Late Mattia Pascal* was indeed improbable. On an impulse Mattia Pascal leaves home and finds himself headed for Monte Carlo, where unlikely good fortune wins him an extraordinary sum at roulette. On his way home a few days later he obtains a copy of his local newspaper and discovers that he has been pronounced dead. His wife and two marshals have identified the body of a man found dead in a ditch as him. Elated to be freed from his wife, his mother-in-law, and his debts, Pascal changes his identity and becomes a professional tourist, eventually settling in Rome. His new life, however, proves increasingly boring and unproductive. He is unable to function freely without avowing his material and social history; he is unable even to report a theft or marry. Better his mother-in-law and a provincial life, he concludes, than this existence with no solid coordinates. He feigns a second death, leaving his coat, his hat, and a note with the words of his alias, Adriano Meis, on the Ponte Margherita over the Tiber and returns home. There, however, he finds that no one but the librarian recognizes him. His wife has remarried and has born a child to his friend Pomino. Pascal takes it all in stride. Laboring to reestablish his civil status, he entertains himself with visits to the grave of his unknown double.

Pirandello is willing to admit that this story might be criticized on the level of artistic technique. It may be poorly constructed or poorly written. But as far as the veristic objections are concerned, they cannot stand, for the simple reason that life itself has a blatant contempt for verisimilitude. It refuses to conform to those categories of probability, unity, order, causality, typicality, and consistency that are foisted on art in the name of life itself—in the name, that is, of "the essential determinants of experience." Happily filled with "shameless absurdities," life has the rare privilege "of being able to ignore credibility."[3] Why then should art be held to task for what is lacking in reality? The logic is askew. "Life's absurdities," Pirandello writes in this appendix called "A Warning on the Scruples of the Imagination," "don't have to seem believable [*verosimili*], because they are real."[4] The absurdities of art, on the other hand, are expected to be believable to convey a feel of reality. And yet the perversity of the logic is such that once these absurdities are made believable they are no longer absurd, and thus no longer true.

Pirandello is not trying to argue that his tales actually improve on the aesthetic of *verismo* by being more faithful to life than the idealized representations of the naturalistic novel. Or not only. He is not claiming that his writing is mimetic in a profounder sense than his critics imagine. He is contesting the very logic of mimesis, the obligation of art to imitate an imperceptible order, the paradox that make-believe must be credible while history is not, that fictions are called upon to embody a "universal human significance and value" not present in facts. Ultimately Pirandello's objection is directed not to a bad mode of art but rather to a bad mode of history, one spurning its own principle of verisimilitude. Like Ivan Karamazov, he is denouncing a life that is none, saying, if this is the show, then I turn in my ticket, like the protagonist of *Henry IV,* relinquishing his historical life to act out the ordered and coherent fiction of the eleventh-century king at Canossa. "It must seem for real, don't you understand?" cries one of the characters playing a part to humor this "king" to another. "Exactly!" Henry IV answers. "For real! That is the only way to stop truth from becoming a mockery [*Perché solo così non è più una burla la verità*]."[5] Ironically, history must conform to the inexorable logic of a fiction to recover the semblance of reality it lacks, a semblance without which the very notion of truth itself collapses.[6] If Pirandello's hero Mattia Pascal is named Pascal, it is not by accident but by aesthetic choice, the kind of choice he lacks in his actual life. It is chance that offers Pascal the opportunity to change identities; chance that wins him the fortune that finances his travels; chance that causes him to change trains in Alenga and be spared his debts. *The Late Mattia Pascal* is not composed in the manner of the worst of novels, as some early critics charged; it is but the reality the novel represents, disdaining all thought of credible progression.

That this is so, and that art must therefore rethink its foundations, is all the fault of Copernicus. Before Copernicus came along and the earth was not made to turn, "a detailed narration, full of tiny incidents [*oziosi particolari*]," was still agreeable (*FMP* 323; *LMP* 5). Now, continues Pascal, narrating his own biography, the logic of appearance has been disrupted, making objective evidence suspect. "Hitherto," writes Kant in the Preface to *The Critique of Pure Reason*, alluding to the Copernican revolution, "it has been assumed that all our knowledge must conform to objects." But now that this objectivity has lost its self-evidence, one can approach the task of inquiry only "by assuming that objects must conform to our knowledge."[7] Life has forgone its apparent order and plan, allowing no events to be described with certainty. It is no time for writing books, declares Pascal, "not even in jest," for there is no longer any objective perspective from which to do so. "Our stories," continues Pascal, this namesake of the philosopher who theorized the smallness of man in the infinite universe, have become "like the biographies of worms" (*FMP* 322–24; *LMP* 4–6). The "necessary illusions" enabling the writing of epic narratives—including computable probability, hierarchical order, and unequivocal cause and effect—have been lost, according to a development recounted in the "lanternosophy" of Pascal's Roman landlord, Anselmo Paleari.

The theme of this "highly specious philosophical concept" of lanternosophy is elementary. Unlike plants and animals, humans are born with the sad privilege of feeling themselves to be alive. From this feeling there results the "fine illusion" by which "we mistake for external reality our inner feeling of life, which varies and changes according to the time, or chance, or circumstances." Variously colored by "the glass that is given us by illusion," this life sensation illuminates the contours of one's waking experience. A subjective feeling supplants, as it were, the objective forms of the empirical world, allowing nothing to be seen as it is in itself. In different groups, individuals, moods, and epochs, different colors predominate, and sometimes it even happens that cultural lanterns are suddenly extinguished by violent gusts of wind. At that point the darkness is broken by an indescribable scuffle of tiny, individual lanterns: "some go this way, some that, some try to move backwards, others in circles. Nobody can find the path." And it is at one of these times, Paleari explains, that Europe is now caught. It is an epoch of transition, in which the common light of a shared idea has withdrawn and has left only sparks. "Darkness and confusion! All the big lanterns have been blown out" (*FMP* 483–89; *LMP* 162–66).

At the very moment when reality is pronounced dependent on the conceptual light by which it is illuminated (the "Copernican turn" of the sixteenth and seventeenth centuries), that same reality announces its independence, its defiance of all luminous projection. The lights lose their power to enlighten. The structure of scientific revolutions indicts the very notion of normalcy. All norms of behavior appear to be only corrolaries of arbitrary metaphysical paradigms. What, after all, is "normal life," Pirandello asks in his appendix to *Mattia Pascal*, but "a system of relationships which we select from the chaos of daily events, and then arbitrarily call *normal?*" (*FMP* 582; *LMP* 258). The concept of the normal, or the typical, has its home only in the archaic context of common sense, according to which the earth is immobile, one's head points upward, and the stars are small. At one time hierarchies were still possible, even natural. After the Copernican reversal, however, anomaly becomes the rule.

This, then, is the context in which Pirandello defends "the paradoxical incredibility" of his fictions against critics' demands for treatments of "man in general" and "universally human significance and value" (*FMP* 582; *LMP* 258). Wherever Pirandello looks for this man in general he finds only aggregates of individuals and points of view. Types and patterns continue to be foisted on the world by only an antiquarian yearning for narrative order.

Pirandello addresses the relation between empirical reality and aesthetics at length in his treatise *On Humor,* which

---

he wrote primarily to secure an academic position. In the course of history, Pirandello writes, causes "are never so logical, so arranged, as they are in our ordinary works of art, where everything is, basically, arranged, pieced together, ordered for the purposes the writer has in mind." A sincere modern writer—say, a humorist instead of an epic novelist—would be unable to acknowledge either heroes or successful conclusions of intentional design.[8] A Pirandellian artist "knows what legend is and how it is made, knows what history is and how it is made: 'compositions' all of them, idealizations more or less, and perhaps the more they have the appearance of reality the more [they are] idealized."[9] "Normal" consciousness endorses a world of fixed associations, a habitual network of ideas and feelings established within a chaotic flow. As conceived by everyday consciousness, experience is a phantasmic process of abstraction, selection, and arrangement. At the root of the process lies a basic derealization of facts. Logic acts as a "filter-pump," conveying the contents of the heart to the brain. On its way through the filter feeling "is cooled, purified, idea-if-ied [*si i-de-a-liz-za*]." From these swarming feelings ("mutable and varying in accordance with the times, with events, and with fortune") the filter abstracts ideas, then classifies and semantically combines them. This idealizing process tends "to fix what is mobile, mutable and fluid," imparting an absolute value to things relative and a permanent status to what is temporary (*U* 162–66; *H* 139–44). It is not long before action turns into a script in a theater of self-performance, in a play of ego ideals and ego impositions, according to a dialectic of life and form which Adriano Tilgher first detected in Pirandello in 1923.[10]

What begins to recur is a fossilized, derivative order of those selfsame habits that critics have begun to demand from art—the *Seinesgleichen* of *The Man without Qualities* with its cut-and-dried forms and patterns. Typification is the central and virtually ineluctable failure of both art and everyday life, as Pirandello recognized with Simmel, but a failure that art could at least attempt to resist.[11] Reality assumes forms only in "the appearances it creates for itself." As these appearances change with different points of view, one begins to recognize that the thing represented "can never be either 'such and such' or in 'such and such' a way, in any stable or sure manner." In the final analysis what has *not* been given to us is reality, and "it does not exist; rather, we are obliged to create it ourselves if we intend to exist" (*Uno* 800; 3 : 8).

All this runs smoothly until the economy of images is seen for what it is. When that occurs the protagonist is jolted from an imaginary order into a nameless reality. Once "someone," *Uno*'s Vitangelo Moscarda becomes "no one."

There is a passage in *On Humor* which describes this type of recognition and establishes the knot between the real and its representation that Pirandello's writing attempts to cut:

At certain moments of inward silence, when our soul strips itself of all its habitual pretences, and our eyes become more acute and discerning, we see ourselves in life, and life in itself, as in a kind of barren and troubling nakedness; we feel ourselves assailed by a strange impression, as if, in a flash, we became aware of a reality different from that which we normally perceive, a reality dwelling beyond human vision, outside the forms of human reason. At that moment, with intense clarity, the organic unity of daily existence, as if suspended in the void of that inner silence of ours, seems to us to have lost all sense and purpose; and that different reality seems to us horrible in its impassive and mysterious harshness, since all our habitual artificial associations of feeling and imagination are split apart in it and disintegrated. The internal void expands, transcends the limits of our body, becomes a void around us, a strange void like an arresting of time and of life, as if our inner silence were plunging into the depths of mystery. With a supreme effort, we seek to regain our normal consciousness of things, to reunite things with their habitual associations, to reconnect our ideas, to feel ourselves alive again as before, in the familiar way. But we can no longer have faith in this normal consciousness, these reconnected ideas, because we know now that they are a trick of our own for living and that underneath there is something else, which a person can face only at the price of death or madness. It has been but an instant; yet the impression of it remains with us a long time, the impression of a kind of dizziness, in contrast with the stability, albeit illusory, of things— mere pretentious or wretched appearances. Then life, which goes its familiar petty round among these appearances, seems to us to be no longer in earnest, to be, as it were, a kind of mechanical phantasmagoria. And how is one to attach any importance to these appearances, or show them any respect? (*U* 160–61; *H* 138)

One recognizes the hand of the historical Pascal and also of Copernicus in details of this sketch: the sense of dizziness accompanying the spinning volatility of things; the feeling of a reality existing outside the bounds of reason; the expansion of an internal void into a void surrounding us. Suddenly daily existence loses its cogency, making experience appear mechanical and phantasmagoric, as if composed of a series of masks: "a puff and they are gone, to give way to other masks," even to that mask within oneself which one calls one's self. "And nothing is true!" Yes, the sea, the mountain, the rock are true, but man can only simulate "whatever it is that, in good faith, he thinks himself to be." He "cannot stop posing, even in front of himself . . . and he imagines so many things which he needs to believe true and take seriously" (*U* 160–61; *H* 139). The resulting reduction, say of a person into a series of attributes, eventually fuels a reaction, a rebellion against this reification and its stifling of subjective possibility.

The most appropriate place to begin tracing this reaction is among figures straddling the divide between history and art: Pirandello's six characters in search of an author, allegories for concrete subjective fact caught up and immobilized in a phantasmagoria.

In the stage directions to *Sei personaggi in cerca d'autore* (1921; *Six Characters in Search of an Author*), Pirandello stresses that the six characters of his play are not living persons but "created realities." He advises the actors portraying them to wear masks "cut in such a way as to leave the eyes, the nostrils, and the mouth free." The result will be a unique combination of historical life and symbolic form, material and idea.[12] The changeless essence of these *personaggi* should present itself in sharp contrast to the shifty and volatile personae of the living actors, who are various persons as the occasion provides. Being "immutable constructions of the imagination," the six characters should convey the impression of figures "constructed by art and each immutably fixed in the expression of his own fundamental sentiment, which is *remorse* for the Father, *vengeance* for the Step-daughter," and so on (*Sei* 54–55).

The quintessentiality of these characters has often elicited precisely those encomiums of art against which Pirandello had begun to react at the start of his career: the "eternal significance" of Don Abbondio, Sancho Panza, Hamlet, and the typicality of artistic operations.[13] The father first proposes this reading when he tries to describe the uniqueness of his family members' nature. The characters have an identity, the actors do not; the characters have absolute significance, the actors are purely contingent. Whoever has had the luck to be born a character, the father tells the director, "cannot die" (*Sei* 58). If living creatures *have* form, the aesthetic character *is* form, or the very thing to which life itself aspires: the distinction of history transformed into narrative. "However sad my lot and horrible the facts," says the character voluntarily living as Henry IV, however "bitter the battles, painful the developments: being already history, they no longer change, they can no longer change, do you understand? Fixed forever: you can settle into it [*vi ci potete adagiare*], observing how every effect follows obediently on its cause, with perfect logic, and every happening unfolds precisely and coherently in each one of its details. I mean the satisfaction of history, the pleasure of history, which is so great!" (*E* 355; *HE* 56).

What is seldom remarked about these paeans to formal perfection is the price that one pays for such sublation. The character, Pirandello writes in the preface to *Six Characters*, is a creature who has been "embalmed alive." And the paradoxes do not end there. If the father has achieved an incorruptible form, it is only by means of a "most lamentable chance event [*per un caso sciaguratissimo*]." He has been caught soliciting a prostitute in a brothel, and she turns out to be his stepdaughter. He has been apprehended in an aspect "such as I never intended to assume [for my family], in a shameful and fleeting moment of my life." Purely by accident he has been personified as this character by which he will henceforth be defined, this mask of remorse to which he is destined beyond every shift of time. The father knows that he cannot be equated with such a personification, no more than any living person can be said to be "'this one' we believe ourselves to be in each one of our acts." This is something we realize only when

we remain suddenly hooked and suspended in one of our acts: I mean we realize that the entirety of our being was not in that act [*ci accorgiamo . . . di non esser tutti in quell'atto*] and thus that it would be an atrocious injustice to judge us by that act alone, to keep us hooked and suspended, held up to execration, for an entire existence, as if this existence were fully summed up in that act! Now do you understand the perfidiousness of this girl? (*Sei* 43, 72–73)

The stepdaughter's perfidy is that of idealization, or abstract interpretation. If these immutable characters are enabled to be, it is only by not being allowed to become.

We might now return to the accusation by Pirandello's critics that he was "unable to give a universally human significance" to his works. By this they meant that idealization failed on the level of moral statement. The reader was unable to see what general message might be culled from Pirandello's stories and plays. Now Pirandello is prepared to give his first reply to the charge:

What if the significance consisted precisely in this, that a man or woman placed, by themselves or by others, in a painful situation, socially anomalous, absurd if you like, remain in it, bear it, play it out [*la rappresentano*] in front of others *as long as they themselves do not see it,* whether through blindness or incredible good faith; for, as soon as they see it, as though a mirror had been set in front of them, they can no longer bear it, they feel all its horrors and break it, or if they cannot break it, feel it will kill them. What if it were precisely in this that the significance consisted, that a socially anomalous situation is accepted, even when seen in a mirror, which in this case holds our own illusion up to us; and then we play it out, suffering all its pain, as long as the performance is possible behind the stifling mask that we have put on ourselves or that others, or cruel necessity, have forced on us; in other words, as long as there, beneath this mask, some keenly felt feeling of ours [*un sentimento nostro, troppo vivo*] isn't hurt? Then the rebellion finally breaks out, and that mask is torn off and trampled underfoot. (*FMP* 582–83; *LMP* 258–59)

The "anomaly" of the situation Pirandello describes consists precisely in its normative rigidity. It is socially anomalous, he stresses, insofar as it transforms human interaction into a relation of roles. Something in the very dynamics of communicative action reifies its own participants. The universal significance of Pirandello's stories, then, consists in this self-composition of characters "not freely but by necessity . . . in an anomalous, unbelievable, paradoxical situation; a situation . . . they finally shatter" (*FMP* 582–83; *LMP* 258–59). In the social, psychological, and metaphysical defect of this fictitious construction lies the significance of his tales for man in general.

The rebellion breaks out with the characters' apparent recognition of the incompatibility of their individual countenances and "society's view" of them. The recognition generates a kick knocking apart that "whole theater" in which each person is "voluntarily the marionette of himself." Purposely means not only voluntarily but also in the rounds of practical, teleological activity. As long as the performance is possible by means of the mask, no tragedy occurs, for such characters make no critical reflection on the life that is theirs. However, if the mask wounds a live feeling, it is torn off and trampled underfoot. Here another dimension seems added to the "universal significance" of Pirandello's stories: the discovery of Mattia Pascal and others of "their naked individual face beneath that mask" (*FMP* 582–84; *LMP* 258–59). The moment in which things become stripped of their habitual pretenses produces a vision of life in its barren and troubling nakedness. Or does it? The statement calls for suspicion, and it makes all the difference in the destiny of Pirandello's rebels.

That there is a peripeteia in nearly each of Pirandello's tales is sufficiently clear; the question involves the nature of its anagnorisis.

In *Mattia Pascal* one day a man becomes aware of the un- reality of everything that has defined him as what he is—his birthplace, his indigence, his wife, and even his "wandering eye." Profiting from a series of fortuitous events, he rebels against the marionette he has been thus far. The moment de- scribed by *On Humor* in which a silence threatens to engulf the world of natural consciousness acts as a dramatic junc- ture and catalyst. Holding up a mirror to his condition, the drastic defamiliarization of Pascal's everyday world has a lib- erating effect. Who is not struck by Pascal's elation to be freed from the burden of his past, as though it signaled the start of a free adventure in self-making?

I was alone now, and no one on earth could be more alone than I, with every tie dissolved, every obligation removed, free, new, and completely my own master, no longer bearing the burden of my past, and with the future before me, which I could shape as I pleased. (*FMP* 404; *LMP* 83)

Now that I had cut off all memory of my previous existence, now that my spirit was firmly determined to begin a new life from this point, I was filled and uplifted as though with a fresh infant hap- piness; it felt as though my consciousness had become virgin and transparent again, my spirit alert and ready to profit from every- thing for the construction of my new I. (*FMP* 408; *LMP* 87)

The reader of *Mattia Pascal,* like the protagonist himself, ex- pects that all possibilities of being will change with Pascal's unexpected liberation from his ties. Thanks to a malfunction in the very system of identification, Pascal has become free to construct his person anew, to attune his consciousness to who he truly is, or wants to be. And yet in the course of the narrative what happens is the reverse. Pascal fails to encoun- ter that coveted "individual countenance" that gives the lie to its social reflection. Far from a naked face, the mirror presents only a "naked mask" (*Maschere nude* is the title of

Pirandello's collected plays). The face is just another disfiguration. Pascal is as repulsed by his new, clean-shaven look as by his previous appearance.

The difficulty Pascal encounters in constructing an alternative to the puppet show is not just of an epistemological order, a difficulty of knowing who he is. A more serious obstacle is existential. He finds himself historically incapable of fleshing out an alternative, nonidentificational order of experience. Pascal's unconstrained life as the fictitious Adriano Meis lacks all the coordinates of an empirical existence: a bank account, an entry in the public register, and the basic rights of a citizen that follow from the ability to prove one's identity. Without a calling card he can construct neither a self nor a life. The freedom he experiences proves far too empty and metaphysical. Instead of freedom "it could better have been called solitude and boredom [noja]." He had smashed the marionette of himself only to have become a shadow. "But it had a heart, that shadow, and couldn't love; it had money, that shadow, and everyone could rob it; it had a head, but only to think and to understand that this head belonged to a shadow, and wasn't even the shadow of a head. Exactly so!" The simulated death of a factitious character has resulted in the simulated life of a fictitious one, indeed, in nothing other than a living death. Had he thought it was a stroke of luck to be dead? Well, now he was dead in the deepest sense. "Dead? Worse than dead . . . the dead can no longer die, while I could: I am still alive for death, and dead for life." An artificial character has been replaced by an "almost non-existent [inconsistente] identity." "Madman that I was!" he reflects. "How could I have believed that a trunk can live when cut off from its roots" (FMP 511, 524, 521, 445, 549; LMP 189, 200, 197, 125, 224).

We shall soon have an occasion to ponder the significance of these "roots" prefigured in money, the heart, and the head. But first we must recognize that the attempt at unmasking has failed, revealing no reality beneath the illusion. An equally ironic turn had occurred in conjunction with the Copernican correction of Ptolemaic geocentrism, that event ordinarily understood as a definitive unveiling of the cosmos. The whole astronomical stage was kicked apart, Pascal admits, but to be replaced by what? By a truer picture? One should recall that the Copernican revolution exposed the fallacy of common sense with the aid of the telescope. Designed to improve man's vision of the universe,the telescope resulted in something quite different:

> While our eye looks from below through the smaller lens and sees as big all that nature had providentially wanted for us to see small, what does our soul do? It jumps up to look from above through the larger lens, and as a consequence the telescope becomes a terrible instrument, which sinks the earth and man and all our glories and greatness. (*U* 164; *H* 142)

Far from offering an accurate perspective on the objective world, the Copernican revolution has performed just another in a series of distortions. If the stars were enlarged, the stature of the viewer was proportionately diminished. The "scientific universe" was essentially the effect of a lens, making this most positivistic moment in Europe just a projection in Signor Paleari's lanternosophical history.

Can we draw any conclusions from these reflections? Pirandello's fictions indeed bespeak a rebellion against the phantasmagoria. His characters recognize the real world as no more than an apparent world, truth as a fiction, the face as a mask, the normal as a species of anomaly, the objective as a subjective projection. But the expected liberation does not follow. Pirandello has often been called a pessimist precisely because none of his works offers a clear affirmation to replace the negation, a "knowledge" to supplant the illusion. Here, too, we should not be led to believe that the dramatic peripeteia occasions a revelation of the "naked individual faces" beneath the stripped-off masks.[14] "Life in the raw, nature without any (apparent) order, bristling with contradictions": this, Pirandello had said, is the ultimate subject of his fictions, as against the false idealizations of history (*U* 166; *H* 144). Unwilling to forgo the concepts of reality and truth,

Pirandello would simply be redefining them as their opposite. Like Nietzsche in Heidegger's reading, he would be turning them on their head, assessing reality as illusion and illusion as reality, normalcy as abnormal and abnormalcy as normal. But this reading does not hold. In neither Pirandello's nor Nietzsche's case can "life in the raw" preserve any meaning, no more than the notion of a face beneath a mask can. Once the true (that is, ideal) world has been abolished, as the fable runs in Nietzsche's "History of an Error," so has the apparent world from which the real was once distinguished.[15] What is left at that moment are no longer two separate worlds but a single one in which the opposition no longer holds—or an infinite multiplicity of worlds. And in this single/multiple (in any event, nondualistic) world, the contradictory sets are repealed.

This repulsion is alluded to in what Pirandello calls the second significance of his fables, the most satisfactory rebuttal of the claim that his art lacks universal validity. Admitting that his fictions are invariably set in the contrast between reality and illusion, Pirandello asks, "what if the *universally human* significance and value of some of my fables and characters . . . consisted first of all in the significance and value to be assigned that first contrast that, thanks to one of life's constant jests is always revealed as non-existent?" (*FMP* 582; *LMP* 258). Triggered by an insuperable opposition, Pirandello's fiction shows that same opposition to be a false one, a pseudocontrast. The ultimate significance of his fables would thus lie not in the antithesis between fact and fiction, or between the individual's countenance and society's view of it, but rather in the revelation of the impropriety of these mutual oppositions. If the apparent world is unreal, so is the distinction between it and a real one. The same may be said of the entire conceptual bureaucracy that classifies Western experience: life versus form, thing versus idea, ego versus other, truth versus error, tragedy versus comedy. Pirandello's work cancels the autonomy of the terms. The ultimate phantasmagoria is not habitually perceived empirical reality (beyond which the truly real might be fleetingly sensed), even if Pirandello often travels in this direction.[16] The phantasmagoria is precisely the either/or. Supporting and enabling these antinomies is a conceptual mechanics that Pirandello attempts to unbalance. Fact and fantasy are two dimensions of a single lie.

What then of the unmasking moment of Pirandello's fiction? A troubling nakedness had suddenly come into view, in an experience that Musil's Törless describes as that of trying to lip-read the words of a paralyzed man and not being able to do it (GW 6:89; YT 119). One had a "strange impression" that in a flash a different reality starkly contested the mechanical phantasmagoria of life as commonly perceived. This voiceless world does not allow itself to be approached as a "thing in itself." It is a hypothesis suggested by a failure at the heart of the mechanical phantasmagoria, the sign of a missing link in the chain, a chink in the armor. Like Conrad, Pirandello's first interest lies in the effects, or defects, of these disruptive moments on the constituted phantasmagoria. If this deconstruction holds, then the debates between subjectivism and idealism, idealism and realism, and other such antinomies in Pirandello must be radically reassessed.

Subjectivism, or the doctrine that things are only what they appear to be to a person, is the traditional explanation not only for Pirandellian lanternosophy but also for the entanglement of perspectives in his plays—the failure of characters to understand a single phenomenon in a common way, their inability to mean the same things by their words, the very resistance of their feelings to language, and their stubborn conviction of their personal rightness against all objective evidence. To say subjectivism, especially at the beginning of the century, is also to suggest idealism and ontological relativism, two positions that must be carefully distinguished from each other.[17] Ontological relativism finds the nature of a phenomenon to be relative to the structures that render it intelligible. Things in themselves lack a definitively discernible identity. If subjectivism implies relativism, it does not necessarily extend so far as idealism. Idealism takes the subjective element in cognition to the point of considering all known beings to be constructs of mental processes. Consciousness stands as the foundation and formative matrix of empirical reality. In its most extreme form idealism turns into solipsism, or the belief that nothing exists independently of the creative power of the individual ego.

Versed as he was in the philosophical issues of his time, Pirandello added his voice to the contemporary debate.[18] In his reflections as well as his fictions the very conceptual oppositions on which the debates were based begin to disintegrate, ceding to the possibility of a "third way" for which thinkers like Lukács express such scorn.

Eric Bentley and Anthony Caputi have both called attention to a central passage in Pirandello's essay "Sincerity and Art" which posits objective data as the a priori element of conscious activity.[19] "For me," Pirandello writes,

the world is not only an ideality, that is, it is not limited to the idea that I make of it for myself: outside of me the world exists for itself and with me, and in my representation I must determine *to realize it* as much as I can, creating for myself something like a consciousness [*coscienza*] of it in which it lives, in me as it does in itself, seeing it as it sees itself, feeling it as it feels itself. Then there will be no need for symbol or appearance: everything will be real and living.[20]

We can note that Pirandello aspires to consciousness of the world as it "lives in itself," an aspiration that implies the existence of objective reality prior to consciousness of it. Something like "life in the raw" seems to exist after all (even if it acts curiously in the manner of a subject, "seeing" and "feeling" itself). Artistic consciousness of this external world allows everything in it to be "real and living," just as it is in itself, so much so that all imitations and symbols now appear as intolerable acts of fictionalization. Indeed, Pirandello "hates" symbolic art, for in it

representation loses all spontaneous motion to become a machine, an allegory; a vain and misguided [*malinteso*] effort, for the very fact of giving allegorical sense to a representation lets it clearly be seen that it is held to be merely a fable, which has, in itself, no truth, neither imaginative nor effective. (*Sei* 36)

We shall have occasion to return to this opposition between (allegorical) symbol and (historical) image once we have understood the crux on which this paradoxical identity of meaning and image seems to hinge: the meaning of a conscious realization of the world. In both of the above statements Pirandello turns away from idealism and its inevitably symbolic idiom toward a realist aesthetic. And yet obstacles remain to this turn. How can one see the world "as it sees itself" when subjective perception plays the distorting role that lanternosophical philosophy attributes to it? And how can the world live "in me as it does in itself" without a definitive carryover from one to the other? What does it mean for an aesthetic representation to "realize" the world, as though it were not real on its own? No sooner have we anchored Pirandello in a reflective epistemology (by which mind directly reflects experience) than he begins to set sail. We are led outside the subject/object duality to the question of the consciousness in which they are united, an issue that, Caputi notes, is central to every aspect of Pirandello's work.[21]

In the passage from "Sincerity and Art" Pirandello speaks of the realization of the world in a representation. It does not sound as though this representation is merely a reproduction of something whose form is already and autonomously given. This representation seems more like an act of making, a poetic *creation*. In the realization of experience in an image or a form, experience begins to appear as whatever and however it is. The realized phenomenon is not an object independent of a subject; it is a "not me" in "me," a form in which the phenomenon lives "in me as it does in itself." This realization is a phenomenalization, not merely a reflection; it is a subjectively experienced objectivity, an objectivity *made* subjective.

When, Pirandello asks, does an independent object turn into an aesthetic fact?

When I try to contemplate it as an object in me, when it begins to will itself [*a volersi*] in me, just as I will it for itself [*qual'io per se stesso lo voglio*]; when it ceases to be mere theoretical contemplation in me and becomes action, when its mere theoretical form becomes practical, technical form, that is, free, spontaneous, and immediate movement of form itself, no longer objectification, but subjectivated [*subiettivata*]. Only then, and not before, will I have created the aesthetic fact, art.[22]

In the aesthetic fact the object "wills" itself by means of the subject. The subject and the object become what they are through the agency of the other. Theory becomes practice and practice theory. It is precisely within the parameters of this discussion that Pirandello's celebrated polemic with Croce occurs, a polemic that goes a long way toward elucidating what Pirandello means by a "conscious realization."[23]

Pirandello's main objection to Croce's view of the aesthetic process concerns what Pirandello considers its mechanicity. For Croce art presents theoretical knowledge of experience, or direct and immediate intuition. The problem with this view, in Pirandello's reading, lies in the fact that it denies that any secondary mediation or refashioning of the original intuition is needed to transform it into an aesthetic fact. Croce, writes Pirandello, "does not want to distinguish at all between perception and intuition . . . nor does he want to distinguish between intuition and imaginative representation." According to Croce, "the distinction between reality and non-reality is secondary and extrinsic to the nature of intuition."[24] In Pirandello's view, to the contrary, aesthetic representations can be fashioned only at a *recognized junction* of reality and nonreality, of objective and subjective, of fixed and imaginary. Art does not consist in a "mechanical objectification of the qualities" of a perceptual intuition but rather "in the subjective interpretation of these qualities" ("Art and Science," *SPSV* 174). Otherwise put, an objectified intuition in itself is not artistic. It must be further reworked. Art arises when one expresses "the subjectification of this objectification" ("Towards an Aesthetic Logic," *SPSV* 924). Art, the creation of form rather than the "intuition of content," is therefore "*the intuition of an intuition*. It is not all in *material-form,* as Croce sees it, but in *material-form-material*" ("Art and

Science," *SPSV* 178). Art is the material representation of material form, a form whose content is the very conjunction of form and content, and it is this quality alone that distinguishes deliberate aesthetic creation from constrained and mechanical perception. Art is free, and it requires decision, while intuition itself does not. Thus, if Croce makes too easy an equation between expression and intuition, form and content, subject and object, Pirandello complexifies the relation. To be sure, he also unifies them, but it is a unity that cannot be called a single intuition of theoretical knowledge.

Croce is able to equate artistic expression with a theoretical rather than a practical act only after "having rent the network [*compagine*] of consciousness." From the start he "cut apart the various activities of the spirit, which exist in an intimate, inseparable bond and in continuous reciprocal action." For Pirandello these activities of the spirit allow for no purely theoretical and no purely "objective," immediate, or unadulterated representation. Consciousness is objective and subjective at once, occupied by feelings, desires, and memories as much as by concepts, perceptions, and ideas, "none of which has priority over the others." All exist "in intimate connection and in continual reciprocal action." In fact, only by a working out of this continual reciprocal action can something like aesthetic expression arise, "something like a consciousness of [the world] in which it lives, in me as it does in itself." When we have reestablished the unity of consciousness,

considering it no longer purely in its representational function but in its double aspect, objective and subjective, we find that its conditions are immediately altered, the representations are altered by the subjective elements of feeling and impulse, that quality of *fixity* is lost which they [the representations] had on their own, isolated by means of abstraction. ("Art and Science," *SPSV* 167, 174, 170)

In one and the same move Pirandello worries both the objectivist and subjectivist epistemologies of consciousness. For consciousness is not primarily an actively imaginative faculty. It is a locus of intersection, a place of practico-theoretical realization which constitutes the abstractions of both subject and object. By positing a world in itself, Pirandello avoids the trap of idealism; by emphasizing the objectification of objects *by subjectification,* he avoids the trap of that reflective epistemology according to which an already constituted empirical reality is merely mirrored in a secondary mind. *Between* these improperly distinguished realms of subject and object, in a space where neither is entirely itself, the process of understanding occurs.

Pirandello addresses the same issue in different terms in *Mattia Pascal.* Here what interests him is not artistic intuition so much as simple cognition. As before, Pirandello characterizes consciousness as an active realization of the world, not as an independent theoretical act. Consciousness is an arena encompassing multiple "minds," the site of a practicotheoretical interaction. Tito Lenzi, a minor character in the novel whom Pascal meets in his travels, begins his famous soliloquy on consciousness by rebutting precisely the notion that consciousness is an autonomous faculty:

Consciousness? Why consciousness is of no use, my dear sir! It can never suffice as a guide. That might be possible, but only if consciousness were a castle, so to speak, and not the village square [*se essa fosse castello e non piazza, per così dire*]. That is to say, if we could conceive of ourselves in an isolated way, and if our consciousness weren't by nature open to others. Basically, in consciousness, as I see it, there is an essential . . . that's right, essential relationship between myself who does the thinking and the other beings of whom I think. And therefore consciousness isn't an absolute which is sufficient to itself, if I make myself clear. When the feelings, the inclinations, and the tastes of these others, of whom I think and you think, are not reflected in me or in you, we can never be satisfied or calm or happy. So much so that all of us struggle to have our feelings, our thoughts, our inclinations, and our tastes reflected in the consciousness of others. And if this doesn't happen because, let us say, the air of the moment refuses to carry the seeds and make them flower . . . the seeds of your idea into the mind of others, why then, my dear sir, you cannot say that your own consciousness is sufficient. (*FMP* 424; *LMP* 103)

This passage obviates the whole question of subjective idealism by depicting consciousness as already containing those objectivities that seem to lie outside it. And yet, relativism has returned in the same gesture, for single, stable, and definitive knowledge is as unattainable in this model as in a solipsistic one. The ego is now permeated by the events it attempts to grasp, corrupted by the "other" from which it strives in vain to set up a distance. And that other (presumably objective) reality is itself infused with subjectivity, feeling, and willing. The world, realized in conscious form, appears as it exists in itself and for me, living within "me as it does in itself." How can we get a firmer grasp on this paradoxical conjunction of an "I" and an objective experience that determines its inherent constituents?

An analogy for this in-itself-for-me can be found in the work of Max Scheler. In *Formalism in Ethics and the Material Ethics of Values* (1916), Scheler characterizes the realm of objective, eternal value as "the good-in-itself-for-me" (*das An-sich-Gute-für-mich*). Paradoxical though it sounds, this equation of an "in itself" and a "for me" actually makes sense in the domain of ethics, where the very idea is to secure a universal judgment from a subjective point of view. A value is good in itself, according to me. Every judgment of value must necessarily be qualified by the phrase "for me." Although Pirandello is talking less about evaluation than cognition at large, the key to his complex description of consciousness may lie precisely in this question of evaluation, which philosophers after Nietzsche came to view as an inalienable dimension of comprehension itself, including even the "disinterested" comprehension of positive knowledge. Perhaps, Pirandello suggests, this evaluation is no less immanent to consciousness as a whole (even if this casts into doubt his insistence that aesthetic consciousness carries no ethical implications).[25] Taking a step back from Scheler to a historically earlier moment, we can find another gloss on this conjunction of the objective and subjective in an Italian dissertation written in 1909, at the same time as Pirandello's "Art and

Science," namely, Carlo Michelstaedter's *Persuasion and Rhetoric.*[26]

Like most philosophers indebted to Schopenhauer, Michelstaedter ties knowledge to the desires of a will in a voracious world. No immediate knowledge of the overall dynamic of this will is possible: "in the infinite infinitesmal fluctuation of variations nothing can have consciousness of this fluctuation." In actual practice the will arrests and segments this fluctuant experience in accordance with its desire. "At every moment the will is a will for determinate things." Consciousness develops essentially as a means of serving the will by discriminating value. "Determination is the attribution of value: consciousness." From these axioms there follows another, directly addressing itself to the self/other relation elucidated by the soliloquy of Tito Lenzi: "Nothing is for itself, but in relation to a consciousness." In a world of willful striving, every phenomenon is both other oriented and other determined, both evaluating these others and being evaluated by them. The final axiom in this argument brings us closer than ever to the metaphor of consciousness as a village square: "Life is an infinite correlativity of consciousnesses."[27] Every activity of the mind occurs within a network of related objectifications. All acts of perceptive will confront each other in dialogue or argument as the case may be. As a practical arena, life is an infinite correlativity of consciousnesses in which each in-itself is from the start for-others, and these others are interdependent. The scene is a *piazza:* a place of both random and planned encounters, of discursively relating subjects, of harmony and discord, of influx and efflux, of action and reaction. And the composition of this piazza cannot be stable.

What loses its force at this point is that Cartesian model of understanding which lies at the very heart of subjectivism: namely, the idea of "mind" on the one side of the divide and "life" on the other. According to this model, experience transpires as a meeting between an ego and a world that the ego freely and autonomously contemplates, as immune to its effects as a castle to marketplace bustle. When, on the contrary, consciousness is itself that meeting place, or piazza, the antinomy between subjectivism and objectivism breaks down. Consciousness of the world can then only be the articulation of a *bond* between ego and world. Subtending the very activity of conceptual thought, we might say (and negating the possibility of thought's disinterestedness), is an always already determinate relation of ego-and-world. To understand this more clearly, let us move to another moment in the history of thought, leaving Michelstaedter for a philosopher much closer to the workings of Pirandello's fictions: Wilhelm Dilthey.

Dilthey was the chairman of philosophy at the University of Berlin during the years Musil did his doctoral work. Fifteen years earlier, in 1888, when Pirandello arrived to do his own studies at Bonn, Dilthey had already written his acclaimed *Introduction to the Sciences of the Spirit* (1883). He had also had a significant influence on Theodor Lipps, the philosopher under whose tutelage Pirandello conducted his own research. The importance of Dilthey in this discussion consists in his reassessment of the Cartesian duality in terms of historicity, or his assimilation of consciousness to lived experience. According to Dilthey, the empirical reality of life can never be viewed as a pure object (whether an object of direct intuition, as in Croce and Henri Bergson, or of an intellectual postulate, as in Descartes).[28] That so-called empirical reality objectively conceived by philosophers already incorporates the mind which is categorically distinguished from it. Thematic theoretical knowledge is only an offshoot of *Verstehen,* or of understanding as a basic apprehension of meaning, purpose, and value in experience as historically lived.[29] It is out of the hermeneutical processes of practical conduct that the very concepts of mind and world first develop.

Admittedly, everyday consciousness believes in a distinction between ego and world. But the distinction is derived from the experience of resistance-as-limitation-of-impulse.[30]

One comes to learn the limitations on desire and identifies these limits with the boundaries of an ego. In actual fact, the difference between "me" and "not me" is cut out of a given continuum of experience infused as much by impulses, goals, memories, and projections as by objective data.[31] Lived experience, or *Erlebnis,* is already "a mind-created structure," derived from the permanent basis of a historical setting, or already preselected and shaped by the desires, perceptions, and reflections of a practical agent. "This permanent basis, from which differentiated processes arise, contains nothing which is not vitally related to an I. As everything is related to it the state of the I changes constantly according to how things and people respond to it."[32] What is more, this permanent historical basis is always animated by those systems of shared beliefs and common experience which Tito Lenzi and Dilthey find reflected in rules of conduct, assertions about the passage of life, conceptions of good, and so on. In the guises of custom, tradition, and public opinion, they inform the consciousness and identity even of the person who, like Mattia Pascal, would attempt to break free from them.[33]

Prior to the differentiation between subjectivity and objectivity, then, we have a historico-existential horizon of lived experience. Only later dichotomized into ego and world, this experience is composed of reciprocally dependent structural relations (*Strukturzusammenhangen*) that render the individual no more than "a point where webs of relationships intersect." In fact, one might do better to drop the term *individual* altogether, as Heidegger does, and speak simply of *Dasein,* or "being there." This type of being cannot be understood in isolation but only by addressing the time and place in which it occurs, including

the whole web of relationships which stretches from individuals furthering their own existence to the cultural systems and communities and, finally, to the whole of mankind, which makes up the character of society and history.[34]

In Pirandello's words, written in 1908, the same year as this material by Dilthey:

There lives in our soul the soul of the race or of the collectivity to which we belong; we unconsciously feel the pressure of other people's way of judging, of other people's way of feeling and acting: and as simulation and dissimulation dominate in the social world . . . we too simulate and dissimulate ourselves, doubling and often even multiplying ourselves.

The individual is composed of "so many separate and mobile systems" that one might say that every person is really the product of "several different and conflicting personalities." "Its life is a changing equilibrium; it is a continual awakening and obliterating of emotions, tendencies, and ideas; an incessant fluctuation between contradictory terms, and an oscillation between opposite poles." In short, the oneness of the soul "contradicts the historical concept of the human soul." The soul "that is our life" evolves as the scene of a village square, a struggle and compromise between numerous souls all "fighting among themselves for the exclusive and final power over our personality" (*U* 157−59; *H* 134−37).

Of course, here Pirandello takes the historical conception of the soul so far as to overthrow even Dilthey's holistic hermeneutics (for Dilthey believed that the intersection of structural relationships still resulted in an essentially unified self). He describes something rather more like an anarchic combustion, something more analogous to the logistics of Heideggerian everydayness which keep one from being a self. Apart from their differences, however, Pirandello and Dilthey take the same turn away from the "ontic" separation of subject and object toward an ontology of historicity.

Dilthey's web of relationships offer those roots from which Mattia Pascal realizes the trunk cannot be severed: the heart, the mind, and the financial statements. Recognizing the impossibility of severing the trunk from the roots, Pascal admits to the failure of subjective autonomy. He had mistakenly attempted to fashion "a consciousness and a personality for himself" outside these primal relations, abstracting himself from the only conditions that marked him as a historical being.

From the very beginning one of Pascal's eyes pointed off in the wrong direction, into the realm of ideal and pure identity.[35] When Pascal finally resolves to straighten this eye by means of surgery, he sees that no alternative consciousness can be constituted outside those objective relations in which he has always been caught. Are not human actions intrinsically determined "by the colors, the appearance of the things around us, the various hubbub of life?" he begins to ask.

Naturally, there's no doubt about it—and who knows how many other things! Don't we live, as Signor Anselmo says, in relation to the universe? Now it remains to be seen how many follies this cursed universe makes us commit, for which we then hold our wretched consciousness responsible, impelled though it be by external forces, blinded by a light outside itself.

In an effort to liberate his identity he had cut the threads that bound the puppet to the show, but to what end?

This: the threads had become knotted together again by themselves; and life, despite my guard, despite my opposition, life had swept me off with its irresistible force. Life, which was no longer for me!

From the subjectivist perspective of an I aspiring to itself, the life he had once lived was a nexus of lies. Precisely through his rebellion, however, the ties and lies that Pascal had tried to cut have come back in strengthened form. Once condemned to unconscious deception, he now has to lie knowingly (*FMP* 509, 511, 514–15; *LMP* 187, 189, 192).

The absurdity of Pascal's project is that of "wanting to rebuild himself as an unrelative man."[36] What he discovers after two years of feigned existence is not only that there is "an essential . . . relationship between myself . . . and the other beings of whom I think" but also that the very goal of life lies in developing this relation. This is the value of sympathy: "to have our feelings, our thoughts, our inclinations, and our tastes reflected in the consciousness of others."[37] When this does not occur, as in an alienated retreat to a lofty castle, a person "can never be content or calm or happy."

Like a Conradian character in need of a witness, Mattia Pascal admits to the insufficiency of his deepest subjective convictions. "If everything I had imagined and constructed concerning Adriano Meis was of no use to other people, to whom was it useful? To me? But I could believe it, if at all, only on the condition that others believed it too" (*FMP* 428; *LMP* 107).

The inability to believe without a communal share in the belief marks the difference between Mattia Pascal's final, hermeneutical mode of understanding and his earlier, pre-Copernican hope to discover a *fundamentum inconcussum* for knowledge. Pascal resigns himself to being a subject of modern democracy—a pluralistic form of communicative interaction—rather than of the autocratic rule to which he once aspired.

Let us recall some of the steps that suggest this conclusion. After Copernicus reality has become abnormal, a jumble of viewpoints, a derivative and inconsistent record of selections, abstractions, and rationalizations. Norms have not disappeared; they have proliferated in unprecedented fashion. Once enjoying the privilege of a single universal light, "lanternine" history has broken up into a plethora of sparks, each with its own tint and shadow. This is the epoch in which Mattia Pascal rebels against projections he perceives as *not his own* and endeavors to recover the luminosity of subjective essence. In the course of the action, however, Pirandello dispels the ontology of the subject in which Pascal and his reactionary epoch attempted to seek the new light of the future. What now appears as the real phantasmagoria are not the projected selves and puppet shows so much as the schematic oppositions of subject and object, essence and appearance, which furnish the scaffoldings on which they are built. If there is anything more real than this conceptual phantasmagoria, it is the actual interaction of the historical piazza. The vision of consciousness as a piazza instead of a Cartesian castle corresponds to the communicative action of a post-Enlightenment democracy. Like Pirandello himself, Pascal comes to acknowledge the inexorability of this fact only after seeking to avoid it, only after admitting that no historical alternative seems to work. *Mattia Pascal,* whose central theme Croce slightingly summed up as "The Triumph of the Civil State," is in many ways an allegory for this acquiescence in democracy and its conditions for knowledge.

A scene in Chapter 11 of the novel finds Pascal roaming around Rome bemoaning the infelicities of his new fledgling *libertà.* Staggering with the dizziness of his condition, a drunk vagabond spies the crestfallen Pascal and gently shakes his arm. "Be happy!" he says, repeating the phrase and accompanying it by a movement of the hand which seemed to mean, "Why do it? Why think? Don't bother about anything!" After some astonishment Pascal imagines answering the drunkard by quoting the saying of a little "imperialist lawyer" he once knew: Citizens cannot be happy unless ruled by a benevolent absolute monarch. "You don't know these things, door drunken philosopher," Pascal thinks to himself,

they never even cross your mind. But the real cause of all our sufferings, of this sadness of ours—do you know what it is? Democracy, my dear, democracy, that is, the rule of the majority. Because when power is in the hands of one person alone, this one knows that he is single and that he has to please many; but when the many govern, they think only of pleasing themselves, and what you get is the most absurd and hateful of tyrannies: the tyranny masked as freedom. Absolutely! Why else do you think I suffer? I'm suffering precisely from this tyranny masked as freedom. . . . Let's go back home! (*FMP* 448–49; *LMP* 127–28)

Some readers will no doubt be reminded of Pirandello's support for fascism in the 1920s and 1930s. In truth, his struggle with the relativism of the piazza had an earlier and more philosophical beginning. The problem with democracy was not only its ironic nourishment of generalized egotism but also its forfeit of a single, firm vantage for value. The problem in knowledge and politics alike was the demise of the "absolute monarch" of pre-Copernican days. Already by 1893 Pirandello laments that "no one is able to establish a stable and unshakable point of view."[38] At this stage Pirandello still hopes that this chaotic drama might yield a systematic reorganization. Ethics, he writes, appealing to Herbert Spencer, "needs an intrinsic foundation":

The norms of conduct must have a necessary nature, founded on relations of natural causality. . . . *Being, knowing,* and *acting* [*operare*] are the three laws that must become one with each other and unify themselves [*immedesimarsi e unificarsi*].

Only when being, knowing, and acting become one can one adopt ethics as a "normative governance in life." Only then will it be possible to accomplish the "invariability, universality, and absoluteness of an ethical-juridical law." But what is needed before all else, he writes (anticipating Ulrich's ideal of precision and the soul), is an "exact conception of both life and man."[39]

Franco Zangrilli has noted that, in the first decades of his literary career, Pirandello was trying vigorously to solve the problem of relativism in culture and morals.[40] The protagonist of the story "When I Was Mad" attempts to regain his reason by writing a treatise *On the Foundation of Morals.*[41] Gregorio Alvignani, a minor character of Pirandello's first novel, had devoted himself to a similar project, feeling the need to undertake "a large, eloquent examination of modern consciousness."[42] For some time he had been working on a study to be called *Future Transformations of the Moral Idea,* the "moral idea" presumably being single, whatever its ramifications. Yet Spencer and the positivistic program begin quickly to slip away, for the work for which Alvignani is drawing up notes in the present time of the novel is called *Relative Ethics.* The process of democratization is irrevocable, the piazza too intricate in its interconnections. Being, knowing, and acting cannot be subsumed under a positive law of natural causality. They are shaped by an influx and efflux of elements, of which none can presume to open onto the piazza like the window of a castle, no more than a citizen can live as an aristocrat in an age of democracy.

Democracy and conscious fluctuation may thus be read as

interchangeable metaphors. Epistemologically speaking, hermeneutical historicity underlies the conceptual categories on which the philosophy of subjectivity, the politics of tyranny, and the pursuit of positive knowledge have based their respective projects. This is that structural network of will, thought, and feeling, which is *coscienza* itself, the "light" in which, along with the mechanical phantasmagoria, the subject and object first come to shine. And, as *Mattia Pascal* shows, a failure to recognize this reflexive historicity as the very fabric of consciousness can only cause misery. Pascal gives up his freedom. He goes back to his debts, his wife, and his mother-in-law in a symbolic "reincarnation."

We may now be in a position to understand why Pirandello aspires to consciousness while considering that same consciousness as impossible to fix; why his ultimate interest is the "objective world" though that world is irremediably subjective; why he speaks of the conscious realization of the world as occurring in art. A realization of the conscious world can only take the form of an unstable relation, a multiplicitous and "abnormal" process shaped as a continuous and creative mediation of subject and object. In fact, it is not by chance that Dilthey characterized art as a development of that same *Verstehen* displayed in lived experience, operating by means of a selection and ordering of structural relations. Art involves the construction of a unique language game out of the literal and symbolic references of linguistic play in general. As expressed by Pirandello, this formal *Verstehen* that could easily have been expressed in a poem or play implies the more extensive opportunities of a novel, constructed as it typically is by a dynamic exchange between subjectivities and objective settings, by data relativized by their own articulation, by wholes and parts that mutually determine each other. Pure philosophical consciousness will no longer do, no more than it will do for Mattia Pascal to abstract himself from his ties and construct a purely theoretical self.

And yet the game of life is homologous to the game of the novel, and its forms are instances of realized experience, only when considered from outside itself. Only from the assured perspective of existential distance, as taken for instance by Henry IV, does experience appear to be eternally settled, with each effect bound to its cause. The game of an evolving historical present, however, is at best a novel in the process of construction, an *attempt* at a novel, a game in which the rules of narrative order contrast with others possessing altogether different types of logic, often developing in contradictory and random ways. The same problem appears in Pirandello's plays. As Franco Ferrucci notes in his reading of *Six Characters* as a "drama of incompleteness," the characters of this play knock at the door of the author's mind with the intention of "*exiting* rather than entering life." Concerned with fractures and fissures, Pirandellian drama diagnoses the impossibility of coherent incarnations.[43] We might say that definitive aesthetic realization—as espoused by *verismo,* Croce, Lukács, and Dilthey—can only be effected by an image representing a coincidence of the particular and the typical, existence and essence, mask and face, subjective and objective conditions. Completely realized consciousness is that which is achieved by "classical" art or history, where a normative principle finds perfect embodiment in formal expression.

Pirandello's criticism of this type of realization concerns not only its disingenuous claim to theoretical knowledge but also its mechanistic relation to lived experience. What is excluded from such pictures is the historical *arena* of realization, the dynamics of conscious activity. Art that poses as a mirror of life fails to realize (or express in its form) the mirror of reflection itself, or the drama in which the mirroring occurs.[44] In psychological terms classical or objective "aesthetic intuitions" leave out the inevitable *non*coincidence between the potentialities of subjective desire and the most satisfying existential *Strukturzusammenhang.* In historical terms they fail to detail the obstructions of plot by means of everything contingent, improbable, and unpredictable. In artistic terms they leave unspoken the process by which the artist *manages* an intuition into a satisfactory expression. In art, Pirandello had said, the very material of the intuition is itself turned into form, just as the fragment that Conrad snatches from time is given a unique representation for the reader. "The impression, having become (internal) expression, must become again impression, elaborated material" ("Art and Science," *SPSV* 175). At that point the reconstructed unity of the impression is shown *as* reconstructed in an art that thematizes itself. When Pirandello calls on art to realize consciousness of the world he asks for consciousness not of objects but of consciousness.

To put it another way, if Pirandello had offered in his fictions a representation of typical or normative experience as Croce, Lukács, and the verists would have liked, he would have performed only a rudimentary aesthetic function, expressing an "objective realization" of the world. Moreover, such an objectification would have transcribed a coincidence of form and content, a narrative order in the sequence of events, a clear organization of appearances and essences. Pirandello believes, however, that there are more complex relations, more accidents and fortuities, more resistance to plan and logic in history than the novel is traditionally used to treating. Consequently, what becomes peculiar to Pirandello's fiction is not merely that it bends its prose to transcribe experience not exhausted by plan but that it actually tests the "novelistic logic" of life formation, reflecting on the "laws" of the formative process. Once consciousness articulates those dimensions of its activity that are traditionally excluded from the aesthetic act, the aesthetic image finds its purpose beyond the objectification of content. It becomes "free, spontaneous, and immediate movement of form itself" ("Aesthetic Logic," *SPSV* 927). If an image is an "achieved aesthetic form," then aesthetic formation is a process overcoming the very fixity of its image relations, allowing for infinite interpretations. Objective narrative order is unable to realize historico-aesthetic consciousness.

Pirandello's marionettes had rebelled against this very type of order, unable to endure their lives within it. As Lenzi's disquisition on consciousness had claimed, this ontological model makes too categorical a separation between such things as theory and practice, objective data and their subjective interpretations. To no avail, the marionettes had rebelled against one term of the pair in the hope of attaining the other. They had kicked apart the puppet show only to find it reconstructing itself, revealing the seemingly autonomous terms of the opposition to be reciprocally joined. Pascal decides to reconnect himself with the determining rules of the historical *Strukturzusammenhang*. And yet he does so without the naiveté he once possessed as an unconscious player. Rather he lives his old life, or relives it, as a reincarnation, with a new distance and freedom, writing not a third-person narrative but an autobiography. Equally self-reflexive, neither Pirandello's fictions nor his characters succeed in discovering an alternative to the phantasmagoria (in the form, for example, of a radically alternative literary or biographical style). Instead they adopt a modified attitude to the one that is given, a new method of playing and not playing the part, of questioning and questing to offset the one-sidedness of every representation.[45]

Up to this point, Pirandello's marionettes have rebelled against their roles, recognizing at last that the theater cannot be abolished. What remains to be analyzed is the essayistic existential condition, or the consciousness of consciousness, inspired by this failed rebellion.

Part Two

Conscious
Essayism

4

Joseph Conrad

The Ethos of Trial

The "feeling of unreality" accompanying the crtical dismantling of delusion in Conrad's fiction serves more than a negative function. Far from abolishing reality, this "doubt of the
ground" elevates it to the status of a desideratum, a goal still
to be achieved. In this sense the ubiquitous crises of Conrad's
fiction mark a turn from an unpersuasive and everyday certainty to a profound and inarticulate feeling of existence.
This dialectic is clear in a passage from *The Rescue* (1920) to
which J. Hillis Miller has already drawn attention.[1] Lingard,
who is passionately in love, senses life and existence to be
mutually exclusive:

It seemed to Lingard that he had been awake ever since he could
remember. It was as to being alive that he felt not so sure. He had no
doubt of his existence; but was this life—this profound indifference,
this strange contempt for what his eyes could see, this distaste for
words, this unbelief in their importance of things and men? He tried
to regain possession of himself, his old self which had things to do,
words, this unbelief in the importance of things and men? He tried
to regain possession of himself, his old self which had things to do,
mere consciousness of life, and which in its immensity of contradictions, delight, dread, exultation and despair could not be faced and

yet was not to be evaded. There was no peace in it. . . . If this was existence then he knew that he existed.[2]

Try as Lingard may to regain possession of his habitual feelings and responsibilities, he is "seduced away" by a tense feeling of existence.

How can we understand this sense of existence, which not only militates against pragmatic, functional consciousness but seems even to result from its failure? It is filled with an "immensity of contradictions." It lacks stability and peace, causing delight to come adulterated with dread and exultation with despair. In this existential condition, which can neither be faced nor avoided, things are both themselves and their opposites—but also neither—in irresolvable tension.

The condition returns in one of the most original portraits of all Conrad's fiction: the motley Russian encountered by Marlow in Kurtz's camp. The first thing by which Marlow is impressed is the phenomenal inconstancy of this nameless creature. The Russian possesses no fixed or definitive traits. Smiles and frowns chase each other over his open countenance "like sunshine and shadow on wind-swept plain." Like the autumn sky, the man's face is "overcast one moment and bright the next." His clothes are like those of a harlequin, "covered with patches all over . . . patches on the back, patches on the front, patches on elbows, on knees, coloured binding around his jacket, scarlet edging at the bottom of his trousers" (*HD* 53). He was instability and contradiction itself, like the sea in a storm.

As Marlow ponders this Russian, he begins to interpret him in terms of the very barest of human structures, as though the man represented an entirely unanchored life. "His very existence was improbable, inexplicable, and altogether bewildering. He was an insoluble problem." What unsettles Marlow most about this harlequin's existence is its lack of a constitutive *how*—a historical ground or method, an ethical substance or pattern. "It was inconceivable to me how he had existed, how he had succeeded in getting so far, how he had managed to remain—why he did not instantly disappear." The Russian was a pure adventurer, a person holding everything ordinarily constitutive of a life deliberately at bay. Without homeland, friends, or duties, this skeleton and sketch of a man exuded an essence of living so rarified as to burst into flame:

He surely wanted nothing from the wilderness but space to breathe in and to push on through. His need was to exist, and to move onwards at the greatest possible risk and with a maximum of privation. If the absolutely pure, uncalculating, unpractical spirit of adventure had ever ruled a human being, it ruled this be-patched youth. I almost envied him the possession of this modest and clear flame. (*HD* 54, 55)

Appreciating in him, no doubt, a dimension of his innermost self, Marlow begins to admire this character (for Marlow too was "a wanderer," always ready to clear out "for any part of the world at twenty-four hours' notice" [*HD* 8, 16]. In the figure of the Russian he is privy to a purely utopian motivation, a striving for the mere sake of striving. The Russian's is a life of pure and unappeasable project, of means without ends, of a desire so noble as to overcome the lure of all finite objects. The motions of his indeterminate and unfettered will reveal a simple and accelerating motor drive, a "pushing on" and a "moving onward" past all seductions of power, a readiness to confront the greatest risks without hesitation or reason. The Russian's existence attests to an ecstatic denial of all provisional orders and shelters, feeding on itself in self-transfiguration.

Against the background of the essayals of historical and intellectual stability in such tales as *Lord Jim, Heart of Darkness,* and *The Nigger of the "Narcissus,"* this vision of existence seems to bespeak an almost literal appropriation of the feeling of unreality. With uncanny and inexplicable success the Russian has given his life a formless form, adapting to a universe of self-reversing fortunes. He offers a human correlative of an essayistic world. And this is probably why he ventures as far as he can from the confines of all "civilized" order. In this character the doubt of the ground has generated a new and no longer just critical essayism: a striving beyond everything that can be identified and fixed, a yearning for a different and more essential type of experience, an impulse toward transcendence pure and simple. This utopian projection offers a positive correlative to an otherwise negative essayism, even if the two are inseparable. For, as certainly as utopianism follows from the experience of unbelief, so it *causes* that same experience, insofar as no critical stance can be taken to any shaky ground without a prior sense of transcendence. This positive essayism is the very impulse at transcendence which leads Conrad and his characters to take to sea, glancing askance at the receding land.

No doubt, the very extremity of this positive and active essayism makes it a dubious model for practical ethics. Indeed, Conrad is skeptical of the appeal of the existence represented by the Russian and the passionate Lingard. It recalls the drawback of the second of the two types of Europeans peopling the harbors of the Far East. The first are the categorical *non*essayers—seamen who, finding themselves in the East purely by chance,

had now a horror of the home service, with its harder conditions, severer view of duty, and the hazard of stormy oceans. . . . They loved short passages, good deck-chairs, large native crews, and the distinction of being white. They shuddered at the thought of hard work, and led precariously easy lives . . . [and] would have served the devil himself had he made it easy enough . . . and in all they said—in their actions, in their looks, in their persons—could be detected the soft spot, the place of decay, the determination to lounge safely through existence.

The "soft spot" is a moral and psychological inability to commit to anything but safety, certainty, and ease. This is the degeneracy embodied in Donkin and James Wait, in the sailor that Leggatt murders, in the crew of the *Patna*. By extension, it is also the ethic of the land dwellers described in "An Outpost of Progress," entrenched in their defensive shelters. Lacking will, motivation, and imagination, this first type of character remains subject to lassitude and the shirking of duty. "At length, [Jim] found fascination in the sight of those men" (*LJ* 9). He joins their company when he boards the *Patna*.

But there was another type of seaman, who was in the East strictly by choice, to whom Jim was equally drawn:

Some, very few and seen there but seldom, led mysterious lives, had preserved an undefaced energy with the temper of buccaneers and the eyes of dreamers. They appeared to live in a crazy maze of plans, hopes, dangers, enterprises, ahead of civilization, in the dark places of the sea. (*LJ* 8–9)

These are the kinsmen of Kurtz, Brown, and the Russian, committed to taking risks for the sake of taking risks. Potentially, they are also nihilists, prone at any moment to give up "restraint." Yet, for all of Conrad's reservations about this type, he recognizes a compelling logic in their adventures beyond and ahead of civilization. As little as they may offer in the way of political, social, or moral achievement, their lives reveal an enviable power of motivation. A promise seems to lie in the very propulsion of this mode of living, a promise that it is the *basis* for all achievements of significance. This second type of character embraces the openness of existence against which the defensively structured world is designed to guard. If there is any goal in this pure mobility, it lies perhaps in the liberation of the very means toward goals.

Once the "mere consciousness of life" loses its grip on a mind, the feeling of such an existence begins to hold sway. The task is now to elucidate its essayistic characteristics. Two new traits will accrue to the critical essayism with which we are already familiar: the "projectuality" of a virtually infinite and unappeasable aspiration (the essay as open-ended attempt); and the contest with fate that this project engenders (the essay as a trial of the aspiration itself). Accompanying that critical and dramatic essayal of their own structures of action and thought, Conradian characters also experience an essayism inherent in their wills, eventually accompanied by an essayal *of* that very same will on the part of the unlawful necessities of history. The romantic impulse of the first runs up against the realistic contentions of the second. And at that moment, when "fate compels recognition," as Zabel writes, "a man's conscious moral existence begins."[3]

To understand the projectual connotations of essayism, we must take a closer look at the motivation of Conrad's protagonists and the seduction that leads them afield.

In portraits like that of the Russian, Conrad is alluding to the possibility of stepping voluntarily into an existence already perceived as unsheltered. "Improbable" though this step may be, Conrad endeavors to give it shape. In truth, it is the very same project that draws his narrators into hearts of darkness and into unending analyses of human experience, sensing that the meaning of things does not lie inside them but outside, in the "haze" revealed by the glow of the investigation. And it is the same impulse to overcome the limits of the known that distinguishes Kurtz from his fellow traders. Unlike the chief accountant, Kurtz refuses to feign form in a setting that has none. He has delivered himself to the wilderness. In calling Kurtz's methods "unsound," his colleagues miss the mark, for, in fact, he "has no method at all." Developing a stare "wide enough to embrace the whole universe," he has "peeped over the edge" (*HD* 9, 69). Like Kurtz, Conrad's protagonists are never assaulted by abnormalcy; they seek it out. Whether driven or driving themselves, these seamen and exiles, anarchists and criminals, heroes and adventurers, voluntarily inhabit the fringes of normalcy. Like Conrad himself (who took to sea at seventeen, abandoned his homeland, tried even to abandon life itself, and finally settled on a career he considered more precarious than skippering a ship—namely writing), they seek the extraordinary.

To prepare us for Marlow's trip to the "uttermost ends of the earth," the frame narrator of *Heart of Darkness* draws a portrait of adventure that serves as an analogue to the voyage to come. Considering the interminable waterway leading out of the city of London, he reflects on those numerous characters who at one time or another had followed the Thames out to the sea:

Hunters for gold or pursuers of fame they all had gone out on that stream, bearing the sword, and often the torch, messengers of the might within the land, bearers of a spark from the sacred fire. What greatness had not floated on the ebb of that river into the mystery of an unknown earth? . . . The dreams of men, the seed of common-wealths, the germs of empires. (*HD* 8)

Beyond the political implications of passages like these stands the narrator's respect for the ethos of the characters in question: their voluntary assumption of responsibility (*bearers, bearing*); their lofty ambition (*fame, the sword, the torch, might, the sacred fire*); the implicit productivity of their venturesome quest (*pursuers, hunters, spark, dream, seed, germs*).[4] For better or worse, these are men "of whom the nation is proud." Whether expressed as pure greed or primordial passion, their *feu sacré* drives them outward and onward toward creative achievement. If it occasionally settles for gold, it is the same energy that uncovers the mysteries of "an unknown earth."

What is the real object of these venturers' quest? It is the sense of reality betrayed by the reality principle. Within and by means of their projects these explorers seek a substitute for precisely those structures of life which have begun to smack of unreality, as though this substitute awaited them in everything still undiscovered and unimagined, in still un-domesticated contexts of action, "horizons as boundless as hope." "There is such magnificent vagueness in the expectations that had driven each of us to sea," confesses Marlow, "such a glorious indefiniteness, such a beautiful greed of adventures that are their own and only reward. . . . In no other kind of life is the illusion more wide of reality" (*LJ* 205, 78–79). Those who followed the sea believed they would find, in possibilities systematically excluded by the so-called mere consciousness of life, the reality so conspicuously missing from the reality principle. Their decisions are governed by a professional idealism, a type of *Prinzip Hoffnung,* a faith that whatever the discoveries that await them, they will re-deem the effort.[5] The real goal of this desire does not consist in the gold or the spices or the love of war on which it fastens but in their symbolic correlatives: the dream, the idea, a sign, a call, and the "impeccable world."

In *Lord Jim* and *Heart of Darkness* the dream stands vari-ously for an expression of wish fulfillment, a synonym of self-delusion, or the glimpse of a vision impossible to express in words. In all cases the dream denies both the appeal and the value of a perceived condition of reality, beckoning to characters from beyond the bounds of their familiar world. For Jim the dream is much more than the "exalted egoism" of an "imaginative beggar." It is a compulsion to reject what-is in a yearning for what-is-not. Long before Jim gives up his life for the sake of a fiction, Jewel recognizes the symptoms of the conflict to which he is prey. How, she cries, could Jim re-ject the only certain thing about his existence—namely, her love and the life they had established together—on behalf of a remote and hazy idea? He has been "torn out of her arms by the strength of a dream," deluded by a vaporous fiction. Jewel appeals to Marlow to clarify this compulsion that she fails to grasp. What is this unreal reality that divides Jim in two, she asks, half-desperate, half-mocking. "It is alive? . . . Has it got a face and a voice. . . ? Will he see it?—will he hear it. . . .Will it be a sign—a call?" (*LJ* 253, 212, 191–92). With the last words she hits on the intangibility of the thing. The dream is only a sign, a marker for something missing, a negative indication of positive potential. More than Jim's haunting memory of his shortcomings, it is a compulsion to overcome them.

Marlow recalls Jewel's words when he returns to the sea after his stifling sojourn in Patusan:

I breathed deeply, I revelled in the vastness of the opened horizon, in the different atmosphere that seemed to vibrate with a toil of life, with the energy of an impeccable world. This sky and this sea were open to me. The girl was right—there was a sign, a call in them— something to which I responded with every fibre of my being. I let

---

my eyes roam through space, like a man released from bonds who stretches his cramped limbs, runs, leaps, responds to the inspiring elation of freedom.

Marlow appropriates the same words that Jewel had used to denote something more like a conscience, now giving them a referent outside the self. The object of the dream is the boundless energy of an impeccable world, the vastness of the opened horizon, the inspiring elation of freedom. If Jim betrays his historical reality, he does so to serve the same spirit of transcendence that motivates the Russian. "This is glorious," cries Marlow to Jim, as the two make their way to the ship, "and then I looked at the sinner by my side. He sat with his head sunk on his breast and said 'Yes,' without raising his eyes, as if afraid to see writ large on the clear sky of the offing the reproach of his romantic conscience" (*LJ* 201). Jim will be unable to look up at the sky—or to answer the appeal of transcendence—until he goes to Doramin to be shot.

The dream, a definite sign of something indefinite, is the voice of that potentiality without which the realm of the actual remains paralyzed and static. Jim's mistake is simply that he has equated this dream with a specific ideal (and pursues his fantasy in utter contradiction to the revelations of his concrete acts). But can this really be called a mistake? Like a Yeatsian anti-self, the dream of heroism indicates the innermost truth of Jim's being.[6] It is his calling and his single most intractable ideal, that possibilizing principle without which he, and every voluntary agent, is unable to act. For Conrad, as for Yeats, the reality of experience can be measured by the amount of potential it contains. "He was false," cries Jewel when she recognizes Jim's attachment to his own antithesis. "And suddenly Stein broke in. 'No! no! no! My poor child! . . . Not false! True! true! true!'" In fact, Jim's commitment to his dream is one of the only things defining him as "one of us." And the question his tale leaves lingering is whether in his essays to be himself "he had not confessed to a faith mightier than the laws of order and progress" (*LJ* 213, 206).

This faith is the very will to believe, gauged by the efforts required to maintain it. It returns in Kurtz's Intended, who, hoping that she will hear her name, insists on being told Kurtz's final and dying words. Marlow is forced to comply and thus lie, bowing his head "before the faith that was in her, before that great and saving illusion that shone with an unearthly glow in the darkness." If there is any legitimacy to the Intended's intellectual dishonesty, it consists in its own lucidity, in the fact that it is motivated by a *conscious* desire for an ideal. "I want—I want—something—something—to—to live with," she cries (*HD* 74, 75). The "delicate shade of truthfulness" on her features as she makes this appeal marks her deliberate unwillingness to live without such belief. And this is what separates her from characters like Brierly, who is unconsciously deluded, who had always believed in his heroism with unflagging conviction. Unlike the conviction of Kurtz's Intended, Brierly's had not been wrested from conditions announcing the opposite.

If Jim and the Intended were true, it was not because of their faith in a "saving illusion." It was because they lacked such faith, or because they demanded this kind of illusion, insisting that it be proved true. Here lies that same objectless idealism of those who had followed the sea. And here too is the knowledge embodied by Kurtz's pronouncement "the horror," for one of the things Kurtz realized in his confrontation with death was that, if all objects of belief were utterly fictitious, the will to believe was not. And his pronouncement itself was "the expression of some sort of belief; it had candor, it had conviction, it had . . . the appalling face of a glimpsed truth. . . . It was an affirmation, a moral victory" (*HD* 69–70). This moral victory is a tragic one, manifested by the willingness of characters to pursue belief at the risk of perdition.

If Jim responds to the dream by refusing to accept his limitations, Marlow does so by venturing into the Congo. Marlow repeatedly apologizes to his audience for attempting to represent a dream. When he gets back from his voyage, it is clear which of his faculties the jungle most sorely taxed:

"It was not my strength that wanted nursing, it was my imagination that wanted soothing" (*HD* 70).[7] What does Marlow mean by imagination? The imagination is what projects people beyond the confines of their everyday lives. It is, writes Kierkegaard, "what providence uses in order to get men into reality, into existence, to get them far enough out, or in, or down in existence. And when imagination has helped them as far out as they are meant to go—that is where reality, properly speaking, begins."[8] In Musilian terms reality results from the sense of the possible, on the capacity to think that "here such and such might, should, or ought to happen" (*GW* 1 : 16; *MWQ* 1 : 12 [4]). In the absence of the imagination there is no reality but only a mechanical phantasmagoria. And the Congo helps dissolve this phantasmagoria, revealing less about an alternative to the world than about the reality Marlow thought he was leaving behind.

The productive setting of the Congo is further replicated in the reaches of Patusan where Jim tries to become what he is. "Do you notice," asks Marlow, emphasizing the unreality *not* of this fairy-tale world but of its opposite,

> how, three hundred miles beyond the end of telegraph cables and mail-boat lines, the haggard utilitarian lies of our civilisation whither and die, to be replaced by pure exercises of the imagination, that have the futility, often the charm, and sometimes the hidden truthfulness, of works of art?

If both the East and the West are constructed by lies, there is a difference. The lies of England are "haggard" and "utilitarian" while those of Patusan offer "pure exercises of the imagination," possessing both the appeal and the truthfulness of works of art. The so-called lie of interpretation proves responsible not only for the delusions of fact and fiction but also for the access to this still ineffable truth. In fact, as Marlow claims, all our illusions may really be "visions of remote, unattainable truth, seen dimly." And this may be the intuition that incites him "to tell you the story, to try to hand it over to you, as it were, its very existence, its reality—the truth disclosed in a moment of illusion" (*LJ* 172, 196). The venturer is analogous to the artist. Both seek the real in an imaginative transcendence of form.

Sixteen pages later Conrad locates the dream at the basis of the human enterprise at large. Jewel had claimed that Jim had fled from his reality

as if driven by some accursed thing he had heard or seen in his sleep. . . . She had said he had been driven away from her by a dream. . . . And yet is not mankind itself, pushing on its blind way, driven by a dream of its greatness and its power upon the dark paths of excessive cruelty and of excessive devotion? And what is the pursuit of truth, after all? (*LJ* 212–13)

The will to power itself is nothing but a dream of unending accomplishment, as is the insatiable compulsion of the will to truth. In its responsibility for every form of commitment, effort, and revelation, here the dream becomes the emblem of an essayism impelling the very motions of the human condition. It becomes the will to realization.

While Conrad defends the formative nature of dangerously following the dream, he still insists on exposing as a delusion the hope of discovering some authentic and definitive being "out there," in a different and undefinable universe. This point is illustrated in the transformations undergone by the idealist Kurtz. While Jim attempted to overcome his own limitations rather naively, Kurtz appeared to have succeeded with a terrible directness, transcending the conventions of his historical heritage to encounter the wilderness of his innermost being. In this freedom he seemed even to have legislated his own values. And yet, aside from the question of what kind of values he has legislated—merely more of the human, all-too-human, machinations of greed—the problem with Kurtz is another one. In his singularity he has become unaccountable. "You can't judge Mr. Kurtz as you would an ordinary man," the Russian hastens to warn Marlow. And that is the problem. The severance between him and humanity is too great. Marlow is willing to concede that everything belonged to Kurtz, "but that was a trifle. The thing was to know what he belonged to, how many powers of darkness claimed him for their own. That was the reflection that made you creepy all over."

True, the seeds of Kurtz's lack of restraint are sown by his imaginative ability. Kurtz is a consummate artist, "a painter who wrote for the papers, or . . . a journalist who could paint," in any event "a universal genius" (*HD* 56, 49, 71). In Kurtz we are privy to a danger inherent to the aesthetic enterprise itself: that of overcoming the limitations of form without achieving a coherent alternative. In the very measure to which Kurtz's behavior does not allow for a standard of judgment, it also lacks all determinable substance. For all practical purposes Kurtz is a "hollow sham," a man who has not found but lost himself.

Conrad writes novels partially out of his sense of the need to situate existence within a dramatic and historical reality. Among the factors informing this context there is one he refuses to overlook: the existence of other selves, or witnesses and judges of one's mode of being. Kurtz comes to some realization of this being largely through the presence of Marlow, a presence rupturing Kurtz's transcendence and offering his life the measure it had theretofore lacked. Marlow contests Kurtz's life in the same way that this life contests the world to which Marlow belongs (and which Kurtz has presumably left behind). But the contact reaffirms that Kurtz still belongs to that world and that he cannot escape its rules.

The venturesome overstepping of empty conventions, the dream pulling a character into an ideal territory—all these transcendent dimensions of human existence are grounded in a realm of facticity, in one's being determined in a certain way, by tradition as well as action, whether one likes it or not. If the "there" belies the "here," the "here" also belies the "there." Jim's defect lies precisely in the fact that he *has* jumped off the Patna. Marlow cannot go ashore for a howl and a dance because he must man his boat. Kurtz may possess excellent ideas, but in the meantime he is cutting off heads. For Conrad as for Sartre, actuality is a truth that mocks one's fiction. And this actuality takes the shape of fate: the resistance of external affairs to the desires of the will. If everything were to go Jim's way, he would no doubt be the hero he aspires to be. But events "conspire" against him, contesting his plans. The first time he has the opportunity to realize his ideal he is unprepared to act. The second time he is seduced by example. The third time he falls prey to a weakness he thought he had suppressed (a weakness, once again, of sympathetic identification, of otherness encroaching on one's attempted autonomy). In time fortune gives the lie to freedom, showing one's touted potential to be only what history enables. Tested by fortune, one is called on to function in the context not of abstract but concrete freedom.

Jim's tragedy is therefore inevitable. It bears witness to the problem of actualizing one's intentions in the present. Jim understands what he was up against when he deserted the pilgrims on the *Patna,* even if he mistakenly believes he can prevail against it: "It is all in being ready. I wasn't; not then. There were boats enough for half of them, perhaps, but there was no time. No time! No time!" What Conrad dramatizes in his fiction is that there is *never* time—never time to make ready for a present that leaps out of the future. In essence Jim may well have been a hero; in practice he was just another person "taken unawares" (*LJ* 53, 59). The greater the desires of the will, the more they must answer to intractable fate. Just as the dream tested all finite stability, finitude now tests the dream.

And yet this vision of fortune as an agent of fateful finitude tells only half the story. In Conrad fortune also functions as the opposite of an antithesis to transcendent ideals, or as the operator of transcendence itself. The disruptive power of contingency and chance intrudes on nothing less than a life conducted as though it were consubstantial with will. Far from contesting the unhinged ideals of Jim and Kurtz, the real function of fortune is instead to originate the very experience of transcendence. Fortune shatters pragmatic and conceptual shelters, the first forms of that illusory transcendence and shaky idealism from which humanity suffers. And this is why Conradian fortune so often appears as a storm. Upsetting the placidity of a life lived in self-prediction, attacking the very laxity of all normal theorizations of experience, fortune confronts characters with the choice of perishing or operating in more deliberate ways. In fact, these eruptions of chance are never mere accidents. They are gifts of destiny, embedded in the very soil of experience. Dramatic reversals of circumstance offer a character the occasion to come into reality, to move into contact with things that a life has willingly or unwillingly sought to exclude. In the simplest of terms, the Conradian crisis shows its protagonists to be incomplete in their systems of security. It summons them to meet their truth beyond that coherent but untested ensemble of ideas, emotions, and practices structuring their functional routines. To become themselves they must overcome themselves; to overcome themselves they must struggle forward into the openness of the future and the unfamiliar. Even as it challenges the delusion of all ideal achievements, Fortune still sounds the note of opportunity.

Conrad thus traces a circular path. On the one hand, his criticism of the security of a life governed by a placid, complacent logic points to transcendence as the proper and irrepressible domain of truth. On the other, he submits this transcendence itself to a withering test of action. In either case the fortunate-unfortunate turn functions to offset the petrification of truth in conscious illusion. One must believe in one's dream, one must believe in one's fact; ultimately one must believe in the *discord* between one's fact and one's dream. In ethical terms one must resolve on one's destiny as insuperable conflict. To live is to be on trial, a trial in which the immanent and the transcendent function as prosecution as well as defense, each suffering repression at the hands of the other, each rebelling against this repression by unbalancing its pseudostability. Critical and utopian essayism are gestures of a single essay.

Only insofar as this essay is maintained does the famous "feeling of existence" hold sway. And this is where the distinction of Conrad's protagonists lies: in their acquiescence in a conflict to which they are destined. Their personal aspirations are complicitous with the impersonal objections of fate. Once he has deserted the *Patna,* Jim becomes destined to the tension that the moment has caused. The more he pursues his ideal, the more he increases his "inward pain," which is all that makes him "know himself." And it is also this pain, continues Stein, that "makes him—exist" (*LJ* 132). Once again it is a gift conferred by destiny and withheld from a whole host of Conradian characters. Captain MacWhirr in "Typhoon" (1919) had never had the opportunity to undergo such trials. He "had sailed over the surface of the oceans as some men go skimming over the years of existence to sink gently into a placid grave, ignorant of life to the last, without ever having been made to see all it may contain of perfidy, of violence, and of terror." "There are on sea and land," Conrad adds with sobering irony, "such men thus fortunate—or thus disdained by destiny or by the sea."[9] Jim's parents suffer a similar exclusion. "Nothing ever came to them; they would never be taken unawares, and never be called upon to grapple with fate" (*LJ* 208). They would never encounter the revelation of "some awful catastrophe." It will be reserved for Kurtz, the captain of *The Secret Sharer,* the crew of the *Narcissus,* and the searching Marlow. If such characters had "mastered their fates," as Conrad suggests in *Lord Jim,* it was not because they had succeeded in controlling their fortunes, but because they had tried.

At the moment when fate compels recognition, to quote Zabel again, "a man's conscious moral existence begins." This conception of a moral existence has little to do with the classical notion of morality as action in accordance with a good. Rather, it envisions morality as constituted by the effort to *determine* a good. A moral existence is one that makes choice possible to begin with. In this sense characters entrenched in their protective shelters do not lead a moral existence; their actions are ruled by automatisms. Existence is moral only when racked by an either/or, when a trial, challenge, or ambivalent situation calls out for a stance. Only in an essayistic condition can a person be said to be moral. And what this may mean, as Musil puts it, is that to act morally is to base none of one's decisions on morality.

In this new description ethical behavior finds its basis not in stolid obedience to a system of belief but in the experience such obedience intends to serve. As with the ancient Greeks, ethos is a matter of character. And this character is equivalent to destiny, the historical configuration of the existence one leads.[10] When Marlow first sets eyes on Jim, he is struck precisely by the appearance of such an ethos:

> He stood there for all the parentage of his kind, for men and women by no means clever or amusing, but whose very existence is based upon honest faith, and upon the instinct of courage. I don't mean military courage, or civil courage, or any special kind of courage. I mean just that inborn ability to look temptations straight in the face—a readiness unintellectual enough, goodness knows, but without pose—a power of resistance, don't you see, ungracious if you like, but priceless—an unthinking and blessed stiffness before the outward and inward terrors, before the might of nature, and the seductive corruption of men—backed by a faith invulnerable to the strength of facts, to the contagion of example, to the solicitation of ideas. (*LJ* 27)

What shows the substance of a person most persuasively is not the rhetoric of facts and ideas but the ability to look temptations in the face. If there is a faith underlying the courage this requires, it does not appeal to a particular code of belief. If anything, it is a faith that enables one to function without such a code, or to bear up under the dissolution of fact as well as idea. Lacking an ideological object, this faith is a faith in the challenge one is undergoing, in its capacity to bring something to the surface, in the validity of the findings. This faith is an *amor fati*, a love of fate.

Of course, as the story of Jim unfolds, no reader fails to recognize the irony of Marlow's first impression of the man (the irony that Jim turned out to lack that "blessed stiffness" Marlow here extolls). But this irony risks masking that other and deeper one that Conrad's fiction never tires to repeat, to the effect that no one, not even a courageous hero like

---

Singleton or the French lieutenant, is ever invulnerable to the inward and outward terrors. The chinks in the armor can always be pierced. In presenting his ethical vision, Marlow does not claim that a character will actually prevail against the risks that are run. In fact, to hedge against too narrow an interpretation, Marlow immediately distinguishes this ethos from unthinking inflexibility:

This has nothing to do with Jim, directly; only, he was outwardly so typical of that good, stupid kind we like to feel marching right and left of us in life, of the kind that is not disturbed by the vagaries of intelligence and the perversions of—of nerves, let us say. He was the kind of fellow you would, on the strength of his looks, leave in charge of the deck.

Conrad's addition suggests that we should not interpret this ethical substance in terms of a mindless clinging to a "few simple notions." Yes, the "good" and "stupid" type of person marching on either side of us might well prevail against the inward and outward terrors. Oblivious to nerves and intelligence and imagination, such a person might even be left in charge of the deck. But what interests Conrad is this heroic spirit in the context of overwhelming pressures. His tales are not about Singleton but, rather, the ordinary crew, not the aplomb of the French lieutenant but the vulnerability of Jim, "a conscientious man on a rack" (*LJ* 27, 394). The difference between Jim and an unflinching hero is the same as the one between essayism and victory, the former representing the effort to achieve such victory. Measured by the ubiquitous crises confronting Conradian characters, the only reading of these traits of courage, readiness, and faith that preserves their relevance is one in which they constitute the very *capacity* to be tested, a readiness to be unready, a willingness to see the challenge through, even if one fails to prevail against it.

Here we might recall that eulogy of the warriors and explorers who followed the Thames at the beginning of *Heart of Darkness*. When Marlow takes over the narrative from the anonymous speaker, the reason for the eulogy becomes clearer. The ancient Romans who invaded the British Isles may not have been very clever, but they were "men enough to face the darkness." "There's no initiation either into such mysteries," Marlow adds, imagining the experience of a commander camped in the savage primitivity of that island. "He has to live in the midst of the incomprehensible" (*HD* 10). To live in the midst of the incomprehensible is to inhabit a condition of unfamiliarity, risk, and hampered vision. It is to be exposed to the underside, as it were, of the conventions and comforts of the kinsmen at home. The conscious endurance of such a situation calls for an ethos much deeper than any intellectual or sentimental conviction. It calls for faith in the contest itself, that willingness to confront the irreducible tensions and ambiguities of character cum destiny which is represented by Marlow's own narrative journeys and research.

Turning that famous bend in the Congo river to perceive the appeal of an unfathomable truth in the incomprehensible uproar of natives on the shore, Marlow finds himself in a position equivalent to that of the Romans. To respond to this truth, Marlow stresses, a person must be able to "look on without a wink." But this means that

he must at least be as much of a man as these on the shore. He must meet that truth with his own true stuff—with his own inborn strength. Principles won't do. . . . No. You want a deliberate belief. An appeal to me in this fiendish row—is there? Very well. I hear, I admit, but I have a voice too, and for good or evil mine is the speech that cannot be silenced. (*HD* 38)

"Deliberate belief" sounds almost oxymoronic, as though it required the birth of a conviction upon the spot. And, in a sense, this is exactly what it does require: a capacity to believe in the absence of belief, to place one's faith in the stress and strife of the present situation. Insofar as one's principles falter in these situations, this deliberate belief can no longer be a mere belief in an X or a Y. Rather it must be a willingness to be convinced by the situation at hand, which no thought can equal and which cannot be legitimated by any theoretical system—in short, a readiness to hear and look on an autonomous, unique, and abnormal occurrence that calls for unsupported decision.

Presupposing the rupture of preconception, the deliberateness of this belief entails the acknowledgment of the trial with which one is faced. The belief mustered at such moments is a belief in one's power to *come* to a decision, to be able to will in such conditions rather than not will at all. And this kind of belief can arise only as sheer power of motivation. This is that "voice," or that ability to speak, on which words, interpretations, and values depend, the speech that "for good or evil" cannot be silenced. Otherwise put, trial governs belief and not the other way around.

This ethos finds additional elaboration in Marlow's evocation of seventeenth-century traders. The emptier the object of their quest, the more impressive the energy that informs it:

Where wouldn't they go for pepper! For a bag of pepper they would cut each other's throats without hesitation, and would forswear their souls, of which they were so careful otherwise: the bizarre obstinacy of that desire made them defy death in a thousand shapes. . . . It made them great! By heavens! it made them heroic; it made them pathetic, too, in their craving for trade with the inflexible death levying its toll on young and old. It seems impossible to believe that mere greed could hold men to such a steadfastness of purpose, to such a blind persistence in endeavor and sacrifice. . . . To us, their less tried successors, they appear magnified, not as agents of trade but as instruments of a recorded destiny, pushing out into the unknown in obedience to an inward voice, to an impulse beating in the blood, to a dream of the future. (*LJ* 138–39)

What Marlow respects in these traders is no more than their "steadfastness of purpose" and "blind persistence in endeavor and sacrifice." By minimizing the ends to which they strive, Conrad maximizes their tenacity of resolve. What would happen, one wonders, if they had no object on which to focus their energy? Then we would have essayism in its most taxing condition. And that, no doubt, is when something like a few simple notions, or conscious moral principles, might also begin to take shape. What is more, these principles would be the very same courage and faith, accompanied by such values as human solidarity and fidelity in the "community of toil," insofar as this essayistic condition would appear to be universal, underlying and belying the ideologies by which people presume to act. Expressed or unexpressed, this essayistic ethic would offer the very prerequisite for moral behavior, shifting the emphasis of all ethical science from the autonomous validity of intellectual beliefs to the work their formation requires.

There are two passages in *Heart of Darkness* which associate work not with the habitual distraction from objective reality but with a reality entirely of its own, indeed, a reality that responds to the first. One concerns a book Marlow finds in an abandoned hut in the middle of the jungle, *An Inquiry into Some Points of Seamanship* by a certain Towser or Towson. "Not a very enthralling book," Marlow admits, in fact, "dreary enough" reading,

but at the first glance you could see there a singleness of intention, an honest concern for the right way of going to work, which made these humble pages . . . luminous with another than a professional light. The simple old sailor, with his talk of chains and purchases, made me forget the jungle and the pilgrims in a delicious sensation of having come upon something unmistakably real.

In the methodless setting of the jungle the handbook certainly suggests a surreal attempt to shackle the paradoxes of the real to a rational method. And yet what speaks for the other type of reality revealed by the book is its earnest attempt to achieve a singleness of intention in a setting that allows for none. It is this very quest for method which constitutes the reality of that "right way of going to work." "I don't like work—no man does," says Marlow in a second passage which uses reality in this sense of ethical behavior; but in work lies "the chance to find yourself. Your own reality—for yourself, not for others—what no man can ever know" (*HD* 39, 31).

What is this unique reality that no other person can ever know? It is the struggle one undergoes in the project, the

---

strength of one's motivation, the weight of the challenge, the discipline one has imposed on one's actions. One's own reality is the still undetermined possibility the labor reveals. Otherwise put, what work reveals is not the fruit of one's application, which is visible to all, but the nature of the application. And this means one's commitment to achieving potential. Moreover, the achievement of potential lies in the revelation of potential, not in the qualities coterminous with its actualization (the development of a skill, know-how, and so on). Inasmuch as work means methodical commitment to a project, there is little irony in the fact that the manual on seamanship belongs to the man of pure project, the motley Russian.

It now becomes clear that the values ordinarily conceived of as merely the means to accomplish ends—namely, courage, resolve, perseverance, work, integrity, and faith—are the ends in question. Performing a withering critique of all goals to which humans apply themselves, Conrad still succeeds in rescuing the instruments on which such goals depend. What matters in the realm of ethics is not moral certainty but the attempt to achieve it, not truth but the will to truth, not success but the striving on which it is based. The ethical virtues are propaedeutic. As the essay becomes the paradigm for action, the valorous conduct of the contest becomes the most for which one can hope. When Ulrich's sister asks why he bothers with teleologically impossible tasks, he answers "I do my duty. . . . Perhaps like a soldier" (*GW* 3:957; *MWQ* 3:348 [30]).

Call it stiffness, will, or self-overcoming, the *arete* in question is the last to attend a self that destiny has divorced from all but its barest structures. Or perhaps it is no self at all but, rather, an effort to acquire a self, a prelusive, essayistic activity in the service of a distant goal. The honesty, readiness, and courage for teleologically suspended projection bespeak not the "qualities" developed without a man but the "man" without qualities.

That redemption lies in this essayistic aquiescence is suggested not only by Marlow's eulogies of Jim, Jewel, and Kurtz but also by meditations like the one when he is trying to explain why he needed to visit Jim in Patusan. He had wanted assurance that Jim's trials had not gotten the better of him, forcing him to "go out" in an improper way. "I was about to go home for a time; and it may be I desired, more than I was aware of myself, to dispose of him—to dispose of him, you understand—before I left. I was going home." As Marlow ponders this notion of going home, at first it seems synonymous with achieving peace of conscience:

We wander in our thousands over the face of the earth, the illustrious and the obscure, earning beyond the seas our fame, our money, or only a crust of bread; but it seems to me that for each of us going home must be like going to render an account. We return to face our superiors, our kindred, our friends—those whom we obey, and those whom we love; but even they who have neither, the most free, lonely, irresponsible and bereft of ties,—even those for whom home holds no dear face, no familiar voice,—even they have to meet the spirit that dwells within the land, under its sky, in its air, in its valleys, and on its rises, in its fields; in its waters and its trees—a mute friend, judge, and inspirer. Say what you like, to get its joy, to breathe its peace, to face its truth, one must return with a clear consciousness. (*LJ* 135–36)

One should neither mystify nor demystify this talk of the spirit of the land. Home, Marlow notes, involves more "the girls we love, the men we look up to, the tenderness, the friendships, the opportunities, [and] the pleasures" ordinarily associated with the hearth. If Marlow's amplification of home to a spiritual principle may strike some as "sheer sentimentalism," this is only because "few of us have the will or the capacity to look consciously under the surface of [the] familiar emotions" that the hearth contains. In its fuller sense, home is the context for the ego, the arena of everything that precedes, transcends, and outlasts the individual will. It is what, in the form of inexorable external necessity, affirms or denies one's desire. In short, it is the very horizon of human freedom, constituted by the customs and traditions into which one was born, the conditions in which action takes place, and the practical intentions of one's conscious and unconscious decision.

What is interesting about this passage about home is that it comes to attribute the greatest recognition of home to those who have no home. No one, the passage continues, is more aware of the realm of the historically given than those who are truly uprooted, who have few deceptive externals standing between them and their fate. Characters cut off from the "mere outward condition of existence" best understand what it means to render an account to everything that the will itself cannot determine:

> I think it is the lonely, without a fireside or an affection they may call their own, those who return not to a dwelling but to the land itself, to meet its disembodied, eternal, and unchangeable spirit—it is those who understand best its severity, its saving power, the grace of its secular right to our fidelity, to our obedience. (*LJ* 136)

In other words, it is the very distance taken by characters like Jim and the Russian from the normative structures of their original community, from the vox populi of both conscience and town, which puts them in contact with the mute spirit of valleys and trees. In this larger sense of homecoming, going home means first going *away* from home. If homecoming means reconciling oneself with the land to which one is destined, then the first step toward such reconciliation lies in an ethos of critical-utopian essayal—in an active encounter with this spirit as "disembodied" from the land as the souls in question. To render an account to this inspirer and judge of one's trial is to vouch for one's service to it.

It is thus not surprising that Marlow's own homecoming entails not disposing of Jim, as he intends to do, but sealing the bond between them. Marlow has his homecoming in reclaiming this deserter as "one of us," in recognizing that the two of them will remain eternally tied "in the name of that doubt which is the inseparable part of our knowledge." The home to which they belong is the trying ground "from which

[man] draws his faith together with his life." All of us "feel it," Marlow remarks, even though few recognize it consciously. Though he no longer had any home, Jim, too, "felt confusedly but powerfully, the demand of some such truth or some such illusion—I don't care how you call it, there is so little difference, and the difference means so little." And so too does the difference between living and dying, for the going out that this living entails is also a manner of dying. Careless of "innumerable lives," the spirit of the land had allowed better men than Jim "to go out, disappear, vanish utterly without provoking a sound of curiosity or sorrow," often taking to drink and degenerating into a "blear-eyed, swollen-faced, besmirched loafer." But Jim "did not go out," at least not in this sense. Acquiescing in the projection to which he was destined, "he came on wonderfully, came on straight as a die and in excellent form" (*LJ* 135, 136−37).

5

Robert Musil

Conscious
Utopianism

In the first volume of *The Man without Qualities* General Stumm ponders the generalized loss of a Weltanschauung in the modern age. Considering the theoretical gaps that such worldviewing entails, the narrator does not bemoan the loss. He is concerned, rather, with its implications. He turns to his protagonist, one of those intellectuals, General Stumm reflects, whose thoughts never came to rest because they were always beholding "that eternally wandering element, the final, undefined factor in all things, which never finds its proper place anywhere." A person who accepts the loss of a Weltanschauung is faced with an option:

He must either entirely give up the habit of thinking about his life, something in which many people indulge, or he gets into that strange state of conflict [*sonderbaren Zwiespalt*] in which he has to think and yet apparently never can reach the point of satisfaction. (*GW* 2:519, 520–21; *MWQ* 2:267, 268 [108])

This remark contrasts thinking with the inability to bring thought to conclusion. The very aim of thinking—the resolution of perplexity—is at odds with the interminable labor it requires. In fact, it may even be that the passage indicates a misgiving about the inconclusiveness of intellectual inquiry, a misgiving that occasionally leads Musil to envision the possibility of a mystical reconciliation with the world in which everything is "already decided" and all demeanors show love and abandon.[1]

A closer reading of this passage suggests, however, that the very distinction between decision and indecision is hard to sustain. When the clause after *Zwiespalt* is read as restrictive, the "strange conflict" ensuing upon the loss of a worldview becomes one that *necessarily* entails thinking without resolution. Thinking would thus constitute the natural outcome and record of the conflict itself. This second reading would draw this conflict, or *Zwiespalt*, quite close to that condition of alertness, ecstasy, or overtaking of the mind which Musil finds characteristic of the mystical state. Born from "a tension analogous to erotic force, a nameless force of concentration," mystical or ecstatic union possesses only a single opposite—not interminable, essayistic activity but "rigidification" (*Erstarrung*), the rigidification, that is, of habitual, everyday consciousness. This ecstatic, or other, condition (*andere Zustand*) is characterized by "awakening and ascension" (*Erweckung und Aufstieg*),[2] a condition experienced as much by the thinker as by the lover or religious enthusiast: "The dancer or listener, abandoning himself to the musical moment, the contemplator [*der Schauende*], the one possessed [*der Ergiffene*], is detached from all 'before' and 'after'" ("Cues," *GW* 8 : 1151; *PS* 205). In every instant of this heightened awareness "one recognizes the absolute irrelevance of everything one had previously thought with an unmoved mind [*unberührtem Verstand*]." The essayistic labor of an agitated mind would then be one of the ways, and perhaps the only methodical one, of articulating this ecstatic "ethical condition" that needs no "ethical action" ("Commentary," *GW* 8 : 1018, 1017; *PS* 56).

In truth, the strange discord ensuing upon an awareness of a final, undefined factor in all things, Musil writes, can result just as easily in a condition of "complete unbelief" as in one of "complete subjection to belief." Complete unbelief suggests an unending delinquency of knowledge, subjection to belief a supreme and perhaps mystical wisdom. Mystical experience consists in a timeless confluence of subject and object in a "third" condition. In the nihilistic alternative of complete unbelief, this third condition is still the glaring fact, even if it now manifests itself as the utter incredibility of all objects of consciousness. The two cases are faces of a single condition, in which the scaffolding of subject and object, sign and significance, has collapsed, revealing instead a nonpicture in which no phenomenon can be perceived in its finite and definitive nature. What occasionally gives Ulrich the sense of a realm in which everything is already decided, "soothing to the mind as mother's milk," is thus neither thought nor feeling but rather a type of experience which is "neither true nor false, neither rational nor irrational." And one can no more gain a conviction from this experience than "one can make a truth out of the genuine parts of an essay" (*GW* 2:520–21, 1:255; *MWQ* 2:268, 1:303 [108, 62]).

In neither state, neither that of the eternally resolving essay nor that of a mystical "decidedness," can one accept any either/or, any "simple logic," as Maurice Blanchot puts it. And not even "two at once, the two that always end up affirming each other dialectically, or compulsively."

When the domination of truth ceases—that is, when the reference to the true-false dichotomy (and to the union of the two) no longer holds sway . . . then knowledge continues to seek itself and to seek to inscribe itself, but in an other space where there is no longer any direction. When knowledge is no longer a knowledge of truth, it is then that knowledge starts . . . like knowledge of infinite patience.[3]

In this paradoxical condition suspending the structures of cognition, one inhabits a formless situation, a space *between* the alternatives, the excluded middle, the "neutral," the sway of the pendulum.

These variable readings of the *Zwiespalt* indicate that Musil is unwilling to draw a rigid line between categories of experience which would appear at first glance to be antithetical: ecstasy, eros, and the plenitude of pure presence on the one hand; insatiable longing, scientific research, and will to power on the other.[4] Heeding Musil's own claims that there exists in humans only a single consciousness in which intellect and feeling cannot be separated, we might say that he, like most thinkers of the previous hundred years—from the German idealists to Simmel, Klages, Bloch, Pirandello, and Bergson—labors to repair a conceptual rift that might have been avoided from the start.[5] Yet, aside from Heidegger, none of Musil's contemporaries were able to thematize that "single condition" in which the oppositions between art and science, feeling and intellect, ecstasy and method represent only second-order distinctions. In Heidegger it comes to appear that the discordant condition arising with the absence of a worldview is actually more primordial than any worldview, more primordial even than eros and reason. Whether signified in art or researched by thought, this *Zwiespalt* attending paradoxical experience underlies all feelings, thoughts, decisions, or operations that are based upon it. In Heidegger's difficult language this *Zwiespalt* is a condition of resolve (*Entschlossenheit*) responding to the openness, or "disclosedness" (*Erschlossenheit*), of the world, markedly distinguished from the calculated enclosure of experience in a picture.

How close is the resolve of which Heidegger speaks in *Being and Time* to Musil's conception of a conflict in which one must think without reaching the point of satisfaction? We must bear for a moment with Heidegger's argument.

Resoluteness is a condition produced by "the call of conscience." Whence comes this call, and what is its message? The call arises out of the fissures of a structured world, in which everything seems to have its place and the subject is wont to act on the basis of rules of thumb. This is the world of *das Man*, of Musil's *Seinesgleichen*, Pirandello's phantasmagoria, and Conrad's slumber. A call jolts the subject away from this order, speaking as it were of a fault in its foundations. The self's familiar modes of dwelling had been a "listening away" from itself, a *Hinhören* now broken by the call. What gets called in this call? "'Nothing' gets called *to* this

Self." A *Rest* is disclosed: an absence and a lack. Conscience speaks only in the language of silence, saying nothing and yet summoning the self from this nothing to its "inmost *potentiality*-for-Being-itself [*Selbstsein*können]."[6] At the very moment that the call awakens the subjective desire to be oneself it evokes a feeling of uncanniness, or of not belonging (*Unheimlichkeit*). This is the condition of resoluteness, or *Entschlossenheit*.

Resoluteness is not to be confused with a choice from among determinate possibilities, or concrete options, which is called a decision [*Entscheidung* or *Entschluß*]. What one chooses here is not an option but a condition in which options first arise. "One would completely misunderstand the phenomenon of resoluteness," writes Heidegger,

> if one should want to suppose that this consists simply in taking up possibilities which have been proposed and recommended, and seizing hold of them. . . . The *indefiniteness* characteristic of every potentially-for-Being into which Dasein has been factically thrown, is something that necessarily *belongs* to resoluteness.[7]

Resolve is a condition of undecidedness and indeterminacy of vision in which one gazes beyond options to the factors that make them possible. In both Heidegger and Musil this undecidedness is the historical basis for all committed decisions. If Ulrich lives "vaguely" and "undecidedly," it is not out of indecision but rather out of a compulsion to that "loosening and bind of the world" which goes by the name of *Geist:* the active determination of the configurations of choice, and even of the resolved situations that present options to begin with.[8]

To make a choice in the ordinary sense of the word is not to determine one's options but merely to select from those already given. The nothing disclosed by resolve, in contrast, is a silence accompanying whatever logic determines these options, "some factor unknown," Musil writes, which would "make a decision possible" (*GW* 1:151; *MWQ* 1:176 [40]). It is something that lies beneath, between, or outside the alternatives. As a character in *The Enthusiasts* puts it, "life always makes you choose between two possibilities, and you always feel: One is missing! Always one—the uninvented third possibility."[9] Here absolute faith and an absolute absence of faith are linked, even if Ulrich is unable to intellectualize the link. Still he knew that "all the decisive moments of his life had been associated with . . . a sensation of amazement and loneliness." Crucial and decisive moments in the lives of other characters of the novel are described in analogous terms, as, for example, when Diotima is trying to decide whether to engage in an adulterous relationship with the Prussian Arnheim. It was not entirely unjustifiable, the narrator remarks, "that this undecided condition, which was so markedly distinct from the simple coarse-grainedness of connubial life, by her was called passion" (GW 1:155, 2:596, 425; MWQ 1:181, 2:365, 148 [40, 116, 94]).

What does this disclosive event of resolve entail for ethical procedure? Before all else it means, as Ulrich explains to his sister, that "we oughtn't to demand action from one another, but to start by creating the preconditions for it" (GW 3:741; MWQ 3:99 [10]). One can respond to the silent call of conscience, Heidegger writes, only by "choosing to choose" a kind of "Being-one's-Self." To understand the call of conscience is not to choose conscience (which, being silent, cannot be chosen) but to choose having a conscience. "'Understanding the appeal' means 'wanting to have a conscience.'"[10] In Ulrich's words, "in order to acquire intellectuality and spirituality one must first of all be convinced that as yet one had none" (GW 2:365; MWQ 2:75 [84]). The kind of Being-one's-Self that one chooses by means of resolve can no longer remain closed to the openness that comes into view at the very same moment, that Erschlossenheit that is "forgotten" in the course of habitual, everyday functioning. When operating in accordance with stable truths and life organization, like Pirandello's marionettes, "we conceal the fact that to affirm a particular truth presupposes that we are open to choice and truth in the first place." In the related terms of Ernst Tugendhat, only in the possibility of self-responsibility can something like a self be constituted at all.[11] And responsibility itself is "that for which I must answer when I am without any answer and without any self save a borrowed, a simulated self, or the 'stand-in' for identity: the mandatory proxy." Blanchot's condition of "subjectivity without a subject" is also that of the man without qualities: structured from the outside in, determined without having determined, committed but with no clear commitments.[12] It is a condition proleptic to action. Only in this condition can preparations can be made for a conscious ethic.

One of Musil's formulas for this type of condition is "active passivism." One feels like "a stride that can be taken in any direction" and views everything actual as only a single instance of its own potential. Relinquishing one's greediness for experiences, one comes to look upon them "less as upon something personal and real and more as upon something general and abstract." One considers them "with as much detachment as if they were something painted or as if one were listening to a song." Accordingly, an active passivist is not interested in what happens but only "in the significance attached to it, in the intention associated with it, in the system embracing each individual happening." Before making a choice such a person would first have to invent its purpose. So long as "no idea occurred to him, no decision would occur to him either." Events would now be evaluated not by their plots but their spirit: their ability to make accessible "some new content of life [instead of] only distributing what was already in existence" (*GW* 1:250, 2:364, 368, 364; *MWQ* 1:297, 2:73, 79, 74 [62, 84]).

In a broad historical perspective this means that what a person does "is never the decisive thing—it's always only whatever one does next. . . . But what matters after the next step? Obviously the one that follows after that." To live in such a way would be to follow a "morality of the next step," looking first around and outside of things, to their potential concatenations with others. Insisting on maximum motivation in action, an active passivist "does not say No to life, he says Not Yet" (*GW* 3:735–36, 2:444; *MWQ* 3:92, 2:172 [10, 97]). Every event inspires new thought.[13]

On one level the essayistic condition projecting subjectivity into a realm of theoretical possibility emblematizes a loss of sociohistorical direction at the beginning of the century; Ulrich is only an emblem of his time. On another level the strange conflict alludes to a problem underlying every thought or action, which, when contextualized, appears as no more than "an intermediate state" and "medial condition" (*GW* 2:474, 573; *MWQ* 2:209, 336 [101, 114]). It is history itself, and not only its participants, that takes shape in a perpetual play of perhapsness and not-yetness. Musil links these two levels of resolve in a series of contiguous chapters which culminate in the question of whether a new logic can be found for this kind of intermediacy.

In Chapter 57 of Book 1 Diotima is struggling to find an idea to symbolize the destiny and future of Austria. What she always discovered when engaged in this type of activity, however, was that as soon as she had hit upon a convincing idea "she could not help noticing that it would also be a great thing to give reality to the opposite of it." While she found it impossible to live without "eternal verities," she discovered "that each eternal verity exists twice over and even in a multiplicity of forms" (*GW* 1:229; *MWQ* 1:271 [57]). When Count Leinsdorf asks her whether she has chosen a guiding theme for their Universal Austrian Year, she answers that she has invited a circle of distinguished writers to her house to discuss the matter. She will wait and see what suggestions they put forth. "'That's the very thing!' His Highness exclaimed, instantly won over to the idea of waiting and seeing. 'The very thing! One can't be too careful.'" Like Diotima, the present time was suffering from the semantic complex called "redemption," the narrator remarks. It "was expectant, impatient, turbulent and unhappy, but the Messiah for whom it was hoping and waiting was not yet in sight" (*GW* 1:231, 2:521, 403; *MWQ* 1:273, 2:267, 121 [57, 108, 89]).

On this initial level the active passivism of the epoch

allegorizes a particularly exacerbated suspension of belief, which Heidegger alludes to in the phrase "the No more of the Gods that have fled and the Not Yet of the God that is coming."[14] On a deeper level the conflict or suspension is already grounded in the fact that historical evolution is *always* "swinging to and fro" between "the two poles of this Neither-Nor." History, in its indecision, "revokes everything it has done and puts something else in the place of it," building up "great spiritual connections" only to let them collapse once again after a few generations (*GW* 1:248, 251; *MWQ* 1:295, 298 [62]). Change almost always occurs through the uneconomical principle of trial and error, through a utopian thrust that no sooner disrupts an established equilibrium than it provokes a resettling of elements, as in the principle of Le Chatelier.[15] If history is a tragic process of institutionalization, as Simmel, Pirandello, and other contemporaries of Musil believed, it is also a ceaseless process of transformation in which "no ego, no form, no principle, is safe" (*GW* 1:250; *MWQ* 1:295 [62]). It is marked by the dual nature of existence as *Geworfenheit* and *Entwurf:* a "thrownness" into the facticity of a given situation and a "projection" or pressing forward into possibilities. Human existence "is thrown into the kind of Being which we call 'projecting,'" which means that existence is always more than it factually is, "for to its facticity its potentiality-for-Being belongs essentially."[16] Being is always underway.

A typical response to this state of affairs can be seen in the vignette of Chapter 56. A representative of a committee charged with reviewing the wishes, suggestions, and petitions of citizens concerning the Imperial Jubilee pays a visit to Count Leinsdorf to deliver the proposals. After reading them one by one, Count Leinsdorf hands them back to the representative: "All this is excellent," he declares "but one can't say either yes or no so long as we have nothing settled in principle as to the focal point of our aims." Having already anticipated such a reaction from the count, the *Ministerialrat* had, in fact, marked with his gold-cased pocket pencil the formula "*Ass.*" at the bottom of each letter. "This magic formula, which was in use in the Kakanian civil service, stood for *Asserviert,* which means as much as *Awaiting further consideration,* and was an example of the circumspection that does not lose sight of anything and does not try to rush anything." While on the surface this *Ass.* serves to satirize the bureaucracy of the empire, it also has further implications. What the civil service uses as a means for deferring action is a strategy central to existence itself:

How little it means, for instance, that monarchs on their accession take an oath that still includes swearing to wage war against the Turks or the heathen becomes apparent if one bears in mind that never yet in the history of mankind has a sentence been completely cancelled out or completely finished, as a result of which progress at times hurtles among at a bewildering rate. And yet some things, at least, get lost in government departments; in the world nothing does. Hence *Asservation* is one of the basic formulae in the structure of our life.[17]

When a proposal strikes Count Leinsdorf as particularly urgent, he forwards it to his friend Count Stallburg at the court "with an enquiry whether it might be regarded as what he called 'provisionally definitive.'"[18] In time the "provisionally definitive" proposition returns, but still with no categorical yes or no. Leinsdorf decides that at one of the next meetings of the executive committee an interdepartmental subcommittee should be set up "to study the matter" (*GW* 2:225– 26; *MWQ* 1:266–267 [56, 57]).

In Chapter 58 Ulrich approaches the count with the proposals that he himself has received. Ulrich has gone further than the *Ministerialrat,* organizing them into one neat pile labeled "Back to——" and another labeled "Forward to——." Ulrich imagines two possible answers to these petitions, one introduced by the regret that "the present moment is not yet suitable. . . " and the other soliciting further details "concerning the restoration of the world to Baroque, Gothic, and so forth." Sensitive to the irremediable losses the West has suffered from progress, the count becomes piqued by Ulrich's light treatment of the "Back to" requests. "'My young friend,' he said, 'in the history of mankind there is no turning back of one's own free will!'" But this was more than he wished to express, for it meant that if there was no turning back then "mankind resembled a man being urged forward by some uncanny *Wanderlust*, a man for whom there is no returning home and no arriving anywhere" (*GW* 1 : 233, 234; *MWQ* 1−276, 277). As Ulrich says fifty-seven chapters later, it amounted to a "striving onwards where there was no way" (*GW* 2 : 581; *MWQ* 2 : 346 [115]).

This is the world's unconscious essay, perenially un-decided between regularity and accident, necessity and de-sire, in a system impossible to plot. In Chapter 60 Musil ex-tends the issue to logic and metaphysics. The question of whether or not the murderer Moosbrugger should be consid-ered responsible for his crime provokes the narrator to reflect on the discrepancy between the operations of the real and those of legal judgment:

Natura non fecit saltus—she does nothing by leaps and bounds; she prefers gradual transitions and on a large scale too keeps the world in a transitional state between imbecility and sanity. But jurispru-dence takes no notice of this. It says: *non datur tertium sive medium inter duo contradictoria;* in plain English, the individual is either capable of acting contrary to law or he is not, for between two con-traries there is no third or middle term. As a result of this capacity he becomes liable to punishment; as a result of his quality of being liable to punishment he becomes legally a "person." (*GW* 1 : 242; *MWQ* 1 : 287)

The law of contradiction, according to which a thing is either A or not A, and no third or intermediate condition can exist between them, underlies not only those schematizations of the world by which the man without qualities refuses to be convinced but also those ethical options arrayed in pat-terns of one against all. Is there any different solution? Per-haps. Perhaps precisely in a philosophy of the dangerous perhaps.

The belief in opposite values, writes Nietzsche, is "the un-questioned faith of the metaphysicians of all ages"; it has not occurred to even the most cautious among them "that one might have a doubt right here at the threshold where it was surely most necessary":

For one may doubt, first, whether there are any opposites at all, and secondly whether these popular valuations and opposite values on which the metaphysicians put their seal, are not perhaps merely foreground estimates, only provisional perspectives . . . frog perspectives, as it were.

It may even be, Nietzsche continues, heralding attempts to find a new way of thinking, that what constitutes the value of all good things

is precisely that they are insidiously related, tied to, and involved with these wicked, seemingly opposite things—maybe even one with them in essence. Maybe!

But who has the will to concern himself with such dangerous maybes? For that, one really has to wait for the advent of a new species of philosophers, such as have somehow another and converse taste and propensity from those we have known so far—philosophers of the dangerous "maybe" in every sense.

And in all seriousness: I see such new philosophers coming up.[19]

What might this philosophy of the dangerous Maybe entail? Perhaps a new language for the relation between yes and no. But *maybe* also suggests a hypothesis, a thinking that ventures beyond obvious options. Maybe is the mode in which to venture a guess. The hypothesis of Nietzsche's Maybe is that philosophy might forgo the law of contradiction for a different approach to phenomenal reality. Musil's passage on law takes the hypothesis a step further: such an approach might change our very conception of ethical responsibility. Here we might venture an additional guess, anticipating the details of the argument that follows. A responsible response to experience would address the intermediate space excluded by opposites; the projectual nature of historical construction and destruction; the latent "ideality" of facts, or the utopian motivation of decisive action; and the essayistic production of the empirically possible. All of this would be the basis for a conscious ethic, even if this ethic should be the first to admit that it can be no more than propaedeutic.

Musil begins to reflect on these issues as early as the date in which the historical action of *The Man without Qualities* is set. In an essay immediately preceding the outbreak of World War I, Musil confesses to being a "conservative anarchist." [20] A conservative anarchist is one who imagines that new principles of cultural organization might arise from precisely the "interior disorder" already apparent in history:

such an illogical disorder of life, such a relaxing of once-binding forces and ideals should constitute an excellent field for a great logician of the values of the soul. For, in its combination of contradictory elements, this existence is extraordinarily daring, even if only out of inconsistency and cowardice.

All that is needed is an additional step, the courage to push the whole process further in the direction it is leaning:

to become even more daring, but consciously [*noch kühner aus Bewußtheit zu werden*]. Precisely here, where every feeling peers in two different directions [like Pascal's eyes], where everything drifts, nothing is held to and everything loses its combinatorial capacity [*Kombinationsfähigkeit*], we should put to the test and reinvent all inner possibilities and transfer at last the advantages of unprejudiced laboratory-technique from the natural sciences to morality. And even today I am convinced that, in a single bound, we would thereby overcome the slow and backpedaling development from cavemen to today and enter a new era. (*GW* 8:1010–11; *PS* 33)

In this new type of "putting to the test" the practices, encounters, and relationships of haphazard historical scenes would be allowed to generate unanticipated combinations. The new type of thinking which Musil imagines, and which his protagonist attempts to articulate in the course of the novel, would begin by recognizing the functional mechanics of the actual world. No longer would an ideal, theoretical standard be offered as a solution to the tensions, contradictions, rigidities, and contingencies of its evolving system. Instead of a revaluation of values, one would aim only at a "transvaluation," a rethinking of the materials and a re-management of staff. What Musil calls for is not the imposition of a theoretical scheme on history but a hermeneutics of what history already contains. Ulrich and his narrator both reach the conclusion that what is needed in this time of need is not "a new world" but a new understanding of the existing one, a new sense of historicity, contingency, and function. It would simply be a matter of confronting "an epoch that has come into the world buttocks first and only needs the Creator's hand to turn it up the other way" (*GW* 1:306; *MWQ* 1:364 [72]).

There have long been technical means of making useful things out of "corpses, sewage, scrap and toxins," Ulrich tells Bonadea; "it is just about time it became possible for psychological technique to do something similar." One would develop a hermeneutics of complexity to replace the metaphysics of simples. Things would be viewed not as valuable in themselves but as variables in a formula always open to revision. The present would be "a hypothesis one has not yet finished with," a set of conditions and formative arrangements harboring yet undetermined relations (*GW* 1:263, 250; *MWQ* 1:312, 297 [63, 62]). A philosophy of relativity, multiplicity, and pragmatic possibility would supplant that unequivocal reference from phenomenon to rule on the basis of which moralities have typically built their institutions. Not the "what" of things (no longer determinable in itself) but their "how" would determine their value. An action would now be ethical only by virtue of the *way* it is done, by virtue of its far-reaching effects and the relations it establishes with its context at large. Essentially, this replacement of the idea of fixed identities by mobility of function aims to promote an ethical condition in which acts acquire motivation.

Musil's essayistic hypothesis envisions a new principle of daring in thought as well as action. Theoretical audacity would have the courage to operate on the basis of what it has attempted to exclude from its typical operations: duplicity, ambivalence, and relativity. Precisely because both feelings and thoughts are pulled in two different directions one should reconsider their aims. The type of thinking in effect in "statal bourgeois society," Musil writes in an essay from the previous year, is unequal to the task. The reason by which it is governed is a prudent, calculating, and perhaps even cowardly one,

concerned above all with its own security; it asks only whether what it affirms is true, never whether this truth is also useful; in fact one could say that beneath the dominion of its uniform valuation the concept of the *value* of truth has degenerated and become nearly incomprehensible.

What Musil envisions, rather, is a reason

which would give up producing amply proven points of knowl-edge—that is, the type that renders it possible to laminate iron, to fly in the air, and to procure nutrition—but would strive, on the contrary, to discover and to systematize such points of knowledge as would indicate new and daring directions to feeling, even if these remained pure plausibilities, a reason, therefore, in which thinking existed for the sole purpose of offering an intellectual framework [*intellektuelles Stützgerüst*] to certain still uncertain ways of being hu-man. ("Spirituality," *GW* 8 : 988–89; *PS* 22)

Concerned as much with value as truth, this new type of rea-son would bring to bear upon ethics the pragmatic, experi-mental, and relativistic methods that have worked so well in scientific procedure. It would operate in the manner of an es-say: projected toward the attainment of a whole that can never be encompassed, testing the valences of all present phenomena, and liberating the complexity of every "simple" issue.

How would one enact such a new type of reason? A pre-liminary model can be found in the precinct of Nietzsche's "dangerous Maybe." Nietzsche baptizes his "philosophers of the future" *Versucher,* meaning attempters or essayists.[21] What is it that these essayists attempt to determine? The "Whither and For What [*Wohin? und Wozu?*] of man." They are, in Musil's words, "conscious utopianists," assuming something like "the task of transforming the world's haphaz-ard state of consciousness into a single will" (*GW* 1 : 251;

MWQ 1 : 298 [62]). They view reality not as a fact but a mission.

Let us bracket for a moment the goal of this ambition and examine instead what the goal requires in the way of ethical procedure. Before these "furtherers of humanity" can discover new directions for human action, they must be radical skeptics. Soon this same skepticism turns the *Versucher* into "active nihilists," or into their culture's "bad conscience," who apply the knife "to the chest of the very *virtues of their time.*" The skepticism of these "artists of destruction and dissolution" is in no way indecisive. Rather, it is a skepticism of "audacious manliness" (*die Skepsis der verwegenen Männlichkeit*), the symptom of a strength that reaches "for the future with a creative hand." It is a skepticism underwritten by critical decisiveness rather than irresolution, "the certainty of value standards, the deliberate employment of a unity of method, a shrewd courage, the ability to . . . give an account of themselves," making use of "the preliminary labor of all philosophical laborers." And, needless to say, these *Versucher* will also be "men of experiments. With the name in which I dared to baptize them I have already stressed expressly their attempts and delight in attempts [*das Versuchen und die Lust am Versuchen*]."

Preparatory human beings in every sense (*vorbereitende Menschen*), these pioneers will direct their labor to enabling a new age in ethics. Ironically, this new age will not be different from the one to which their procedures already belong, for it is an age, Nietzsche writes, that will "carry heroism into the search for knowledge" (that will seek rather than achieve such knowledge), an age, in other words, resolved on its perpetually propaedeutic activity. Henceforth one will determine value by the question of "how much and how many things one could bear and take upon oneself." Here dissolution, dismantling, and experimentation all serve the purpose of constructing paradigms for new ways to be human. Unlike his contemporaries, Musil was less impressed by the domineering will of these Nietzschean *Versucher* than by the proleptic activity for which they stand. With unprecedented originality, he focused on the experimental nature of the cultural *Versuch*, to the point of wondering whether his predecessor's vision was not even too indeterminate.[22] The "transvaluation of values" necessitated by an epoch born "buttocks first" entails not a new legislation of values so much as that internal reshuffling that Musil upheld in his own notion of conservative anarchy. Let us now return with these materials to the hypothesis of active passivism, looking for the particularly active implications of the propaedeutic demeanor.

Active passivism is bent on discovering and theorizing the potential "solutions" inherent in any historical moment. This is the experimental ambition of intellectual research. *The Man without Qualities* opens, we remember, with Ulrich's decision to take a vacation from life. He resolves to stand back from habitual and preconstituted organizations of life to scrutinize them as a scientist might ponder a phenomenon never seen before. He views every present as a means to an end, a beginning and a potential turning. His task is to break free from the principle of repetition and imitation.[23] The present now appears as a pre- and posttext, a conditional result of the past simultaneously prefiguring a future. Its already given not-yetness bears witness to a movement of perennial aspiration in perennial sclerosis, of unenvisioned identity in multiplicity and multiplicity in ostensible identity. This is the situation of a new type of "systematicity" which cannot and should not seek to be closed, as the various Weltanschauungen of the metaphysicians and philosophers have tended to be in the past.

It is in light of this situation that not just the value of occurrences but also "their essence and nature" appear to Ulrich as "dependent on the circumstances surrounding them, on the ends they served, in short, on the whole complex—constructed now thus, now otherwise—to which they belonged." All things

took place in a field of energy the constellation of which charged them with meaning, and they contained good and evil just as an atom contains the potentialities of chemical combination. . . . In this manner an endless system of relationships arose in which there was no longer any such thing as independent meanings, such as in ordinary life, at a crude first approach, are ascribed to actions and qualities.

Nothing is either itself or not itself, either A or not A; it is, rather, an element in the network to which it belongs, a network that is one among possible others. Morality now requires not the immobility of rigid commandments but rather "a mobile equilibrium continually demanding exertions towards its renewal" (*GW* 1 : 250–51, 252; *MWQ* 297–98, 299 [62]). The goal of any transvaluation of values is the activity of transvaluation itself: a developing, multiplicitous, and unfinishable process synonymous to ethical evaluation itself (as opposed to the unequivocal dictates of reason). Wholeness must be sought in productive incompleteness.

To live hypothetically would thus be to essay the opportunities of the historical present. This is the constructive configuration of a philosophy of the dangerous Maybe, the essayistic activism of constructive guesswork. To live hypothetically would be to concentrate on the capacity "to think how everything could 'just as easily' be," a capacity equivalent to the quest for potential. Unpersuaded by any current reality principle, a possibilitarian (*Möglichkeitsmensch*) does not say, "Here this or that has happened, will happen, or must happen," but rather, "Here such and such might, should, or ought to happen." Such people live in a finer web than ordinary realists, namely, a web of "haze" and the still unmanifested "intentions of God." To call them escapists or dreamers is only to miss the real meaning of possibility. "A possible experience or a possible truth does not equate to real experience or real truth minus the value 'real'"; it has in it "something out-and-out divine, a fiery, soaring quality, a constructive will" (*GW* 1 : 16; *MWQ* 1 : 12 [4]).

Possibilitarians are thus ethical activists, contesting the repetitive order of selfsame events and "recalculating" the sums passed on by tradition. If it is true that all possibilities depend on reality, it is no less true that the same possibilities go on repeating themselves until someone comes along "to whom something real means no more than something imagined. It is he who first gives the new possibilities their meaning and their destiny; he awakens them" (*GW* 1:17; *MWQ* 1:13 [4]). Like the man without character of the homonymous story, Ulrich is a deliberate and self-conscious "pioneer" and "precursor" (*Vorlaufer*), a catalyst whose significance has not yet been grasped.[24]

Both ethically and ontologically, the purpose of possibilitarianism is to promote virtuality, in the Renaissance sense of *virtù:* dynamic preparedness, creative ability, ingenuity, resourcefulness, and abstract skill, which also means "character" as a precondition for decisive action. Character is not the summary of a person's qualities but the ethos they serve. Here the ethos is one of purposive resolve, a virtue of the means. The idea is that if the means are in order, the ends will take care of themselves. In the meantime, the end is precisely to potentiate these means.

This is the key with which we must understand Ulrich's consecutive attempts to become "a man of importance" (*GW* 1; *MWQ* 1 [9–11]). In a juvenile quest for heroism and power Ulrich had first joined the cavalry. As soon as he discovered however, that the only objects of military domination in the military were horses and women, he quit the service and turned to civil engineering. There, he thought, one could order the world on a grander scale, mastering that psychotechnical skill without which all commanding intentions fall flat. But Ulrich is again disappointed, for civil engineering only points out the rift between the staggering advancement of the human intellect and the primitive emotions it serves. What qualities has he acquired so far? A will to command and specialized knowledge of the machinery in which action is caught. His military discipline has succeeded in producing a "conception of hard, sober intellectual strength that makes mankind's old metaphysical and moral notions simply unendurable."

He hated people who could not live up to Nietzsche's words about "suffering hunger in the spirit for the sake of the truth"—all those who give up half-way, the faint-hearted, the soft, those who comfort their souls with flummery about the soul and who feed it, because the intellect allegedly gives it stones instead of bread, on religious, philosophic and fictitious emotions, which are like buns soaked in milk.

Ulrich possesses an ethic before he has even discovered its proper means of expression. "He hated this blend of renunciation and foolish fondness that makes up the general attitude to life, a blend that is as indulgent towards life's contradictions and half-measures as an elderly maiden aunt to a young nephew's loutishness" (*GW* 1:46, 27; *MWQ* 1:48, 25 [13, 7]). Intellectual flaccidity is really lack of nerve.

Ulrich turns to science to discover a more rigorous methodology for the ethic he has revealed all along: "If for 'scientific attitude' one were to read 'attitude to life,' and for 'hypothesis' 'attempt' and for 'truth' 'action,' then there would be no considerable natural scientist or mathematician whose life's work did not in courage and revolutionary power [*Umsturzkraft*] far outmatch the greatest deed in history." Scientific research is proleptic to effective action, "a kind of training" requiring that "all useless questionings should be met with a 'not yet,' and that life should be conducted on interim principles, though in the consciousness of a destination that will be reached by those who come after us" (*GW* 1:40, 46; *MWQ* 1:41, 48 [11, 13]).

When Ulrich graduates from this third attempt to be a "a man of importance" he does not abandon the scientific method; he stretches it to cover more than it is used to treating. Ulrich transfers its micro- and macrological analyses from the study of amoebas and rain clouds to the domain of the soul. Ulrich insists that the proper sphere of application for the audacious new ideas of science is not machinery but action. If one could teach people to think in a new way, he reflects, they would also live differently (*GW* 1:41; *MWQ* 1:41 [11]).

If the real goal of Ulrich's attempts at greatness is a transvaluation of values, then it must begin in precision of thought. The single most common cause of that recurrence of the same which erases the possibility of original decision is "demi-intelligence" (*Halbklugheit*)—the habit of thinking inexactly. Inexactitude is a way of overlooking "decisive differences" (*entscheidenden Unterschiede*). A part is taken for a whole, "a remote analogy for the fulfillment of truth; and the emptied-out skin of a great word [is] stuffed according to the fashion of the day." A perception of decisive differences, on the contrary, would discriminate the complexity of empirical phenomena. The real thinker, as Ulrich's father writes in a letter, distinguishes "an 'or' where the layman simply puts an 'and'" (*GW* 2:498, 1:318; *MWQ* 2:190, 16 [100, 74]).

This discriminatory power is complemented by another: the effort to lift particulars into a higher form of conceptual order, a synthesis that both the idiot and the poet are unable to make. While the idiot is quite familiar with the notions of "father and mother," he fails to grasp the concept "parents." And it is this idiot's deficiency that is turned into the poet's virtue:

> The element common to both cases is a mental condition that cannot be spanned by comprehensive concepts or refined by distinctions and abstractions, a mental condition of the crudest pattern, most clearly characterized by its way of limiting itself to the use of that simplest of coordinating conjunctions, the helplessly additive "and," which for those of little mental capacity replaces all more intricate relationships. It seems that the world itself, despite all the mind it contains, is in a mental condition not far removed from that of idiocy. The conclusion is hard to avoid if one tries to understand all that goes on in this world, in its totality. (*GW* 3:1015; *MWQ* 3:415–16 [37])

True though it be that this treatment of "idiot and poet" enacts that very overlooking of decisive differences which Musil criticized earlier, even here there is a difference. Musil, a poet, uses his "and" deliberately: to decisively identify a structural similarity, an "intellectual framework" on which things might be built.

It is along the lines of this vision of a "utopia of exact living" that Ulrich finally adds his own resolution to the pile of propositions and "dots" entertained by the executive committee of the Collateral Campaign: "What you should do is found . . . a terrestial secretariat for Precision and Soul. Until that is done, all other objectives remain unattainable, or at best they are sham objectives." The goal of this utopian project is to endow feeling with the same articulateness enjoyed by thought. In afterthought Ulrich would have liked to explain to the executive committee that by the Secretariat for Precision and Soul he hardly meant " 'a life of research' or a life 'by the light of science'; what he meant was a 'quest for feeling' similar to the quest for truth," only with the difference that in this case objective truth was no longer the issue (*GW* 2:596−97, 3:1039; *MWQ* 2:366, 3:443 [116, 38]). Even in the positivistic age of psychoanalysis, the methodologies of reason had simply not been brought to bear on the complexity of the soul.[25] With the signal exception of Nietzsche, the procedures of the most advanced theoretical sciences had yet to be applied to ethics.[26]

Exactness would aim at intensifying the individual's capacity for achievement to the highest degree, at developing a practical vocabulary of the imagination. The precision in question would be of a "fantastical" rather than "pedantic" type (*GW* 1:247−48, 2:592; *MWQ* 1:294, 2:360 [62, 116]), aspiring to actualize the latent possibilities of a given situation instead of merely fitting things to rules. No doubt this would mean less diffusion of morality and soul and more select and extraordinary accomplishments. An entire life opus, for example, might add up to no more than three treatises, poems, or actions:

In other words, what this could come to would be remaining silent where one has nothing to say, doing only what is necessary where one has no particular business in mind, and—what is most important of all—remaining indifferent wherever one has not that ineffable sensation of spreading out one's arms and being borne upward on a wave of creativeness!

One would confine one's consumption of morality to a minimum, acting with passion or conviction only in exceptional circumstances and "in all other cases thinking of one's action not otherwise than one thinks of the necessary standardization of pencils or screws" (*GW* 1:245–46; *MWQ* 1:291, 292 [61]). One would relinquish all talent and be left with genius.

The time has come to reckon with the type of systematicity entailed by this utopia of exact living. In his essays from the period of the war Musil had called for a "systematization" of knowledge in such ways as to indicate new and daring directions to feeling, for a great "logician" of the values of the soul to take this "illogical disorder to life" into hand. Even Ulrich's program of "conscious essayism" had envisioned the transformation of the world's haphazard state of consciousness into a "single will." With the question of systematicity goes that of synthesis. Ulrich, Musil wrote to Adolf Frisé, is a character who "does everything in his power to unite in himself many of the best elements of his time which have never been synthesized."[27] What is not yet clear is just how the logistics of this new type of systematicity would differ from those of the past. After all, the repetitive order of history follows directly from its slavish entrapment in systems. History has been diverted and reverted, suppressed and repressed, by precisely those formative principles that promised to provide the groundwork for ethical motivation—moral norms, figures of thought, rules of logic and law, dogmas of religion—with the result that we have ultimately acquired more regularity in matters of feeling than in those of thought.[28] What kind of new systematicity does Musil have in mind, and how does it differ from those enforcements of repetition that have held court in the past?

A preliminary answer can be found in the fact that Musil invokes Nietzsche, the essayist and aphorist (rather than, say, Leibniz or Kant), as the only German attempt to systematize life. What is the difference in their modes of procedure? "Kant can be true or false; Epicurus or Nietzsche are neither true nor false, but alive or dead. For what operates in the realm of their work is less the principle of the excluded middle than the Hegelian principle of the search for synthesis" ("Blei," *GW* 8:1023). What distinguishes Nietzsche and Epicurus is the *search* for synthesis, the tentative nature of their work, articulated in "living" thoughts that elude the distinctions of yes and no upon which systems are ordinarily based. This search for synthesis cannot be systematic in the rational sense. If anything, it can only transcribe a logic of illogic.

To understand the difference between the two procedures in question, let us look at the distinction Musil draws between morality and ethics. The instinct that guides a moralist, he writes, is a logical one. A moralist does not change the language of values but elaborates a language that is already in place. Ethical thinkers, on the other hand, are "masters of men." "Names: Kung-su-tse, Lao-tse, Christ and Christianity, Nietzsche, the mystics, the essayists. . . . They have an affinity with the poet. . . . Their contribution to ethics concerns not form but matter" (*TB* 1 : 645). The articulation of ethics always involves a new "conception of humanity," whether an anthropology, a sociology, a psychology, a metaphysics, or even that "higher humanism" in which all are combined. We might say that the discipline of ethics involves a study of volition and of the structures in which it operates, a study that is missing in moral reformulations of unchanging truths. In the higher humanism of ethical thought, every diagnosis is also a prognosis, every view of humanity simultaneously a new scaffold for action.

Ethics contains a built-in relativity, requiring a precise formulation of theoretical issues and the practical conditions attending them.

"I like this"—changes not only with regard to the "this" but also with regard to the "me"; one likes various things, there are various pleasures; what is common is a vague thing like pleasure. Here lie the insecurities of the usual feeling-psychology of value.

Seeking, like post-Machian science, a means by which "to regulate behavior without laws," ethics allows the vagueness of desire to be channeled into the forms most appropriate to the situation at hand. "The entire task is: life without systematics and yet with order. Self-creating order. Generative

---

order. An order not set from *a* to *z* but progressing from *n* to *n* + 1" (*TB* 1 : 646, 649, 653). This generative order informs the only morality in accordance with this perpetually moving series: the morality of the next step, in which every decision is taken only in consciousness of its dual character as conditioned and also conditioning.

Morality is closed and reactive, ethics active and open. The difference concerns the approach that is taken by a "formal system" to the "natural system" it attempts to address. Two different approaches can be distinguished by systems theory.[29] On the one hand there exist "algorithmic" descriptions of a natural system: descriptions aiming to explain the observable nature of a set of empirical facts (the world as an atomic whole, an Armageddon, a battle of Olympians). An algorithmic description might also be called a predicative interpretation, or one stating that "P is the case." To a predicative interpretation one could oppose a predictive one, understanding the word *predictive* in two ways: (1) attempting to foresee and enable conditions in the natural system which do not yet exist, and (2) positing the intellectual scaffolding, or precondition, for a predicative statement. In the first and primary sense a predictive interpretation would construct a model for a *potential* operation of the natural system. When fed back into the "natural" and observable situation, this model or interpretation would furnish the situation with a direction it might not otherwise have.

In this sense a predictive model is based on an anticipatory rather than a reactive logic, an interpretation of the potential teleology of natural events.[30] A reactive interpretation, on the other hand, begins and ends its claims with what is already the case. Its purpose is to describe an actual state of affairs, not to make a new one possible. While the reactive system is characterized by "feedback" from interpretation to existing phenomena, the anticipatory system is characterized by "feedforward" from interpretation to phenomena not yet in existence. The reactive, predicative system is based on a mechanistic, homeostatic conception of experience; the predictive, anticipatory one on the notion of adaptation, a sense that there are countless potential relations between "effector" and "reactor," or cause and effect, of which the currently observable relation is only one.

Another important difference between the two types of formal system involves complexity and simplicity. A reactive interpretation articulates only a "subsystem" of the system it observes. It tries to pass off a subdescription as a description of the system at large. This is what Musil means by demi-intelligence. It is also why he speaks of the unsystematicity of history at large, which has consistently failed to synthesize its own subsystems. A reactive system is reductionistic. It assumes that all conflicting formal interpretations can eventually be reduced to a single, universal one, and that formal and natural systems have an immediate and one-to-one relation. Its models tend to be constructed as autonomous "Archimedean points" outside, and immune to, the natural systems they address. An anticipatory system, on the other hand, tends to be complex, both intrinsically and in its relation to the natural system. It employs not a single meter of measurement but many. If it too can never articulate more than subsystems of the natural system under consideration, it constructs a number of these subsystems and theorizes their interrelations. Moreover, these anticipatory systems are strictly dependent on the natural system, changing in relation to the observables in question. This is the complexity that Musil remarked in the ethical situation of "I like this," where the paradigm "like" changes in relation to the "I" and also the "this." "Not: what is this, but: how do I behave in relation to it" (*TB* 1 : 650).

Two parables in *The Man without Qualities* illustrate the complex hermeneutical tie between a formal and a natural system. "In every minute of our lives," Arnheim remarks,

we are moving among institutions, problems, and requirements of which we know only the last bit, so that the present is continuously reaching back into the past. If I may put it so, the floor of time is always giving way beneath us and our feet go through into the cellars below, while we imagine ourselves to be in the top storey of the present!

To the pastness of the observable present one must add also its futurity:

The train of events is a train unrolling its rails ahead of itself. The river of time is a river sweeping its banks along with it. The traveller moves about on a solid floor between solid walls; but the floor and the walls are being moved along too. (*GW* 2 : 565, 445; *MWQ* 2 : 325, 174 [114, 98])

The natural frameworks on which one might have hoped to build a lasting system require continual intellectual adaptation. Cognizant of the utopian nature of its own theoretical projection, the anticipatory resolve of predictive modeling can only be an unending formulation of paradigms for comprehension, tools for reality organization, heuristic plausibility arguments, tentative frameworks for potential action.

Through this excursion into systems theory three dimensions of essayism come more clearly into focus. One is the notion of projectual, anticipatory, and paradigmatic thinking, all alluded to in the idea of constructing intellectual frameworks for daring new ways to be human. The second is the notion of a complex system, complex to the point of being uncompletable. The third is the notion of theorizing the relation between the formal and the natural systems.

We have observed the first of these functions, the projectual nature of the essay, in the context of anticipatory resolve, hypothetical living, possibilitarianism, and propaedeutic virtue. It goes without saying that this projectuality also finds expression in the "open" and interminable composition of Musil's novel as well as its rhetoric of speculation: its construction of precisely those heuristic, anticipatory logics and paradigms for action that its literary essayism intends to discover, including the utopia of exact living, active passivism, the morality of the next step, precision and soul, and dozens of others. Such metaphors enact Musil's own principle of constructing scaffoldings for ethical direction. They exemplify the literary-theoretical mission of the essayist: "to discover constantly new solutions, connections, constellations, variables, to set up prototypes of courses of events [*Geschehensabläufen*], enticing models of possible human behavior, to *invent* the inner man" (*GW* 8 : 1029; *PS* 64).

Alongside the propaedeutic virtue promoted by Ulrich's ethical training and investigated by the novel, the projectual nature of the essay is further reflected by the workings of science. Post-Newtonian science not only provides a method by which to engage in a new hermeneutics of experience; it also offers a means for utopian development. More than that determination of universal laws which Mach had critiqued in classical mechanics, this new type of science consists in practical realizations of symbolic dream. The experimentalism of post-Machian science is an intellectual reflection of procedures already operative in nature: on-the-wayness, self-revision, transmutation, and adaptation. Science represents the activity of "a man whose imagination is geared to change":

If the realization of primordial dreams is flying, travelling with the fishes, boring one's way under the bodies of mountain-giants, sending messages with godlike swiftness, seeing what is invisible and what is in the distance and hearing its voice . . . , then modern research is not only science but magic.

Theoretical science discovers and liberates the creative possibilities latent in things themselves. To Ulrich and his colleagues it appeared that science offered "the very well-spring of the times, the *fons et origo* of an unfathomable transformation" (*GW* 1 : 247, 39; *MWQ* 1 : 293, 39 [61, 11]).

The second ambition of essayism to which systems theory calls our attention is the possibility of a complex formal system. And here the literary essay has even more to offer in the way of a model than any strictly scientific procedure, especially concerning multiplicity, relativity of perspective, and the flexible correlation of differences. To transcribe the complexity of an issue an essay must begin by dismantling its ostensible unity, taking it from many sides. The "whole" that an essay can never definitively articulate can nevertheless be evoked by a cumulative conjunction of parts. A complex formal system can "be approximated, locally and temporarily, by appropriately chosen simple ones."[31] The essay embarks on this process of formalization by making the phenomenon appear in a polymorphous way. If this phenomenon is A, it is also B, and C, and D, and E. We are familiar with Walter's description of Ulrich as internalizing precisely this type of polymorphousness:

When he is angry, something in him laughs. When he is sad, he is up to something. When he is moved by something, he will reject it. Every bad action will seem good to him in some connection or other. . . . So every one of his answers is a part-answer, every one of his feelings only a point of view. (*GW* 1 : 65; *MWQ* 1 : 71 [17])

To live in the manner of an essay is to cultivate a pluralism impossible to reduce to a unified system. The fixed "unity of the soul" envisioned by law and morality here cedes to a model of "the subject as multiplicity."[32] The organizational principle of Ulrich's subjective complexity is co- rather than subordination, a self-generative order insuring that no feeling or thought will suppress another through a hard and un-yielding logic. It was a "flexible dialectic of feeling" that allowed Ulrich to discover "defects in what was generally approved of" and to defend "what was beyond the pale." While the fate of such a person can always be forced one way or another by a "really hard counter-pressure," until this happens it will be hard to recognize a motivating passion in this kind of temperament. Ulrich is a model of maximal *disponibilité*, resolved on self-expansion. In the conscious essayism by which he lived "man as the quintessence of human possibilities, potential man, the unwritten poem of his own existence, materialized as a record, a reality, and a character, confronting man in general" (*GW* 1 : 151, 251; *MWQ* 1 : 176, 298 [40, 62]).

What is at play in Ulrich's psychology as in a literary essay (and even history, though not deliberately) is an active mutability, "which has nothing to do with progress, or with the conversion to new points of view, or with internal uncertainty," but rather with that type of plurivocity of interpretation overlooked by exclusive schemata. An essay, Musil emphasizes, embraces "many things that common opinion considers mutually incompatible, not out of indeterminacy but out of overdetermination [*Überbestimmtheit*]" ("Blei," *GW* 8:1023, 1024). It is this overdetermination, or hyper-precision, of particulars which is served by the complexity of essayistic form. This is the "rich ambiguity of existence" (*die vieldeutige Charakter des Daseins*) that Nietzsche endeavors to rescue from reductive worldviews. As the world becomes infinite all over again, meanings proliferate. And this is when calls can be made for human experimentation on an unprecedented scale, for journeys into still undiscovered horizons. Humanity itself now represents the "as yet undetermined animal."[33]

The "overdetermination" of a phenomenon by means of multiple perspectives envisions the possibility of a synthetic comprehension in which nothing is true or false. In reconstructing its object the essay focuses on that object's intrinsic and extrinsic relations. While examples could be drawn from the overall construction of *The Man without Qualities* just as easily as from the three dozen essays Musil published between 1911 and 1931, let us observe how this works in one of Ulrich's reflections.[34] Although Diotima was convinced that Ulrich's opinions closely resembled her own, she always found that he developed them in a way that "missed the point." Here the two of them are discussing the nature of love, or rather, *she* has spoken of love and Ulrich is expected to respond. No sooner does he do so than he finds himself speaking of bouncing balls and bees on a windowpane:

Nowadays we still say: I love this woman and I hate that man, instead of saying they attract me or repel me. And to come one step nearer to precision one ought to add that it is I who awaken in them the capacity to attract or repel me. And to take yet another step nearer to precision one ought then to add that they bring out in me the qualities that make for that. And so on. One can't say where the first step is made, for the whole thing is a functional interdependence like that between two bouncing balls or two electric circuits. And of course we've known for a long time that we ought to feel like that too, but we still prefer by far to be the cause, the first cause, in the magnetic fields of feeling that surround us. Even if one of us admits he's imitating someone else, he expresses it in such a way as to make it seem an active achievement. That's why I asked you, and why I ask you, have you ever been immoderately in love or angry or desperate. For then, if one has any power of observation worth mentioning, one realises one is no better off than a bee on a window-pane or an infusorium in poisoned water: one undergoes an emotional storm, one dashes blindly in all directions, one runs a hundred times up against the impenetrable, and once, if one is lucky, one escapes through an opening into freedom, and afterwards, of course, in a rigid state of consciousness, one explains it as the result of planned action. (*GW* 2:473; *MWQ* 2:208 [101])

Adapting Adorno's terms, we can observe that Ulrich's thinking "does not advance in a single direction"; rather, "the aspects of the argument interweave as in a carpet" (*EF* 160). Why else would Diotima accuse Ulrich of missing the point? This point is either the stereotypical concept Ulrich begins by questioning (the selfsame unity of love) or else an exemplary and summary metaphor he refuses to offer. What he presents instead is a series of analogies, a correlative nexus of hyperprecise and interdependent hypotheses that lead from *n* to *n* + 1 to an untotalizable whole. The same pattern occurs with those unities of plot, character, and thought in the novel at large.[35] These seemingly autonomous logics of reality construction are only reciprocally related subsystems; the characters of *The Man without Qualities* are semantic fields in which body, circumstance, and mind conspicuously intersect; dramatic occurrences exemplify conceptual principles and vice versa (not-yetness, for example, thematically compounded by chapters 56 through 60 of Part 1); thoughts and events echo each other in a vast symbolic system.[36]

"What it comes to," the narrator comments, "is that truth is not a crystal one can put in one's pocket, but an infinite fluid into which one falls headlong." If one wants to understand the action of the sexual murderer Moosbrugger, one would have to cross-reference a list of studies which would look like this:

AH. —AMP. —AAC. —AKA. —AP. —ASZ. —BKL. —BGK. —BUD. —CN. —DTL. —DJZ. —FBgM. —GA. —GS. —JKV. —KBSA. —MMW. —NG. —PNW. —R. —VSgm. —WMW. —ZGS. —ZMB. —ZP. —ZSS. Addickes *ibid.* —Aschaffenburg *ibid.* —Beling *ibid.* and so on. . . . One need only think of each of those abbreviations linked up with hundreds, or at least dozens, of printed pages, each page linked up with a man with ten fingers . . . and for each of his fingers ten disciples and ten opponents . . . and one gets a faint picture of what truth is like. (*GW* 2:533–34; *MWQ* 2:284–85 [110])

Each of the scholarly studies advances the possibility of summary knowledge an additional step. Even so, such knowledge requires more than the elaboration of individual ideas; it requires their correlation. General Stumm explains it as the need for "some sort of railway time-table that would make it possible to get cross-connections between ideas going in every direction." If events in the realm of history amount to "a chaotic succession of unsatisfactory and (when taken singly) false attempts at a solution," thinks Ulrich, these attempts might nevertheless "produce the correct and total solution, but only when humanity had learnt to combine them all." Granted that each of these part-solutions (*Lösungsteilungen*) is "stupid," could it be, he wonders, that "all of them together are fertile?" (*GW* 2:490, 461, 358, 490; *MWQ* 2:230, 194, 66, 231 [103, 100, 83, 103]).

This overdetermination and correlation has its human counterpart in that "theorem of human amorphousness" which Musil counterposes to contemporaneous calls for a revival of Renaissance, baroque, classical, and Gothic man.[37] What makes Ulrich, the embodiment of this theorem, one of the most extraordinary characters in modern fiction is his theoretical sensitivity. Each of his experiences evokes a thought, a feeling, a memory, an investigation, a speculation on the possible relations of this event to others. Ulrich is a dynamic principle of responsivity, a coherently changing measure of the occurrences around him. He is a laboratory of meaning, a psychic conjunction of echoes. What he finds enhanced in his "mystical union" with his sister is precisely this principle of correlativity, which the world as a whole fails to achieve. Their relation is marked by the mutual suggestivity of their thoughts and actions. Their conversations always awakened something in the spirit "followed by a response that was its superior degree . . . so that one had an impression of a process of ceaseless gradation. . . . The last word never seemed to be able to be uttered, for every end was a beginning, every last result the first of a new opening" (*GW* 4 : 1416). While it seldom causes the complete integration of immutable love, this responsiveness is love's sine qua non—that ethical condition that requires no ethical act since it already entails continuous motivation of the spirit. As long as Ulrich responds to the world in this way, he is as close to the *unio mystico* as he is likely to get. In another unpublished chapter of the novel, this time on "the utopia of the motivated life," the ethical model for this cosmic "analogism" is that transformation of a landscape into a "motif" within a painter, without the slightest engagement of will or intention (*GW* 5 : 1914–20).

Inevitably, overdetermination, multiplicity, and correlation involve art. In fact, in some ways art represents a more satisfactory model of systematicity and synthesis than science.

In the radical aesthetics that Musil shares with the various avant-gardes of the beginning of the century, art asserts a polemical independence from "normalized" understandings of experience. Instead of idealizing preestablished views of the world, art supplants them. It leads "towards decisions that cannot be decided [*zu Entscheidungnen, die sich nicht entscheiden lassen*]." "Extract the meaning from all poetic works," Ulrich says to Walter, "and what you will have is a denial . . . negating all valid rules, principles, and prescriptions on which society is based, the very society that is so fond of these poetic works":

Ultimately a poem . . . cuts the meaning of the world clear, where it is bound to thousands of ordinary words, cuts it loose, and so makes it into a balloon that goes floating up and away. If we call that beauty . . . then we ought to see that beauty is an unspeakably ruthless upheaval, far more cruel than any political revolution ever was. (*GW* 2 : 367, *MWQ* 2 : 77 [84])

If art transcends the limitations of rational and historical logic, it is largely by means of analogy, or metaphor (*Gleich-nis*).[38] Transcribing possibilities not contained in the mechanical calculus of options, a metaphor joins two signs into a third with no literal sign of its own. At its best a metaphor cannot be broken down into a figurative truth and a literal falsehood. It is an unequivocal expression of equivocal meaning, both a name for the phenomenon in question and also a symbol. In Rilke's poetry, for example, "everything is a metaphor and—nothing just a metaphor."[39] The impression on a reader, says Musil, is that of "clear stillness in a never-pausing movement, . . . an almost painful tension." In the flux of our sensations these phenomenal metaphors form a knot "that is tied differently from all others," one that "does not allow itself to be grasped and resolved entirely." No solid border exists between one thing and another (*GW* 8 : 1236, 1237, 1239; *PS* 244–45, 246). As with the combining of concepts which occurs in dreams, metaphors articulate "the sliding logic of the soul," "the kinship of things that exists in the twilit imaginings of art and religion." A metaphor, in short, is an emblem of that radically other condition experienced by mystics, lovers, and children (*GW* 2 : 593, 582; *MWQ* 2 : 362, 347 [116, 115]). This third condition acts as an alternative to the rigid, adequational language underlying the construction of simple, reactive, and predicative systems. And yet this opposition to rational logic is also the inherent limitation of art.

While art bespeaks an ecstatic condition, in the context of history it describes no more than a "utopian reality."[40] Measured by the watch, the mystical state lasts no longer than a smile.[41] Though it may articulate a third possibility between any two, art itself, as a formal activity, represents only *one* of the two that history makes humanly available. It seems to Ulrich that every assertion "comes into the world split into two mutually antagonistic falsehoods"—truth and meta-phor, concept and image, intellect and feeling—and "that between these two there is no third possibility" (*GW* 2 : 582; *MWQ* 2 : 347 [115]). If the existence of such a third possibili-ty is *imagined* by the metaphors of art, it is not actualized in historical terms. Only by admitting to this fact can we begin to approach that third dimension of essayism elaborated by systems theory over and beyond projectual anticipation and hermeneutical overdetermination, namely, the need for an ongoing theorization of the relation between formal and natural systems.

In its historical reception a work of art loses the semantic autonomy it may have seemed to possess in itself. In recep-tion, an unravelable knot of metaphor becomes subject to acts of reading. Announcing an unprecedented *parole* within a *langue*, an artwork still relies on this *langue*, or linguistic logic, in which the metaphor has been coined and will be read. A metaphor concedes power to this sign system at the same moment that it contests it. Measured by their relation to the practical sphere of life, artworks lose their independence from those habitual modes of understanding they actively es-say. And that is why all attempts to translate art directly into life show "a certain tendency towards the allegorical," if we understand that to be "an intellectual relationship in which everything is supposed to mean more than it has any honest claim to mean." Otherwise put, between artistic dreams and reality "there is a glass wall" by which each views its own accuser (*GW* 2 : 407, 581−82; *MWQ* 2 : 127, 347 [90, 115]).[42]

Theories and works of art only offer grist to the dialectical mill. In the realm of historical understanding, art functions only as the promise of an alternative and discursively un-speakable truth. No more autonomously significant than the "literal facts" that its figures oppose, art offers merely provi-sional visions, stipulations in the future anterior. An un-ravelable poetic metaphor does not furnish a clear direction in that space of Blanchot where there is no direction; it only points to a place in which to search for direction. Seek though it may, in Adorno's words, "a true identity of the identical and the non-identical," art cannot actualize such an impossible identity. It can only take "an advance on a praxis which has not yet begun."[43] Read carefully, Musil's defense of the synthetic metaphor admits to the same limitation. Although Rilke seems able "to see in another way," it is merely "a way that . . . leads . . . to the image of a world yet to be constructed [zu einem kommenden Weltbild]." His art points a "way to the future," to a condition not yet in sight, like a scent that precedes its object. Like every formal system, art is always "an unself-sufficient condition, . . . a bridge arching away from solid ground as though it possessed a support in the imaginary" (GW 8 : 1240, 1241, 1154; PS 248−49, 208).[44]

Given the immanent relation of art and history, that aesthetics of the audacious metaphor which synthesizes two dissimilar things into a unified third represents only one aspect of the aesthetic operation.[45] Unquestionably, the distant and unlikely analogies in which Musil excels function on behalf of positive and constructive interpretation:

This phenomenon [of writing "pure poetry" in a consumerist age] is more or less the equivalent of trying to compensate for the hollowness of a hole by putting a hollow dome over it. [GW 2 : 407; MWQ 2 : 126 [90])

Did she confide in him? Was it then he who was encouraging her in her oddities? These questions wriggled like worms in Walter's breast, and he felt almost sick. He became pale as ashes, and all the tension went out of his face, so that it shrivelled up in helpless wrinkles. (GW 2 : 369; MWQ 2 : 79 [84])

Regurgitating gossip filled the void, and time developed little bubbles like a glass of stale water. (GW 1 : 115; MWQ 1 : 132 [29])

This beating of a twenty-year-old heart in his thirty-two-year-old breast seemed to him like the perverted kiss that a boy gives a man. (GW 1 : 123; MWQ 1 : 141 [32])

But The Man without Qualities is equally replete with no less daring but "negative" analogies, functioning primarily to contest or undermine an established understanding:

If in earlier days Diotima had been wakened from her sleep and asked what she wanted, she would have answered, without having to stop and think, that the power of love in a living soul yearned to communicate itself to the whole world. . . . And she would really have meant it. There are still thousands of people nowadays who are something like scent-sprays diffusing the power of love. (*GW* 1:332; *MWQ* 2:33 [78])

"I have tried a lot more experiments of various kinds," the General said, and in his gay and lively eyes there was now a faint gleam of irritation or even panic, "trying to get the whole thing reduced to unity. But d'you know what it's like? Just like travelling second-class in Galicia and picking up crabs! It's the lousiest feeling of help-lessness I ever knew. When you've been spending a lot of time among ideas, you get an itching all over your body, and you can't get any peace even if you scratch till you bleed!" (*GW* 2:374; *MWQ* 2:86 [85])

She set her words carefully, as though stitching them together with black-and-yellow thread, and burned the mild incense of high bu-reaucratic phraseology upon her lips. (*GW* 1:268; *MWQ* 1:318 [64])

She had learnt her everyday wisdom in her parents' house, and it was a stern wisdom, as plain and beautiful as old pots and pans handed down from generation to generation; but one could not do much with it, for such saws were always only one sentence long and then that was the end of it. And at this moment she was ashamed of such childish wisdom, as one is ashamed of threadbare clothes. (*GW* 1:339; *MWQ* 2:42 [79])

It may already be clear that the difference between inflation-ary and deflationary analogies removes nothing from their basic act: the practice of seeing in a different way, even if this different way lacks its own autonomous language. Simulta-neously defining and undefining, structuring and destructur-ing, the "two" functions are ultimately indistinguishable. *The Man without Qualities* is accordingly built of both ironic con-trasts and *Vereinungen* ("unions," the title of one of Musil's collections of stories), of satire and inventive research in perpetual contest.[46]

It is in this constructive/destructive operation of art that its essayism lies. Set against its historical reception, the utopia of art (and of every theoretical or formal system) never functions as a pure recreation of the world. The utopia offers only a plausible critique, a reassessment, a partial remaking, an objection and alternate suggestion.[47] It enacts an exchange in which identities cross. The artistic contestation of the law of contradiction takes the form of interminable labor. The active principle of this labor is to be found neither in unequivocal statements of $A = A$ nor in the metaphoric, but equally identificational, $A = B$; rather, it lies in the *principle* of "metaphoricity" that allows for the crossing over, in the equal sign, known to phenomenologists as the hermeneutical "as" factor.[48] The art form that draws most explicit attention to this principle of metaphoricity is the essay. It adopts an openly dialectical relation to conventional modes of interpretation, particularly those that have forgotten their metaphorical origin. This is its conscious utopianism.

Unlike the discursively autonomous languages of sculpture, poetry, and theoretical philosophy, the essay does not make a definitive leap into the utopian regions of the purely imaginary. It measures the distance between the leap and the ordinary discursive practices that constitute its ground. As Lukács writes, the essay receives its initial impetus from "something already formed." In Musil's case, this something already formed is historical actuality in its traditional interpretations. It belongs to the essence of an essay, Lukács continues, that "it does not draw something out of an empty vacuum, but only gives a new order to such things as once lived."[49] The interpretive tools of the essay are not the fantastic equations of the formal arts so much as the crossings, correlations, and ties already at work in everyday language, now posited as the necessary foundation of daring invention. All concepts being "already concretized" by the discourse to which they belong, the essay "begins with such meanings and . . . forces these meanings on further; it wants to help language . . . to grasp these concepts reflectively."[50] The essay thus "overinterprets," stretching meanings beyond their conventional limits and mediating between their literal and figurative connotations. The essay constructs its discourse by accompanying its reader step-by-step from familiar patterns of figuration to a series of new ones. Here the analogical dive takes off from the solid platform of habitual understanding. The essay reveals both platform and dive, or the movement from truth to metaphor and back again. Instead of positing a radically new measure of the real, it decisively transforms the ones already available.

With this statement we have gone beyond the essay's point of departure (its projectual and utopian thrust) to its final end: hermeneutical theorization. Along the way the essay's articulation of multiplicity contests all definitive signs and symbols, for the different sides from which an essay takes a thing involve not only different qualifications of a functionally dependent thing (a unity such as "friendship" being variably good, bad, harmful, useful, pleasurable, difficult, common, rare) but also different interpretive methodologies. An essay extends comparison beyond actual items or qualities to discursive codes, showing their analogies and contradictions in historical practice—the discourses, for example, of reason and feeling, science and art, analysis and description, or fact and value. Rather than advancing a new form of discourse, it establishes relations among these others, with an eye on the possibility of a "super-relation." This is why an essay, at its most ambitious, turns into that multigeneric transcription of phenomenal reality which is a novel, at least a novel like *The Man without Qualities:* dramatic, discursive, iconic, and metaphoric at once. What could still be emphasized about the aesthetics of this novel is the essayistic motivation underlying its combination of: (1) an essentially conventional dramatic depiction, or "realistic" account, of characters, situations, and actions tied in various chains of cause and effect; (2) an intricate and analytical reflection on this drama, especially of its multiple logics and modes of significance, including irony, satire, and philosophical analysis;

and (3) a utopian attempt to combine 1 and 2 into an ethical poetics.[51]

As form, the Musilian essay enacts the metaphoricity underlying all form, whether this form be historical, theoretical, or artistic. It acts as the "genre of genres," showing how the others work. Its operative model is not the unified significance of a mystical experience or an artistic image but, rather, the actual construction of significance in the aesthetic experience (which appears characteristic of history at large). And this may be why Ulrich declares that one should live as one reads, for what is at work in the aesthetic experience—the reader's as well as the writer's, the artist's as well as the scientist's—is always a stretching of the imagination and of expectation, a dynamic tension, a meeting and contamination of orders, a "fusion of horizons."[52] The same thing occurs in the aesthetics of pleasure and desire, though voicelessly. The bridging involved in this interpretive stretch is a conscious articulation of a Maybe, a historical betweenness, a neither/nor, an encounter between opposing systems.

For all these reasons the essay must ultimately be understood as more than a provisional attempt. As Musil writes in *The Man without Qualites,* the essay is also "the unique and unalterable form that a man's inner life assumes in a decisive thought" (*GW* 1:253; *MWQ* 1:301 [62]). The decisiveness of this form of the inner life consists in its critical step toward the articulation of something still undiscovered, a step in which the only discovery lies. Ulrich is not an artist; he refuses to elaborate the delusions of a mere ideal. The conscious utopianism of the essay has no interest in engaging the intellect in the unnatural task of presenting the beyond as real but only in that of "first rendering it 'possible'" ("Spirituality," *GW* 8:991; *PS* 24). If the physician is interested in a "generally valid causal nexus" and the scientist in "a summary schema of the actual," the essayist is concerned with "the extension of the register of what is intrinsically still possible [*die Erweiterung des Registers von innerlich noch Möglichem*]."[53] If its decisive thinking rejects conviction, it is in the same way that an enactment of the principle of metaphoricity refuses to finish the game, even the game of the novel, by means of a definitive dictum, image, or conclusion (*GW* 1:225; *MWQ* 1:303 [62]).

Though it may aspire to a final and summary interpretation, the essay lacks the naiveté to advance one its own. Ulrich abandons the program of adapting his life to a model, whether that of a profession, a creed, or a religion. The essay does not indulge the notion of attaining "the immediate" through linguistic mediation. Rather, it avows and explores the thetic operations of that same mediation, theorizing the modeling process. Ultimately, it is less interested in a specific object of thought than in how this object is rendered significant. This is the sense in which an essayist is analogous to a systems scientist, "brokering" between the properties of systematic languages and the observable phenomena of which they speak.[54] When an essay breaks a quality or a thing into a series of appearances, it brackets the whole question of the "essence" of this thing or substance or phenomenal whole. If anything, it sees this essence as lying outside the thing, in the phenomenological processes that accord it significance. If essayism has an overriding concern, it is this "phenomenalization," to which it recalls all statements. And this explains part of the motivation of Musil's novel, which concerns itself not with the self-evident logic of historical events, nor with the "autonomy" of human facts, types, experiences, and interpretive strategies, but rather with the shifting orders to which they bear witness.

6

Luigi Pirandello

Cheating the Image

At the end of act 1 of *Henry IV* the protagonist gives us a glimpse of one source of his madness (whether feigned or real). He is held captive to an image. "My real condemnation," Henry cries to Donna Matilde,

> is this—or that—look (*he points to his portrait on the wall, almost with fear*) of not being able to detach myself from this work of magic! . . . you must implore the Pope for me, who is able to do it: to detach me from there (*he points to the portrait again*) and allow me to live this whole poor life of mine, from which I am excluded. . . . One cannot always be twenty-six, my Lady! And I ask you this also on behalf of your daughter: so that I may love her in the way she deserves. (*E* 328; *HE* 34)

Henry requests to be liberated from an image in the likeness of which his soul has been cast for twenty years. It all began when he fell off a horse during a ball and struck his head. When he came to his senses he had already taken leave of them, believing himself to be truly the character whose part he had been playing only in jest: the eleventh-century emperor Henry IV.

What is the meaning of this compulsion of the image and

the obedience it exacts? The image is not a thing but a thing perceived, a percept.[1] It is an unliving and unwilled phenomenal order, a sign into which a thing is transformed the minute it enters consciousness. "Just as I did not create that body [and] did not give myself that name," declares Vitangelo Moscarda in *One, None and a Hundred Thousand,*

so, without the participation of my will, so many other things came upon and within and around me from others; so many things had been made for me and given to me by others, of which I had actually never thought, which I had never endowed with an image, the strange and enimical image with which they were rushing upon me now.

"I was for my friend," Moscarda reflects during a conversation,

what he was for me: an impenetrable body that stood before him and that he represented to himself in features familiar to him, and which meant nothing to me; so much so that I gave them no thought as I spoke, nor could I see them or know what they were like; while for him they were everything, insofar as they represented me as I was for him, one among many: *Moscarda.* Is it possible? And *Moscarda* was everything he said and did in that world unknown to me; even my shadow was *Moscarda; Moscarda* if they saw him eat; *Moscarda* if they saw him smoke; *Moscarda* if he took a stroll; *Moscarda* if he blew his nose. (*Uno* 787−88; 3:2)

The image is the self as heterodetermined. In fact, as Henry IV comes eventually to recognize, what is ostensibly a representation of reality is actually that reality's origin. A form with which he once had the misfortune to identify himself now does the identifying, even the willing.

And thus the image begins to stand for a historical fate. "There comes a moment," Milan Kundera writes, "when the image of our life parts company with the life itself, stands free, and, little by little, begins to rule us." And like a character of Kundera's making, Henry might have also confessed:

I came to realize that there was no power capable of changing the image of my person lodged in the supreme court of human fate, that the image in question (even though it bore no resemblance to me) was much more real than my actual self; that I was its shadow and not the other way round; . . . that the lack of resemblance was my cross, to bear on my own.[2]

Pascal's realization is the same. It was originally the feeling that he was only a shadow of himself that had led him to remake himself as Adriano Meis. Yet the new image had obstructed his behavior no less than the first. Whether that of a king or a modern citizen, the image is an effigy by which a character is compelled to live, as a victim in response to pricks in a voodoo doll.[3]

Is there any escape from this trap of an image pursuing its own independent logic? Finding the Marchesa staring at his dyed hair, Henry suggests that there is. "What does it matter," he remarks to the Marchesa, "that, for you, this dye cannot present the real color of my hair?—You, My Lady, certainly do not dye your hair to deceive others, or even yourself; but just a bit—a tiny bit—your image in front of the mirror" (*E* 325–26; *HE* 32). Neither the Marchesa nor Henry is misled by their embellished reflections in the mirror; it is the image itself that is misled, its malign intentions disrupted. By coiffing and pruning themselves, Henry and the Marchesa resist the pressures on their being of an extrinsic force, "cheating" the will of time as it were. Stripping the normalizing mechanics of representation of its literally definitive power (the "objective look" of one's age), they reaffirm their subjective freedom to determine their own beings (even if by summoning up another fixed and stereotypical image, namely, "the visage of youth"). Only by self-styling can they experience their lives as their own.

These two passages from *Henry IV* suggest a counter-reading of a distinction that has become so pervasive in Pirandello scholarship as to obscure the economy of the image in question. It is a distinction between living and seeing oneself live, between "spontaneous" and "natural" behavior on the one hand and self-consciousness on the other. According to this distinction, one either lives or one sees oneself live; one cannot do both.[4] Action occurs on the basis of clear and distinct convictions, of unquestioned orders of perception and purposive logic, illusory though these orders may be. If one has the misfortune of recognizing this operative code, or of seeing oneself live, one destroys both the illusions and the life they enable. "When I set myself in front of a mirror," says Vitangelo Moscarda, "I became as arrested; all spontaneity came to an end, my every gesture appeared to me fictitious or mimicked [*rifatto*]." Nothing seemed strange to Moscarda's friend about their colloquy because as he spoke he "had no image of himself in mind" (*Uno* 749–50, 787; 1:4, 3:2). His economy of signs had not been disrupted by a sign of the signifying process. But once one sees the mechanics of seeing, what is phenomenally present appears as no more than a representation. Life occurs only "on the condition that you live it without 'knowing,' only *believing*."[5] And this ability to believe depends, in turn, on not doubting one's vital images.

This is the theory as it appears on the surface—the surface, that is, of a "philosophy of life" to which Pirandello gave frequent expression. The spontaneous life forces of natural consciousness are radically essayed by the critical and obstructive effects of its reflexive version, an operation so opposed to the furtherance of life that one suspects this critical mind of being no more than an unfortunate prosthesis. And yet this is the very opposition contested by the passages from *Henry IV*, for, to be able to live the entirety of the poor life from which he is excluded, Henry must detach himself from his image. And this does not mean ceasing to look in the mirror; it means ceasing to identify himself with what he is not.

"To know oneself is to die," declares the protagonist of "La carriola" (1928; "The Wheelbarrow").[6] But this narrative, too, resists the traditional reading of the opposition. "The Wheelbarrow" speaks of a lawyer who comes home one day to find that his wife and his children, his name tag, and his profession appear suddenly alien. What does the lawyer recognize at that moment? Not that self-knowledge is death but that without this knowledge there is no life. When the lawyer "sees himself live" he realizes that "my life, a real life of my own, had never existed" in the forms it had always assumed. "I had never lived; I had never been inside my life; in a life, I mean, that I could recognize as mine, willed and experienced by me as mine" (*C* 718, 716). Who, then, had been in his life if it was not he? Was it someone else? An unconsciously operating part of himself? It was a lifeless image. The "we" of daily life, as Pirandello repeatedly stresses, is only a "clumsy, inadequate metaphor of ourselves."[7]

To take the metaphor literally, as Henry does when he identifies with his delusion of being the king, is the very meaning of madness. In fact, Henry's madness originates long before he actually knocked his head—in his lifelong insistence on the veracity of the image. As a young man, Henry used to demand a one-to-one correspondence between reality and its representation. He was different from the other men who courted the Marchesa, she recalls, in that he exacerbated the most unpleasant experience that an attractive woman can have: that of being fixed on by "two eyes that look at us with an intense and restrained [*contenuta*] promise of lasting feeling." What was unusual about Henry's gaze was its unflinching earnesty. He demanded that his signs of affection be "taken seriously." Although the Marchesa used to laugh at these passionate displays, it was only out of fear, for one "could possibly believe in the promise of those eyes" (*E* 312; *HE* 19). But to believe would have meant forgoing that favorite ploy by which coquettish women evade the desire of their admirer, namely, by deriding such affection as pretense, by cynically rejecting the truth of the image before their eyes. To believe would have meant being incapable of dispelling her lover's gaze as a rhetorical gesture. To find the image credible would have meant having to make an existential decision, having to say yes or no instead of equivocating.

Henry was "exalted" in his commitment to images, a commitment that revealed him to be "rich with life." Endeavoring always to endow the image he presented "with the value . . . how shall I put it? of an act of intelligence," he would never be content until he had convinced himself of the accuracy of the representation. Twenty years later, when Henry speaks of cheating an image that has grown independent of his own volition, it is with the same idea in mind: The image is too important to play with in any but the most serious of spirits. Even so, too intense an expectation from the order of representation invites madness or life paralysis.[8] When, by equating himself with the figure of the medieval emperor, Henry erases the discrepancy between his life and its form, his awestruck friends peer on "that terrible mask of his, which was no longer a mask, but Madness!" At that moment a passing delusion "became fixed, perpetuating itself." One could turn into an idiot, the attending psychologist reflects, one "could go mad" (*E* 313–15; *HE* 20, 22).

The real obstruction to life, we might conclude, occurs not when consciousness spies a rift between its life and the images by which it operates (that perplexing and "paralyzing" act of seeing oneself live, of stripping life down to its troublesome nudity) but, rather, when it allows these images to develop their own autonomous logic.

If this is madness, paralysis, and death, what then is life? What is sanity and health? Logically speaking, both would seem to depend on a recognition of a rift between reality and its representation, one freeing a character from a comic, not a tragic, fate.[9] If such a thing as "a life willed and experienced by me as mine" is possible, it would be predicated on a conscious resistance to all reifying rules, on a figurative and nonliteral reading of metaphors. The sickness of mental incredulity would mark the very beginning of health. Destructive as its effects may seem at first, the perplexing suspension of a convincing world thesis might actually advance the interests of a life whose progression that same thesis arrests, furthering as it were the inherent mobility of a soul.

What is passed over by this opposition between living and seeing oneself live is the fact that life always entails some consciousness, some "seeing," or theorization, of the world (from the Greek *theōrein*, to see). Nature actually transpires in the manner of theater.[10] It is life itself that gives rise to that *sentimento della vita*, or feeling of life, that originates the phantasmagoria.[11] The only real difference between humans and animals is that in humans theorization becomes conceptual, developing into conscious creeds.[12] While Pirandello faults the feeling of life for the very rift between experience and interpretation, the problem has little to do with the discrepancy between feeling and fact or between feeling and its conceptual articulation.[13] The problem concerns the ulterior extension of consciousness, the extension of theory beyond any immediate object of vision. When this occurs, consciousness views not just the world but also its seeing of the world. Recognizing the operations of its own cognition, the mind acquires a new and broader topic. Theory becomes its own object. And this is the real significance of pondering one's image in the mirror. Action ordinarily governed by naturalistic images or reflections is then arrested by a reflection on those same reflections. One's natural and spontaneous *sentimento* then appears as only one possible theorization. And this is the moment of potential liberation, the moment when those "spontaneously" constructed images informing the semiconscious aesthetics of living can cede to *deliberately* figurative activity.

Aesthetic, as opposed to naturalistic, composition presupposes a freedom and "surplus" of the very means of significance. Aesthetics is possible only in the awareness that signs, images, and figures are largely independent of the meanings they convey, that they enjoy a degree of semantic freedom, actively deriving their meanings as much as being passively derived by means of them. When a character's natural vision becomes perplexed by a vision of vision, it means that those signs reveal their semantic indeterminacy and "originality." It means that a revelation of vision itself has occurred, a seeing not just of the content but also of the form of its vision, transcending its most immediate and pragmatic functions.

It may be useful to recall the controversy between Pirandello and Croce on this issue of reflection. Croce, we remember, had no place for the "representation of representation" in art. He considered the "reflective faculty" only to impede the spontaneous expression of figurative intuition. Such was in fact the apparent defect of Pirandello's own art, ceaselessly suspending its spontaneous intuitions in such a way that the art did not seem real. According to Pirandello, however, no purely intuitive faculty could account for artistic creation. Aesthetic compositions require the active involvement not only of intuition but, in the philosophical jargon, also of will and reflection.[14] Reflection participates in the production of art by "criticizing the work progressively as it is composed [*man mano che si fa*]" (*U* 134; *H* 112). It assesses intuitions from a position outside them, seeing what the ideal composition may use and how. Without critical reflection an artwork would never even come to form.

Reflection, then, plays both a destructive and a constructive role. It allows for an escape from an otherwise mechanical economy. In the guise of seeing oneself live, or of envisioning one's vision, reflection is the "soil" that nourishes the seeds of intuition, if it is not part of the seed itself.[15] Theoretical self-transcendence, allowing for the manipulation or rejection of one image in the search for a more significant one, is the very prerequisite of aesthetic construction. The dialectic of theory may thus be summarized in the following way: Whether through reflection or projection, reality is converted into images. When reflection comes to reflect on itself (or projection projects itself beyond all immediately available images) the artistic organization of images becomes possible. Simply put, what is required for aesthetic composition is the very sense of fiction, the intuition that images may be organized in another than ordinary way. Once theorization becomes aware of itself, spontaneous, naturalistic, and mechanical living can be replaced by an art of living. Metaphors will no longer have to be read literally.

The difference between living and seeing oneself live is thus a function of an aesthetic transcendence inherent to life. "There is," says the protagonist of *Quaderni di Serafino Gubbio, operatore*, "a *beyond* in everything [*C'è un* oltre *in tutto*]" (*SG* 519; *Shoot!* 4). Critics have been prone to assign an objective referent to this *oltre,* as though it denoted an unconscious or hidden essence of human subjectivity.[16] We might do better to begin with the literal meaning. *Oltre* means "beyond," in the sense of an unspecified field beyond the boundaries of a determinate range of vision. It indicates not "something" but "something more" (as the translator C. K. Scott Moncrieff has rendered the word), something more than the picture delineated from a particular perspective, something more than a content encapsulated in form. The beyond stands for a possibility undetermined by a given configuration of experience. To sense this beyond is not to possess a "positive" intuition. It is to be projected *outside* the figures of one's positive intuitions.

A few pages later Gubbio associates this transcendent *oltre* with a "superfluity" inherent in human nature, which, "to vent itself, creates a fictitious world in nature . . . and yet one with which [people] themselves neither know how to, nor can, be content, so that without pause they restlessly and longingly alter and realter it" (*SG* 526–27; *Shoot!* 14). Again we should begin with the literal meaning. *Superfluity* means an overflowing of boundaries, the boundaries in this case of a poetic construction. If there is a madness entailed by this superfluity, it lies not in the fact that the superfluity can never be persuaded by the images it constructs but in the fact that it *attempts to be,* that it insists on "adequating" facts and figures. Not only is this superfluity useless (insofar as it never achieves its goal); it is also self-contradictory, ceaselessly contesting its own results.

Impelled by one and the same force, this simultaneous construction and destruction of images makes the dialectic of theory clearer. If life creates form, it is also life that undoes it, perpetually restructuring its own organization. If this life is anything in itself, it is aesthetic transcendence, a continuous "rewriting" in search of ever more adequate articulations. Undoubtedly, there is an unappeasable essayism at work in this ceaseless activity. In fact, this contesting of ostensibly natural images, Pirandello suggests, is a sign of the most "feverish" activity of willful figuration, aiming ultimately at

---

nothing less than the definitive achievement of permanent and unshakable belief (*U* 161–62; *H* 139).

In Chapter 3 we saw some of the effects of this superfluous *oltre* on a living character: the obliteration of a living, thematic logic; the suspension of self-identity; the revelation of all images to be rhetorical simulations. Whatever one had grown used to accepting as simply and unequivocally real suddenly appears in the guise of phenomenal likeness. There arises the perplexing and nearly debilitating feeling of a rift between formal, objective conditions and an uncertain, subjective possibility (the very rift between Croce's expression and intuition). At the same time, however, the experience of the *oltre* offers the promise of new ways of seeing, new modes of theorization, new strategies of figure formation. When, after all, does consciousness trace this dialectical path? When does it peer beyond the boundaries of its figured world? Only when its aesthetic ambition outgrows its available resources. Only here does properly artistic construction, in the sense of deliberate and intentional figuration, turn into a project. Essaying the dead letter of the law, the *oltre* provides an occasion for an interpretive birth. It is at this point that the processes of figuration can finally be seen for what they are: metaphors instead of truths, open instead of closed pronouncements. Needless to say, these new manners of seeing are not likely to settle for new unequivocal images or "last words" on the nature of the real. Rather, they will tend more toward duplicity, ambiguity, and contradiction. Transparently metaphorical and self-effacing, they will point to significances beyond themselves.

L'uomo dal fiore in bocca (1923; *The Man with the Flower in his Mouth*) is the story of a man who actively experiences the forms of his life only after his doctor declares him to be fatally ill. The catalyst for the protagonist's perceptual awakening is that most definitive obstruction of the natural order of life which is death, for the "flower" in this anonymous man's mouth is a nodule of the disease epithelioma. Thanks only to death, the man with the flower in his mouth becomes attached to life like "a creeper round the railings of a gate."[17] And yet it is not to his habitual and carefully arranged domestic life that the man attaches himself ("the perfect order of all the rooms . . . the cleanliness of all the furniture . . . the mirrored silence . . . measured out by the tick-tock of the dining-room clock." No, this normal situation is precisely what now appears abnormal, repressively restricting life's expressive potential. To continue living his routine with his doting wife would be as if the citizens of Messina, knowing that an earthquake were about to shatter them, were still calmly to undress themselves for bed, "folding up their clothes, placing their shoes outside the door, and tucking themselves underneath the bedclothes, to enjoy the freshly-laundered sheets" (*UF* 509–10; *MF* 77–78).

When the man with the flower knows that he is dying he abandons his life and his wife forever: "Sometimes I feel like going over and kicking her, believe you me" (*UF* 509; *MF* 77). On the contrary, he becomes attached to a host of improbable objects, to anonymous and barely perceptible details in the backdrop to personal experience, to gestures that would ordinarily seem lifeless and inconsequential. From an observant and imaginative distance, the man with the flower finds significance in such mechanical activities as the gift-wrapping rituals of shop assistants:

My dear sir, I spend entire days watching them. I can stand in one place for a whole hour, watching them through the shop window. I forget myself while I'm there. I feel as though I were . . . I'd like to be that roll of silk . . . that piece of cloth . . . that red or blue ribbon the young girls from haberdashery measure out by the metre—Have you ever noticed how they do it? They gather it into a figure eight between the thumb and little finger, before wrapping it up. (*pause.*) I watch the customers coming out of the shop with the parcel looped round their finger, or in their hand, or under their arm . . . I gaze after them, until I lose sight of them . . . imagining . . . ah, so many things! You have no idea. (*UF* 505; *MF* 73)

I cling to the lives of strangers, where my imagination may work freely. . . . I take note of every little mannerism of one person or another. If only you knew how my imagination works, and how

---

hard! How deeply I can penetrate their lives! I see people's homes; I live there; I see myself right inside them, until I even become aware of . . . you know that particular odour that nests in every home? Yours, mine . . . But in our own home we're no longer aware of it, because it's the very odour of our lives. Are you with me? Yes, I can see you're nodding. (*UF* 505–6; *MF* 74)

The recognition of death has the same effects as reflexive consciousness. Providing occasions to see oneself live, both call into question not only the images but the very context for images by which characters had governed their lives. Arresting the flow of their seemingly vital logic, death revitalizes the interpretive activity on which the flow was based. What follows this man's recognition of the mechanicity, futility, and mortal limitations of human forms is not the myth of shedding one's skin (as in *Mattia Pascal*) but that of enveloping oneself in as many as possible. The disruption of reality's familiar order reveals its "packaging" and surface subtleties (in the form, for example, of the odor of a home that a dweller doesn't notice). Why this paradoxical rebirth of the very feeling of life (brilliantly imagined in its smell) through the consciousness of death? "Because in the very act of living, life is always so full of *itself*, we can never taste it to the full" (*UF* 508; *MF* 76); because the rupture of significance in consciousness or death enables a reflection on the action that is missing in its mere performance. Not filtered by a normative grammar, signs become uniquely dazzling. For the first time in his life the man with the flower in his mouth begins truly to observe his world.

As suggested by Pirandello's "La destruzione dell'uomo" (1921; "The Destruction of Man"), occasions for aesthetic wonder are provided by precisely the recognition of normative emptiness, by the pressure of "nothing" on meaning.[18] Nicola Petix, the protagonist of this short story, is being prosecuted for having flung a pregnant woman into a river. Why did he murder this woman along with her unborn baby? Because he could not bear the thought of her bringing a creature into the world only to repeat the stereotypes of its parents' unmotivated life. When Petix reflects on the mechanics of this habitual and thoughtless action, the pathway to nihilism becomes irresistible:

To do something merely in order to do it? One would have to inhabit the thing done, like a blindman, without seeing it from the outside; or else assign it a goal. What goal? Merely the goal of doing it? Yes, by God: as it occurs. This today and tomorrow that. Or maybe the same thing each day. According to one's inclinations or abilities, according to one's inclinations, according to one's feelings or instincts. As it occurs.

The trouble starts when one tries to see the purpose of those inclinations, abilities and intentions, of those feelings and instincts, pursued from the inside because one happens to possess them and feel them—when one tries to see their purpose from the outside, which, precisely because it is sought from the outside, can no longer be found, just as nothing can be found any more.

Nicola Petix quickly arrived at this nothing, which must be the quintessence of every philosophy. (*DU* 1046)

Although Petix's obsession with the nothing accompanying the rhetoric of human intentions did not yield the imaginative rebirth of the man with the flower, it was on the threshold of this creative turn that he had stood before committing his murder. Here we would do well to consider the positive significance of the "idleness" that came to characterize Petix's life, viewing it not only from his father's point of view but also his own,

for Petix truly attended university classes for years and years, passing from one course of study to another, from medicine to law, from law to mathematics, from the latter to literature and philosophy: never taking a single exam, to be sure, since he never dreamed of becoming a doctor or lawyer, a mathematician or writer or philosopher: The truth is that Petix never wanted to do anything; and yet, this doesn't mean that he remained idle or that this idleness was shameful. He constantly contemplated, studying in his own way, the fortunes of life and the customs of men. (*DU* 1045)

The nothing with which Petix was obsessed was the echo of the still unactualized fortunes of all images, disciplines, and ideologies. The death of every "one" marks the possibility of a reflective "many."

An analogous development can be traced in *One, None and a Hundred Thousand*. At age twenty-eight Vitangelo Moscarda discovers that his self-image is ontologically unreliable. To make matters worse, there are at least a hundred thousand of these inaccurate images. There were "as many Moscardas as there were people" and "all more real than I, who . . . had no reality whatsoever for myself." The one "authentic" Moscarda he hoped to discover beneath his various masks was a formless abstraction ("unable to give myself an image different from that with which I represented myself"). And yet, although the images with which Moscarda had been identified "had nothing to do with my spirit" (*Uno* 781, 788, 795; 2:12, 3:2), they still offered the only concrete indications of Moscarda's being-in-the-world, which he can choose to accept (like the character Cecè in the play by the same name) or reject. In truth, Moscarda is nothing *more* than the sum of his images.[19] It is this simultaneous specificity and multiplicity of form that is foremost in Moscarda's mind when, like so many other Pirandellian characters, he fails to follow the path his father would have liked him to take.[20]

Not, note well, that I deliberately resisted the path on which my father set me walking. I took all of them. But as for walking, I did not walk. I stopped at every step; first from afar, then increasingly close up, I would circle every pebble I met, and was greatly surprised by the fact that others could pass in front of me without paying the slightest attention to that pebble which meanwhile had assumed in my mind the proportions of an insuperable mountain, indeed, of a world in which I could surely have set up my dwelling.

Moscarda, his spirit "full of worlds," was passed by everyone on that general road. At its end "they had found a cart: their cart; they had been yoked to it with much patience, and now they were pulling it behind them. But I was pulling no cart; and thus I wore neither bridle nor blinders; I certainly saw more than they; but as for setting out, I didn't know where to go" (*Uno* 741; 1:1). Whether because no external resistance

Conscious Essayism

had forced him to develop a strong individuality or because his soul had an internal multiplicity which he refused to repress, Moscarda simply refused "to exist firmly in a particular mode of my own. . . . I had for myself no reality that was truly mine, I was as in a state of continuous fusion, almost fluid, malleable" (*Uno* 780–81; 2:12).

It is in deference to these thousands of subjective possibilities that Moscarda finally decides to reject every fixed self-image and adopt instead a fluctuant mode of life, delivering himself to a "breadth of nature in which he dissolves and disperses himself." Escaping the "closure of subjectivity," he relinquishes his personal attributes to retire to a hospice built by means of his own money (by a redistribution, in other words, of his inherited patrimony).[21] Only in this final solution, ascetic and mystical at once, does Moscarda believe he can bring into play "all the life that was in me, all that I could be" (*Uno* 893; 7:8).

Other strategies for evading a definitive life can be observed in "The Wheelbarrow" and *Il giuoco delle parti* (1919; *The Rules of the Game*).[22] The lawyer of "The Wheelbarrow," we remember, recognizes quite suddenly, "from outside" his life, that he had never been in it. Soon after this initial bewilderment, the lawyer resigns himself to the fact that it is impossible to undo the structures of an already constructed existence. The question then is how, "in the prison of this form, could I . . . gather and activate a different life, a life that was truly mine?" He comes up with a method to deceive the operative image of his existence, namely, the performance of a single, gratuitous act for a minute each day. Carefully locking the door of his office, he picks up the hind legs of his aging dog and prances her around the room for a turn or two. Was his the life of a dog, condemned to a fate he passively and uncomprehendingly accepted? Well, now he would have something of his own to say about this image. The wheelbarrow operation is his creative revenge on the figure of his fate. By perverting its original intentions, the lawyer robs it of its definitive power. While this childish game of carting the dog round the room ultimately amounts to nothing, this nothing is "everything" for the lawyer, "a divine, lucid folly," which "liberates me and vindicates me for everything" (*C* 719, 714). Escaping the normative expectations of his quotidian life for a single instant, the lawyer turns his fate into a conscious destiny. Like the man with the flower, the lawyer effects a semantic transformation of an economy of images to which he is already destined.

The fiction in which Pirandello most explicitly researches this possibility of an immanent transformation of the image is *The Rules of the Game*. The protagonist Leone Gala contends that he has understood "the game": the series of mechanical and normative roles required of a social player. When Gala understands this game he abandons his wife to her lover and lives in an ironical distance from the historical coordinates of his own existence (a distance connoted even by his name: *gala* = festivity; *galla, galleggiare* = floating). He achieves his floating existence with the help of a twofold method. The first involves not actually living so much as "watching others live, and even ourselves, from the outside." To achieve tranquility he advises Guido, his wife's lover, one must first "empty oneself out of life," creating something like the space of "a lucid and tranquil vacuum within oneself" (*GP* 530, 531). Then one must seize the occasion provided by this emptiness, namely, that of reorganizing the constitutive contents.[23]

Cooking, that art of blending banal ingredients into new and more palatable solutions, becomes an emblem of Gala's means of balancing his floating life. When the outside world impinges on Gala's freedom, as it necessarily does, he responds by exploiting the ambiguities any present situation offers. Called on by his wife to duel a man who has offended her honor, Gala chooses her lover to be his second and successfully contrives to have him fight in Gala's place. Needless to say, the lover is killed, punished for having followed the rules too literally, for having assumed that role of wife protector which the husband would play only tongue in cheek.

Conscious Essayism

The Rules of the Game addresses an issue only partially treated by the other narratives we have considered: the question of a satisfying response to an existence in which images have lost their persuasion. *The Rules of the Game* tries to offer a description of a constructive aesthetics of perplexity.

Perplexity is that confusion of images produced by the reflexive intrusion of consciousness on one's habitual figures. The immediate effect of this process is a suspension of literalism, of the "letter of the law." Each of one's feelings or thoughts now evokes its own opposite. When the germ of a feeling falls into the soil of reflection, writes Pirandello, "the plant becomes dressed in a green that is alien and yet its own." The result is that "abnormal" condition, he writes, in a simile worthy of Kierkegaard,

of a person who finds himself constantly almost off key, who is like a violin and double bass at the same time; of a person to whom a thought cannot occur without the immediate occurrence of an opposite and contradictory one; to whom for every reason he has to say *yes*, there arises one or two or three compelling him to say *no*; and keep him suspended, perplexed his whole life long between the yes and the no; of a man who cannot abandon himself to a feeling without suddenly perceiving something pulling a wry face within him, and disturbing and disconcerting and vexing him.

This perplexed uncertainty produces the obligation of operating "beyond" every determinate image and convincing belief, of "not knowing what side to take [*non sapere più da quale parte tenere*]" (*U* 142, 146, 153; *H* 120, 124, 131). "O white campanile," Mattia Pascal announces to the tower of Pisa, "you could lean to one side; but I, between those two [conflicting feelings], could move neither to the left nor the right" (*FMP* 554; *LMP* 228).

Aesthetics means the shaping of materials into a deliberate design, the ordering of an otherwise orderless condition. In truth, perplexity already arises from the failure of a particular aesthetic, namely, that habitual, normative, and naturalistic aesthetic in which a phenomenon is defined by a particular image. But this perplexity is not equivalent to mere paralysis. It is already "a particular way of considering the world," namely, the "material and reason" of an aesthetics that Pirandello calls humorous (*U* 134; *H* 112). Perplexed consciousness is itself an aesthetic fact that responds to an ontological condition (described, by recourse to Alfred Binet and Gabriel Séailles, at the end of *On Humor*), whose logic the humorist merely attempts to articulate.

How can we describe the theory of this perplexity in a way that makes its aesthetic implications clear? Epistemologically speaking, the feeling of being "held between two"—or three or four or a hundred thousand—represents the outcome of the perception of a difference built into, but ignored by, the logic of representation. The difference upon which the equation $A = B$ is based reasserts its primordiality (in order to be equated with B, A must first be perceived as different from B; and if A equals B, it may also equal C or D). The duplicity underlying the equation $A = B$ simply triples and quadruples. Ontologically speaking, the logic of difference (experienced in the form of intellectual perplexity) unfolds inexorably in the superfluous self-transcendence of formal experience. When Pirandello's characters step beyond their mechanical mental orders, they discover no literal replacements. Their deepest and instinctive essay fails. Dissociated from their familiar conceptual structures and projected into a type of "nothing," Pascal and Moscarda are caught between the unviable poles of a neither/nor. The old order of images has collapsed; a new one remains implausible. The characters are caught in between. Pascal, Moscarda, Henry, Petix, and the lawyer remain trapped by a system to which they no longer belong, "naturally inclined" in ways that no longer appear natural.

In this respect the feeling of perplexity consists in a recognition of an epistemological aporia as ontological in its implications as the most radical poststructuralist theory.[24] Identification breaks down. The gaze in that ubiquitous Pirandellian mirror reveals not sameness but difference.[25] Measured against ordinary faith in the referentiality of an image, the perplexed uncertainty of this duplicitous condition con-

---

stitutes a type of madness. And yet, as we have seen, this madness is also the ground for wonder, for critical thinking, for semantic creativity. Perplexity is a sign for the very openness of signification. To express itself, this perplexing transcendence by which experience interminably constructs and destructs itself requires a new conceptual vocabulary, an ambivalence of expression, one resisting the very notion of unequivocal form.

In opposition to the "common lie" by which the reality principle enforces its univocal and monocular visions, Pirandello proposes an "explicit and declared tolerance of dissension and contrast." In the aesthetics of perplexity "each image, each group of images evokes and attracts contrary ones, and these naturally divide the spirit, which, in its restlessness, is obstinately determined to find or establish the most astonishing relationships between these images" (U 155, 141; H 133, 119). The "restless" spirit becomes determined to find or establish "the most astonishing relationships" among these images awakened in contrast. In truth, these images and feelings and thoughts do not simply "awaken" in contrast; they evoke and attract their opposites. In finding or establishing new relationships among images an aesthetics of perplexity aims at renewing hermeneutical production, discovering affinities and connections among articles of faith hitherto considered incompatible. Such an art requires the help of procedures ordinarily suppressed by rationalistic or naturalistic aesthetics: digression, disruption, and contradiction. The artist of perplexity now encourages elements between which categorical logic had allowed no commerce to combine in unimagined ways. And the goal of this new procedure is a hermeneutics of connotation, not of definitive denotation.

Let us state once more that such an art would be interested in nothing so little as the construction of a new logic of experience, an nth repetition of the procedures of ordinary consciousness. It is, in fact, what Pirandello's protagonists find impossible to accomplish in life. And it is no different in the activity of artistic composition. Instead of constructing a new logic of experience, an essayistic art begins by essaying the coherence and validity of its own intuitions. It attacks the referential fallacy according to which an image reflects a phenomenal truth. Rather than attempting to pass off a figure as a fact or a metaphor as a literal statement, it cultivates ostensibly "implausible" tales in an art that reflects on itself. Beginning by researching the variable ways in which meaning is construed, it frees phenomena from the tyranny of exclusive and authoritarian readings.

In addition to the fallacy of objective reference, there is another against which this art will tend to militate: the effort to generalize, typify, or categorize particular events. In a discussion of Taine, Pirandello's aversion is clear: "'Antiquity serenely constrained forms into the harmony of the finite.' There is a synthesis for you. All of antiquity? No ancient Greek excluded? . . . 'The ancient world shrank the supernatural energies into plastic forms.' There is another synthesis for you." If art has any constructive purpose, it is predicated on undoing such conceptual simplifications. Pirandello's art, in particular, aims to divulge a phenomenal multiplicity that resists harmonious, systematic, and coherent organization.[26] Or better: The new organization at which it aims (for such organization is the sine qua non of art) is one that emphasizes the potential infinity of this phenomenal multiplicity. The new type of construction for which its own dismantling of implausible logics implicitly calls is one that must present an unsynthetic coherence, an instable and elastic relation among its elements.

It is therefore clear that digression, disruption, and contradiction are not enough for the aesthetic Pirandello has in mind. At best they produce comedy, not humor. Humor requires that this perception of revelation of tension produce a *feeling* of tension, or the sense of a necessary and ineluctable relation between the contrasting elements. The feeling of tension lies only in an awareness of a fundamental and indissoluble bond between conflicting terms (digression and the main narrative line, free choice and its predetermination, desire and duty, yes and no). What Pirandello in his famous definition of humor calls the "feeling" rather than the "perception" of contradiction (*il sentimento del contrario*) envisions an insoluble link *between* the opposing terms. The feeling of contradiction divulges a C in the relation of A to B. Comedy changes to humor only when, from a reflection on the failure of two feelings to submit to a Tainian synthesis, "another feeling springs forth or emanates" (*U* 135; *H* 113). This new feeling of contradiction is the very sense of the bind, the essayistic fate of being "held between two," without recourse to resolution. The celebrated *sentimento del contrario* does not consist merely in empathy for a character's dilemma but in an affirmation of that dilemma's hermeneutical dynamic.

The critical dismantling of discursive unities thus aims to renew interpretive activity, inciting the spirit to establish connections among images typically kept remote from each other. That "asynthetic" order to which Pirandello aspires with his explicit tolerance of dissension and contrast envisions a new order of complexity in which nothing will present itself as autonomously significant but only as contextually determined, functionally dependent, and conceptually elastic, part of a whole whose wholeness can neither be intuited nor transcribed. The hypothetical unity of this whole will invite repeated and unlimited attempts to interpret its shifting logics. Only now will we have a consciously reflexive aesthetic construction, an inexhaustibly dynamic synthesis, essayistically related in such a way that every part sheds light on the unimaginable whole.

In this mutual mirroring of disparate elements lies a further significance to the word *reflection*. One need only recall the place where Mattia Pascal has chosen to write his autobiography, namely, the Church of Santa Maria Liberale, which has now been deconsecrated and transformed into a library. In the post-Copernican setting of Pascal's autobiography, the categorical truth of a single, authoritative Book (that is, the Bible) has given way to a "veritable Babylon" of texts and opinions. The confusion is "indescribable." And yet, as with the democracy pondered by Pascal when he encounters the drunkard, this confusion of perspectives bespeaks an interrelatedness of each with all. In this Babylon Pascal finds evidence for the most "singular friendships" among rival hermeneutics:

Don Eligio [the librarian] told me, for example, that he had a hard time detaching the three volumes of an extremely licentious treatise, *Concerning the Art of Loving Women,* written in 1571 by Anton Muzio Porro, from a *Life and Death of Faustino Materucci, Benedictine of Polirone, Known to Many as "Blessed,"* a biography published in Mantua in 1625. The dampness had caused the bindings of the volumes to stick fraternally together. It is worth noting that the second volume of the licentious treatise discusses at length the life and amorous adventures of monks. (*FMP* 321–22; *LMP* 3–4)

In this parable of discursive contamination, we have a hint as to how Pirandello will construct his own tales, contrasting not only intuitive contents but also various idioms and levels of articulation. As the logic of literal and objective representation yields to an endeavor to divulge a C in the relation between A and B, the issue becomes the actual restructuration of these constitutive elements by means of their contextual relations (the blessedness of Materucci attached to Porro). Transcending speech *in modo recto,* meaning begins to transpire *in modo obliquo.* One speaks of an X by reference to a Y. In such a system of relative meanings words develop their significances in countless ways. Depending on the network traced, we become able to regard "the terminus as the fundament and the fundament as the terminus." [27]

The astonishing relationships established between dissimilar things can now be casual as well as hypothetical, or based on the weight of an *if.* "If Cleopatra's nose had been longer, who knows what other events the world would have known," reflects Pirandello in *On Humor* (*U* 167; *H* 145). To cultivate an aesthetics of the *if,* in deliberate opposition to the indicative mood of realist living and writing, is to encourage the production of new interpretations. In fact, the consideration "if this, then that," underlies even the most banal daily decisions (where the sequence from "this" to "that" is typically mechanical and repetitive). To worry the habitual links between these given and self-evident "thises" and "thats" is to allow for the discovery of the most astonishing new relationships. As witnessed even by the incidental, episodic plot of *Mattia Pascal*, contingency need not be fortuitous. It can allude to another type of hermeneutic, one countering mechanization. Like reflection and death, the humorist's *if* acts as a principle of transfiguration, interrupting the logic of an imagistic economy to prepare for still unimagined possibilities. Against the order of unequivocal narrative causality (where A necessarily entails B) the *if* posits the possibility of a projective or essayistic causality (in which A might just as easily produce C and D and E). Breaking that reflective mirror in which phenomenon A reflects B and only B, the *if* liberates as yet undiscovered potentialities of speculation. What is more, this essayistic speculation guarantees that no reflection will ever be final. It problematizes the very relation between experience and understanding, enabling one to *read* those images by which one is normally read.

Let us now return from these aesthetic considerations to Pirandello's statement to the effect that persons are always only metaphors of themselves. We now find it to mean more than "The images by which we operate do not accurately represent our subjective being." Nor does it mean that beneath these metaphors lie "souls" masked by their representative images. The metaphoricity refers to neither the operative images nor the souls that act by means of them but, rather, to the activity by which the two are linked in historical decision. This means the bridging of the two in action, the stretching from all intuition to its required expression. The real metaphoricity entails this mediation between the two types of metaphor, the definitive image and the amorphous soul, in an open, dialectical process.

The first act of metaphoricity entails imagistic identification. Whether naive or deliberate, this rhetorical identification eventually reveals a gap between the subjective "fact" and the fiction with which it equates itself, between the I and its representation. From the recognition of this disjunction there arises the second moment of metaphoricity. The feeling of a "real face" is born. There arises the sense of a "central active self" inside oneself which is inadequately served by its historical acts, the unmistakable intuition of "a spiritual something which seems to *go out* to meet these qualities and contents" by which it is defined, "whilst they seem to *come in* to be received by it." [28] The second moment of metaphoricity arises with the "wounding" of the marionette's "self-feeling," the betrayal of what Pirandello calls a *punto vivo,* which is a "God within" (*Uno* 880; 7:5). A realization of the metaphoricity of expressive action inaugurates an effort to banish all metaphors in a quest for one's proper name.

The attempt to transcend the image fails, however, insofar as it is linked to the very logic it battles (namely, the logic of representation, here striving merely for amelioration). The freedom of the wheelbarrowing lawyer and Pascal can only be expressed in an ironic reenactment of the plight they have spiritually transcended. The third moment of metaphoricity begins when these characters relinquish the very notion of a proper name, when both Pascal and Gala resign themselves to the fact that they consist *only* in self-mediation, only in the "cheating" of the functions that fate sends their way. The "central and active self" withdraws as an insufficient hypothesis. If Pascal and Gala have any freedom at all, it is only the freedom to manipulate the *relations* among these images that define them as what they are, in an attempt to determine the final conglomeration as best they can. The third moment of metaphoricity consists in a recognition of destiny as fateful and "improper" interpretation. One "becomes what one is" only by attempting to bridge the distance between insufficient terms, or to coordinate their conflicting demands into an approximate whole. The I is a shifting economy established among the various "me's."

This process is engaged in with quite differing degrees of awareness among Pirandello's characters. Few consciously resolve on it (in the sense, for example, of Musil's Ulrich). Moscarda, for example, ultimately ignores the metaphoric semantics on which his transcendence of self is based. His

     Conscious Essayism

self-identification with the infinite forms of the universe is no less literal than the self-representations from which he had forcibly detached himself: "I am this tree. Tree, cloud; to-morrow book or wind: the book I read, the wind I drink. Al-together outside, vagabond." He has not reevaluated the naming process to which he is historically destined. He has relinquished the very effort to alter his use of language. "Willing nothing," Moscarda felt that he "could no longer speak" (*Uno* 901, 899; 8:4, 3).[29]

The characters toward whom we must look for a deliber-ate ethic of metaphoricity are rather those who continue to speak, and precisely through the lie of the figure. When Mattia Pascal returns to his village to take "practical enjoy-ment of his social non-being," he resolves to do willingly and knowingly what until then had been merely a compulsion.[30] Once a downtrodden marionette, he returns to the theater of his past with a "Homeric laughter" racking his entrails. Has his wife remarried? Has she born a child to his friend Pomino? No matter! He is now free to play with the forms that had once constrained him and to which he had been unfairly subjected: "Ah, now that I was going to be alive again, I could even enjoy telling lies, lots and lots of them, as big as those of Cavalier Tito Lenzi. Even bigger!" (*FMP* 551; *LMP* 226).

This ironical solution is made possible only by a change in attitude—by a recognition of the impossibility of precisely that self-coincidence for which Pascal had yearned through-out his first two lives. His third life is only a partial reinsertion into society and "normalcy." It is a *posthumous* life, in which nothing theoretically his is practically his: "I am far from being in a sound legal position, nor have I regained my indi-vidual characteristics. My wife is the wife of Pomino, and I can't really say who I am" (*FMP* 578; *LMP* 250). Yet now for the very first time he can stage his life within the gratuitous constraints of history.

How can we define this operative space between himself and his roles in which Pascal finds his gratification? Piran-dello represents it as the space of writing, and, more particu-larly, as the space of autobiography—the ongoing mediation of a constructed self by means of a self-constructing one. One need only recall the first-person narration of most of Pirandello's stories to realize that his characters never find expression for their celebrated feeling of life by simply living their lives but only by "writing" them, in the sense of recalling, narrating, describing, and deciphering. Far from a literal rehearsal of events in consciousness, this writing is a creative remaking.[31] The I of autobiography corresponds neither to the subject nor the object of the interpretation in process but rather to the relation between the two. The I is a virtual self, an act of metaphoricity.

A final example of this metaphoricity can be found in the "balance" and the "pivot" espoused by Leone Gala in *The Rules of the Game.* The secret of mental health, Gala explains, consists not only in the double gesture of emptying and refilling oneself but also in the balancing of these two, or in "finding a pivot." A pivot is a structure allowing for motion, enabling rotation around an immovable point. It is a device that makes a rod swivel. The rigid and immovable parts of this particular machine are the roles and rules by which a historical subject is obliged to play. To manage their conflicting demands one must devise a pivot, one "for each random event [*caso*], and a good and solid one, so that fortune [*caso*], which visits you often unexpectedly and violently, shouldn't break it" (*GP* 531). As a means of coordinating roles, the pivot enables an original performance.[32] Once he has understood the rules of the normative game, Leona Gala adopts the mobility of a character assuming and abandoning roles as his reading of the script requires. Gala's existential formula is more convincing in this respect than Moscarda's, for Moscarda presumes to efface the very distance between reality and imagination by an ethic of improvisation. But improvisation is never fully allowed by the "necessitarian" mechanics of performance. If anything, it increases rather than decreases cliché.[33] Unlike Moscarda, Gala spies interpretive freedom only in the constraints of a script. Pivotal living means reinterpreting the facts or the figures already thrown one's way (whether wind, book, wife, or tree).

Having recognized that his possible selves are in fact metaphors, Gala points to the only place in which to locate Pirandello's existential ethic: the figurative space between them. Neither the role nor even the actor, the historical person is, instead, the process of playing, of sliding from one image to another in an effort to make a definitive move.

Conclusion

The fragment is modern, the essay postmodern, says Lyotard, describing the fragment as a commemoration of the failure of language and the essay as a new aesthetic beginning, a renewal of confidence in expressive adventure. If the fragment is haunted by a sense of semantic negativity, the essay engages in a satire of hermeneutical experimentation.[1]

In my own reading the two terms are not quite as antithetical as that. Here the essay is conceived as aspiring precisely to wholeness in fragmentation. Where modernism names the struggle to theorize the theorization of the real, essayism represents its last and conclusive chapter.[2] It aims at the same absolute knowledge whose absence the fragment bemoans, the same generalizability of truth, the same unity of understanding in which the vision and the practice of life might flow together. Historically no less than epistemologically, essayism is a symptom not of happy relativism but of skepticism at odds with its own despair, attending epochs more like Montaigne's and the beginning of the twentieth century than our own.

If any single factor is responsible for the skepticism of this second essayistic moment, it is that questioning of the truth value of ethics, aesthetics, and metaphysics which goes by the name of positivism. Measured by certain and positive criteria of judgment, these humanistic sciences make only pseudostatements. Truth can be attributed only to what can be scientifically or logically corroborated, like mathematics and the operations of amoebas.

Artists tended to respond to this critique of their instruments and highest ambitions in one of two ways. They either continued to elaborate expressive techniques that positivism had tried to discount (symbolism, aestheticism, and mythologism; imagism, realism, and naturalism, even if these latter aimed at the most "positive" types of representation), or they showed a defiant new audacity, wagering that courageous new experiments in form might overwhelm the forces of reason that positivism had rallied against them (expressionism, futurism, surrealism, and Dadaism—the avant-garde in general). In fact, sometimes the two responses cannot even be distinguished, making the difference between "regressive" and "progressive" aesthetic procedures appear to offer merely two moves in a single utopian gamble. Even so, the two moves are there: the quest for immediate and intuitive knowledge, on the one hand, and the destruction of that same dream, on the other.

Conrad, Musil, and Pirandello resist both temptations. They write in full awareness of the epistemological shortcomings of the first, "regressive" move, the one proposing new formulations of old types of aesthetic coherence. I mean the holistic languages of the passions and the senses (Gabriele D'Annunzio and André Gide); Manichean divisions of experience into strong or weak, healthy or sick, authentic or inauthentic (Thomas Mann, D. H. Lawrence, vitalism, voluntarism, and existentialist fiction); the linguistic rigors of mimetic precision (Ezra Pound and James Joyce); the mystical fusions of symbolism, neo-idealism, and Bergsonian intuitionism.[3] At the same time the three essayists also reject the iconoclastic enthusiasm of the avant-garde. Of course, this is not to say that Conrad, Musil, and Pirandello fail to make use of aesthetic techniques developed on both of these fronts. But they never entertain the hope of invalidating or replacing the language of reason, the language, that is, of testable, conceptual truth. They refuse to believe in the autonomy of aesthetic cognition or the self-sufficiency of literary craft, whether mimetic or antimimetic.

In short, Conrad, Musil, and Pirandello take the positivistic threat to artistic knowledge more seriously than all but the philosophers. And this is simply because their writing aims at the same positive understanding of experience invoked by philosophy itself. Unwilling to sidestep the contemporary critique of aesthetics, they meet it head-on. To meet it head-on is to admit, even before lifting one's pen, that one lacks a language with which to write.

Nowhere is this dilemma expressed with more pathos than in *Signs of the Times,* a book written by Gaetano Negri in 1889: "Metaphysical science has fallen forever; reason has succeeded in discovering the extent of its vanity. What has remained standing is the metaphysical feeling, against which reason is impotent."[4] What Negri has in mind with this voiceless metaphysical feeling is that consequence of positivism better known as nihilism: the recognition of the failure of *all* languages of truth, insofar as the stringent new claims of reason finally allow for no definitive statements whatsoever. At the beginning of this century it was not quite so easy to laugh this knowledge to death (with the simple observation that the truth that "there is no truth" cannot logically hold). Yes, one could replace conceptual criteria for truth with pragmatic ones. One could also embrace the new freedom of the imagination. But neither pragmatism nor intoxicating play can cancel the fact that knowledge, morality, and law—to say nothing of the simplest and most everyday decisions—rely on distinctions that become impossible to maintain in good faith (true versus false, right versus wrong, good versus bad). All appeals to the authority of interpretive conventions only avoid the recognition of the original theorists of nihilism and those who attempted to overcome it: that the foundations for decision become theoretically illegitimate.

Essayism accompanies this juncture where reason has

abolished truth but not the will to truth. If anything, such an abolition has only exacerbated this will, resulting, as Musil observes, in the fact that "man is much more interested in metaphysics than he admits today." The "essence of the epoch is that it calls for a utopia."[5] Utopia means "a direction for life, a vision of the whole, a lucid construction and organization of the future"; it requires more than new formulations of old values and cataclysmic experimentations in language.[6] Spurred by a "Cartesian anxiety" to reground the very bases for intellectual operation, the call for utopia demands nothing less than a new approach to history.[7]

To respond to this utopian challenge means neither to bemoan nor to celebrate the absence of truth (the aesthetics of the fragment and the satire, respectively); it means to formulate such truth in its absence. The utopian essay can be engaged in only on the basis of a double recognition; a recognition of the irremediability of the metaphysical feeling (which means merely the desire to guide action by consciousness) as well as of the insufficiency of each of its articulations. Neither a radically new language nor an ingenuous use of the ones we have offers a sufficient means for approaching the task. Otherwise put, a solution to the nihilistic dilemma must be sought in an immanent critique of the understanding itself, in a rehearsal of the self-critical nature of knowledge. Here one is asked to welcome the new pressures that are placed on our cognitive instruments. To respond to the call for utopia is to seek to remunerate the defects of the reigning logics of experience, to order their conflict in an unprecedented way.

In fact, this immanent transformation of the positivistic critique of knowledge is the only answer to positivism itself. In truth, there is nothing "irrationalistic" or "antirealistic" about Conrad's, Musil's, and Pirandello's attacks on moral and representational logic, on reason and common sense, on psychological and social convention (as it might seem by analogy to the work of their peers). On the contrary, their dismantlings of these interpretive idioms reveal more like "a superabundance of realism and rationalism, which, by dint of its own dynamic, penetrates everything fictitious and conventional which logic and reality entail." The essayists simply make an ulterior appeal to that same integrity of thought on which positivism itself had insisted. Their writings bear witness to a type of logic "which rejects conclusion and synthesis precisely through an excess—and no defect—of rationality" and thus finds itself able to "prolong itself infinitely."[8] Here we could take a cue from Adorno and his vision of art as "rationality criticizing itself without being able to overcome itself."[9] What Adorno has in mind is the implicit rejection by aesthetics of the very procedures of conceptual thought. In the art of Conrad, Musil, and Pirandello, however, this rejection is explicit, performed from *within* the same structures of reason (accompanied by no less immanent a criticism of the representations of Adorno's art). In these essayists the "essence of art" as Adorno understands it becomes self-conscious.

Conrad, Musil, and Pirandello may thus be distinguished from their literary peers not merely by the fact that they face up to the ramifications of the nihilistic dilemma (social, moral, and epistemological) but also by the fact that they seek a solution to the dilemma in its own terms. Here all that can be done is to reassess those languages of moral, scientific, and aesthetic knowledge which seemed to have gone wrong, to rethink their possibilities, to relate them to each other in more precise and productive ways. Unwilling to relinquish the metaphysical demand for definitive knowledge, Conrad, Musil, and Pirandello seek a more adequate means for its satisfaction than those we have so far enjoyed, a means that will be as practical as theoretical, as existential as intellectual. (And this search may explain some aspects of the style of their works, which demands discursive understanding of aesthetic representations.) A language for the metaphysical feeling can only be shaped out of the conceptual and imagistic shards we already have. If totalizing organizations of experience have lost their viability, then wholeness must be constituted out of their death. The utopian task is to find coherence in incoherence, reason in unreason, identity in the nonidentical.

Essayism in many ways heralds our own contemporary theoretical climate in which categorical and unequivocal systems of interpretation have ceded their authority to pliant and relativistic new methodologies. Indeed, more than half a century after Conrad, Musil, and Pirandello first envisioned the need for such flexibility, many spheres of intellectual activity have begun to approach their tasks with a subtle new sense of pragmatics and hermeneutical function. Essayism intends essentially to take this development *further* than it has been wont to go, further in the sense of more daring critiques of what counts as evidence, more venturesome experiments in method, more sophisticated articulations of feeling. In fact, on close analysis many of our contemporary methodologies reveal the same mechanicity as the orders against which they crusade—the same glib self-confidence, the same historical predictability, the same moral absoluteness, the same ultimate appeal to subjective conviction. Essayism, in contrast, wishes to rethink not only the determinations of judgment but especially the determination *of* those determinations, the procedures by which decisions are reached.

Here it will not suffice to shift one's labor from system building to micrological mappings of local historical functions (whether cultural, political, psychological, or sexual). Nor will it do to commit these new mappings of function to the age-old service of self-assertion (even where they undermine the economy of the self in question). Otherwise put, what has not always changed in our contemporary transformations of theoretical procedure are the metaphysics and the valuations on which they are based, including that center around which so many issues are made to revolve, the human subject. It was precisely this economy of the subject that Conrad, Musil, and Pirandello had attempted to call into question, believing that it could no longer stand as the fulcrum of theoretical work. Although contemporary research has made numerous efforts to dismantle this subject (relocating its values in tradition, institution, and the suprapersonal creativity of language itself), it is the very same subject that has returned as the first principle of many postmodern essays (variously addressed to the empowerment of the individual, the liberation of desire, and the autonomy of various complexes of mind-history-body).

Essayism does not extol a new liberalism subtended by subjective self-certainty. Nor does it propose new instruments for the old project of self-determination. Rather, it questions the subject still imagined by this liberal project, a subject that appears not only to be an ideological epiphenomenon but also an all too static, even reflex, reaction to complex operations of being-in-the-world. The invitation by Conrad, Musil, and Pirandello to reconsider the operations of this being-in-the-world did not hope to be answered by improved programs for self-realization. If anything, they expected that the subject might begin to outgrow its own self-conceptions, desisting, as it were, from its projects of practical and ideal desire. Where desire entails a hermeneutics of circumstance which neither the subject nor reason nor the state can master, self-determination and authenticity suddenly lose their persuasiveness. Were it possible at all, authenticity would depend less on the affirmation than the negation of desire (even in the form of death); self-determination would be foreclosed by all strategies of personal empowerment; power would be promised only by the recognition of unachievable economies of desire, of the mere virtuality of experience, of ineluctable tests of all personal capacity. The only certainty attending this new subjectivity without a subject is neither a feeling nor a goal but, rather, an ongoing need to take a stance in the world, a need for openness, endurance, and the management of conscious perplexity, a stance that is therefore no stance at all, at least not in the sense of a firm position.

"Anything that does not wish to wither," writes Adorno, "should . . . take on itself the stigma of the inauthentic." Proceeding from a reflection on "the ego as embarrassment," essayism constitutes an effort to authenticate this ineradicably inauthentic life.[10] It can only begin in a phenomenology of this inauthenticity.

Phenomenology means the study of form, an analysis of the ruling metaphors of action and thought. Its aim, as Conrad says of his work, is simply "to make you *see*" (*NN* xiv). But to make you see is simultaneously to elaborate new ways of seeing. Phenomenology is way finding. Analogously, the moral uncertainty of Conrad's, Musil's, and Pirandello's characters signals a therapeutic condition, an "open field" that comes into view when an old order of values is overturned, a condition of perplexity which "precedes and accompanies the revaluation."[11] Essayism aims to serve the possibilities of theorization. "Before what is thought is thought," as Bloch puts it, "what ought to be thought is opined."[12] Essayism is this proleptic effort to opine what ought to be thought. And this is an effort to transform the very paradigms by which we act, including those moral algorithms in which all that changes are the embodiments of the good but not their categorical opposition to the bad. Imagining an active reshuffling of the meanings by which we operate, essayism amounts to an "attempt to see the new in the old instead of simply the old in the new."[13] In more practical terms, it imagines the possibility of a subjectivity enhanced and complexified by the sophisticated operational principles already at work in the technological world, a reparation of the rift between the ultracomplex organization attending the realm of the technical and the stunted mentality to whose service they are put.

Here the decisive factor is no longer morality but ethics, not what but how one believes. Ethics entails the nature of the relation between mind and experience, the hermeneutics at work in conscious action. Needless to say, moral action is in no way precluded by this attention to ethics; it is just that some of its favorite procedures are stymied. Only in bad faith does the essayist participate in the everyday mechanics of ballot box choice—that is, with a nagging sensation of missing precisely what is decisive through the either/or. Essayism is ready to admit that it possesses no vision of a new world order, unless it be an order marked by a striving for order. It is a messianism without eschatology, serving no utopia but that of the motivated life. And this is the utopia enacted by that proleptic and inconclusive experience of the present, that condition of alertness and wonder in which spirit is felt in the form of its absence. This is that condition in which the man without qualities find himself when he thinks of the "strange experience that 'spirit' is as of a beloved by whom one is betrayed throughout the whole of one's life without loving her any the less for that; and this united him with everything that came his way. For when one loves, everything is love, even when it is pain and loathing" (GW 1 : 155–56; MWQ 1 : 181 [40]).

The ideal formulation of goals and meanings which essayism intends to encourage depends on nothing less than a vision of this present, a vision attempting to see "whether a goal and a meaning can be found for what happens to us and has always happened to us" (GW 1 : 247; MWQ 1 : 293 [61]).

List of
Abbreviated
Works

B   Robert Musil, *Beitrag zur Beurteilung der Lehren Machs* (Inaugural Dissertation. Berlin: Dissertationen-Verlag Carl Arnold, 1908).

C   Luigi Pirandello, "La carriola," in *Novelle per un anno II,* ed. Manlio Lo Vecchio-Musti (Milan: Mondadori, 1956).

CP   Luigi Pirandello, *Collected Plays,* vol. 1, ed. Robert Rietty (New York: Riverrun Press, 1987).

DU   Luigi Pirandello, "La distruzione dell'uomo," in *NA* 1.

E   Luigi Pirandello, *Enrico IV,* in *MN* 1.

FMP Luigi Pirandello, *Il fu Mattia Pascal,* in *Tutti i romanzi,* vol. 1, ed. Giovanni Macchia (Milan: Mondadori, 1984).

GP   Luigi Pirandello, *Il giuoco delle parti,* in *MN* 1.

GW   Robert Musil, *Gesammelte Werke in neun Bänden,* ed. Adolf Frisé (Reinbek bei Hamburg: Rowohlt, 1978).

H   Luigi Pirandello, *On Humor,* trans. Antonio Illiano and Daniel P. Testa (Chapel Hill: University of North Carolina Press, 1974).

HD   Joseph Conrad, *Heart of Darkness: An Authoritative Text, Backgrounds and Sources, Criticism,* ed. Robert Kimbrough, 3d ed. (New York: W. W. Norton, 1988).

HE   Luigi Pirandello, *Henry IV,* trans. Robert Reitty and John Wardle, in *CP.*

LJ   Joseph Conrad, *Lord Jim: An Authoritative Text, Backgrounds,*

Sources, Essays in Criticism, ed. Thomas C. Moser (New York: W. W. Norton, 1968).

LMP   Luigi Pirandello, *The Late Mattia Pascal,* trans. William Weaver (Hygiene, Colo.: Eridanos Press, 1987).

LWW   Robert Musil, *Leben, Werk, Wirkung,* ed. Karl Dinklage (Reinbek bei Hamburg: Rowohlt, 1960).

MF   Luigi Pirandello, *The Man with the Flower in His Mouth,* trans. Gigi Gatti and Terri Doyle, in *CP.*

MN   Luigi Pirandello, *Maschere nude,* ed. Manlio Lo Vecchio-Musti, 2 vols. (Milan: Mondadori, 1985).

MWQ   Robert Musil, *The Man without Qualities,* trans. Eithne Wilkins and Ernst Kaiser, 3 vols. (London: Secker & Warburg, 1953–60).

MT   Robert Musil, *On Mach's Theories,* trans. Kevin Mulligan, intro. G. H. von Wright (Washington, D.C.: Catholic University of America Press, 1982).

N   Joseph Conrad, *Nostromo: A Tale of the Seaboard* (Garden City, N.Y.: Doubleday, Page, 1919).

NA   Luigi Pirandello, *Novelle per un anno,* ed. Mario Costanzo, 2 vols. (Milan: Mondadori, 1985).

NN   Joseph Conrad, *The Nigger of the "Narcissus": A Tale of the Sea* (Garden City, N.Y.: Doubleday, Page, 1927).

OP   Joseph Conrad, "An Outpost of Progress," in *Tales of Unrest* (London: T. Fisher Unwin, 1898).

PS   Robert Musil, *Precision and Soul: Essays and Addresses,* ed. and trans. Burton Pike and David S. Luft (Chicago: University of Chicago Press, 1990).

SA   Joseph Conrad, *The Secret Agent: A Simple Tale,* ed. Bruce Harkness and S. W. Reid (Cambridge: Cambridge University Press, 1990).

Sei   Luigi Pirandello, *Sei personaggi in cerca d'autore,* in *MN* 1.

SG   Luigi Pirandello, *Quaderni di Serafino Gubbio, operatore,* in *Tutti i romanzi,* vol. 2, ed. Giovanni Macchia (Milan: Mondadori, 1984).

SPSV   Luigi Pirandello, *Saggi, poesie, scritti varii,* ed. Manlio Lo Vecchio-Musti (Milan: Mondadori, 1973).

SS   Joseph Conrad, *The Secret Sharer,* in *'Twixt Land and Sea* (Garden City, N.Y.: Doubleday, Page, 1926).

TB   Robert Musil, *Tagebücher,* ed. Adolf Frisé, 2 vols. (Hamburg: Rowohlt, 1983).

U   Luigi Pirandello, *L'umorismo* (Milan: Mondadori, 1987). This paperback edition is identical in all respects except page number to the text included in the authoritative edition of

SPSV. In *SPSV* cited passages appear exactly eight pages earlier (that is, *U* 118 is *SPSV* 110).

UF   Luigi Pirandello, *L'uomo dal fiore in bocca,* in *MN* 1.

Uno   Luigi Pirandello, *Uno, nessuno e centomila,* in *Tutti i romanzi,*
        vol. 2.

UWE Joseph Conrad, *Under Western Eyes* (Garden City, N.Y.:
        Doubleday, Page, 1923).

YT   Robert Musil, *Young Törless,* trans. Eithne Wilkins and Ernst
        Kaiser (London: Panther Books, 1971)

Notes

Introduction

1. Robert Musil, *Der Mann ohne Eigenschaften,* in *Gesammelte Werke in neun Bänden* (1930–43; hereafter *GW*), ed. Adolf Frisé (Reinbek bei Hamburg: Rowohlt, 1978); trans. Eithne Wilkins and Ernst Kaiser as *The Man without Qualities,* 3 vols. (London: Secker & Warburg, 1953–1960) (hereafter *MWQ*). In anticipation of the new English edition being prepared by Alfred J. Knopf, I refer to volume and page numbers and also, in brackets, to the chapters from which citations are taken (hence, here, *GW* 1:255; *MWQ* 1:303 [62]). Throughout this study I have taken the liberty to revise the Kaiser-Wilkins translations when I thought it appropriate.

2. Robert Musil, *Leben, Werk, Wirkung* (hereafter *LWW*), ed. Karl Dinklage (Reinbek bei Hamburg: Rowohlt, 1960), 341.

3. Martin Heidegger, *Nietzsche,* vol. 4: *Nihilism,* trans. David Farrell Krell (New York: Harper & Row, 1981), 55.

4. The three most important theorizations of the essay may still be those of Theodor W. Adorno, "The Essay as Form," trans. Bob Hullot-Kentor and Frederic Will, *New German Critique* 32 (1984): 151–71; Max Bense, "Über den Essay und seine Prosa, *Merkur* 1 (1947): 414–24; and Georg Lukács, "On the Nature and Form of the Essay," *Soul and Form* (1910), trans. Anna Bostock (Cambridge: MIT Press, 1971), 1–18. An excellent discussion of the major theories of the essay can be found in John A. McCarthy, *Crossing Boundaries: A Theory and History of Essay Writing in German, 1680–1815* (Philadelphia: University of Pennsylvania

Press, 1989). For additional discussions of the poetics of the essay (especially as "antigenre" and antagonist of form), see Réda Bensmaïa, *The Barthes Effect: The Essay as Reflective Text* (Minneapolis: University of Minnesota Press, 1987); and Graham Good, *The Observing Self: Rediscovering the Essay* (London: Routledge, 1988).

5. George Bataille, *Visions of Excess: Selected Writings, 1927–1939*, trans. Allan Stoekl, with C. R. Lovitt and D. M. Leslie (Minneapolis: University of Minnesota Press, 1985), 171. For a discussion of Bataille's own essayism in the context of a general turn toward the essay characteristic of Walter Benjamin, Jean-Paul Sartre, and other writers of this century, see Michele Richman's introduction to Bensmaïa's *The Barthes Effect*.

6. Lukács, "Nature and Form of the Essay," 16.

7. See, among many references, Friedrich Nietzsche, *Beyond Good and Evil*, secs. 209–12, in *Basic Writings of Nietzsche*, trans. and ed. Walter Kaufmann (New York: Modern Library, 1968), 321–29.

8. Robert Musil, "Über Robert Musil's Bücher" (1913; "On Robert Musil's Books), *GW* 8:996–97. An English selection of Musil's essays has appeared under the title *Precision and Soul: Essays and Addresses* (hereafter *PS*), ed. and trans. Burton Pike and David S. Luft (Chicago: University of Chicago Press, 1990), 26. I have consulted and profited from these excellent translations but in most cases have stuck with my original renditions of the German. Whenever possible, I will identify the location of my citations of Musil's essays in the Pike and Luft edition.

9. Luigi Pirandello, *Quaderni di Serafino Gubbio, operatore* (hereafter *SG*), in *Tutti i romanzi*, ed. Giovanni Macchia (Milan: Mondadori, 1984), 2:526–27. *Quaderni* is translated as *Shoot!* by C. K. Scott Moncrieff (New York: E. P. Dutton, 1926); here p. 14.

10. Martin Heidegger, *Being and Time* (1927), trans. John Macquarrie and Edward Robinson (New York: Harper & Row, 1962), sec. 74.

11. Luigi Pirandello, *L'umorismo*, ed. Manlio Lo Vecchio-Musti (Milan: Mondadori, 1987), 141; trans. Antonio Illiano and Daniel P. Testa as *On Humor* (Chapel Hill: University of North Carolina Press, 1974), 119. (Hereafter these volumes are abbreviated *U* and *H*.) While translations of Pirandello are my own, I have profited from Illiano and Testa's edition as well as from John Patrick Pattinson's excellent abridgment called "The Art of Humor," *The Massachusetts Review* (1965): 515–20.

12. Joseph Conrad, *Lord Jim: An Authoritative Text, Backgrounds, Sources, Essays in Criticism* (hereafter *LJ*), ed. Thomas C. Moser (New York: W. W. Norton, 1968), 57.

13. Friedrich Nietzsche, *The Gay Science*, trans. Walter Kaufmann (New York: Vintage Books, 1974), sec. 319.

14. Nietzsche, *Gay Science*, sec. 374.

15. Robert Musil, "Franz Blei" (1918), *GW* 8:1023.

16. Lukács, "Nature and Form of the Essay," 10.

17. Adorno, "Essay as Form," 160.

18. Lukács, "Nature and Form of the Essay," 6–8.

19. Robert Musil, "Skizze der Erkenntnis des Dichters" (1918; "Sketch of Scriptorial Knowledge"), *GW* 8:1029; *PS* 64.

20. Lukács, "Nature and Form of the Essay," 8.

21. Benedetto Croce, "Luigi Pirandello," *La letteratura della nuova Italia,* 2d ed. (Bari, It.: Laterza, 1945), 6:356.

22. See Milan Kundera, *The Art of the Novel,* trans. Linda Asher (New York: Harper & Row, 1988), 63–64.

1. Joseph Conrad: The Perception of Unreality

1. Albert J. Guerard reads Marlow's adventure as a night journey at the end of which Kurtz represents a type of "Freudian id or the Jungian shadow." Frederick Crews interprets it as an oedipal fantasy. Lillian Feder sees it as a journey into the underworld, in which moral conflict is repositioned in its social and political milieu. See Guerard, *Conrad the Novelist* (Cambridge: Harvard University Press, 1958), 41; Crews, "Conrad's Uneasiness—and Ours," in his *Out of My System: Psychoanalysis, Ideology, and Critical Method* (New York: Oxford University Press, 1975); and Feder, "Marlow's Descent into Hell," in *Nineteenth-Century Fiction* 11 (1955):280–92.

2. Joseph Conrad, *Heart of Darkness: An Authoritative Text, Backgrounds and Sources, Criticism* (hereafter *HD*), ed. Robert Kimbrough, 3rd ed. (New York: W. W. Norton, 1988), 36–38.

3. Michael P. Jones, *Conrad's Heroism: A Paradise Lost* (Ann Arbor: UMI Research Press, 1985), 135.

4. Joseph Conrad, "Preface," *The Nigger of the "Narcissus": A Tale of the Sea* (hereafter *NN*) (Garden City, N.Y.: Doubleday, Page, 1927), xvi.

5. Joseph Conrad, *Within the Tides* (Garden City, N.Y.: Doubleday, Page, 1923), viii.

6. On Conrad as impressionist, see Guerard, *Conrad the Novelist,* 126–77, and Ian Watt, *Conrad in the Nineteenth Century* (Berkeley: University of California Press, 1979), 169–80. Some of the ambiguities attending the relation of truth to sensation and image, particularly as expressed by the Preface to *The Nigger of the "Narcissus,"* are discussed by David Goldknopf, *The Life of the Novel* (Chicago: University of Chicago Press, 1972), 82; and Geoffrey Galt Harpham, *On the Grotesque: Strategies of Contradiction in Art and Literature* (Princeton: Princeton University Press, 1982), 150–56.

7. One of the best examples of this approach to Conrad is Thomas Moser's seminal study of 1957, *Joseph Conrad: Achievement and Decline* (Cambridge: Harvard University Press), which begins its investigation

with "fundamental questions" about Conrad's "world." The first is "to understand what has value" in this world. Establishing that "humanity is important" and that "fidelity is the highest virtue," Moser concludes that, for "Conrad, the moralist, with his simple idea of fidelity," the central dramatic event of the test "reveals whether or not [the protagonist] is faithful to the community" (11–15).

8. It is in this key that Frederick Karl counterposes Conrad to Nietzsche and other "skeptics" who rejected precisely the reality of this moral and metaphysical base. Conrad "did believe in absolutes, and by no means threw in his lot with the philosophical relativist. . . . Rejecting the relativistic implications of Frazer's anthropology as much as he did Nietzsche's form of demonry, Conrad saw human behavior in terms of the individual's commitment to certain absolutes, certain givens." (*Joseph Conrad: The Three Lives* [New York: Farrer, Straus & Giroux, 1979], 28). The statement, of course, is biographical, whereas what Conrad the man may have believed is not the issue here. ("On admire ce dont on manque. Voilà pourquoi j'admire la perseverance et la fidelité et la constance," Conrad confesses in a letter of 26 August 1891 to Madame Poradowski.) When it comes to the work, the most forceful positive reading of Conrad may still be that of Moser, for whom the somnolence-shattering crises of Conrad's stories act as tests of moral character, and protagonists take their place in a "moral hierarchy" on the basis of their performance under exacting conditions (*Joseph Conrad*, 11–15). Conrad would thus be measuring his characters with the yardstick of a preset ideal. Note the assumptions underlying Moser's reading, if only to push for their rejection: that what "has value" in Conrad's work is an answerable as it is questionable; that Conrad is a moralistic writer, in the sense of meting out reward or punishment; that his fiction is primarily concerned with establishing "types" instead of articulating the ambiguities that worry all theories of types.

Other examples of the positive reading can be found in the following samples. Conrad is a writer who "celebrates the values of the *Volk*, its traditional manners and moralities" (Avrom Fleishman, *Conrad's Politics: Community and Anarchy in the Fiction of Joseph Conrad* [Baltimore: Johns Hopkins Press, 1967], 55). Between 1898 and 1910 Conrad's work reveals a developing vision of moral integrity that receives its apotheosis in *Under Western Eyes* (Steve Ressler, *Joseph Conrad: Consciousness and Integrity* [New York: New York University Press, 1988]). Earlier and more skeptical works like *Heart of Darkness, Lord Jim,* and *Nostromo* do not articulate that full Conradian understanding that allows for the successful dramatization of coming to knowledge and "moral growth" in which a character is allowed "to discover and embrace conscience" (147, 144, 150). (Virtually the only character in Conrad to achieve this tragic knowledge, however, is Razumov in *Under Western Eyes*.) Other positive readings can be found in Daniel R. Schwarz, *Con-*

rad: Almayer's Folly *to* Under Western Eyes (Ithaca: Cornell University Press, 1980); Tony Tanner, *Conrad:* Lord Jim (Woodbury, N.Y.: Barron's Educational Series, 1963); David Thorburn, *Conrad's Romanticism* (New Haven: Yale University Press, 1974); and Watt, *Conrad in the Nineteenth Century.*

As may already be clear, the risk of the positive reading is that of side-stepping the complexity of Conradian questions in an effort to furnish his answers. Recalling Karl's apology for Conrad as categorical absolutist, we cannot fail to note that if Conrad's writing submits anything to question it is precisely these "certain gives," or self-evident values, that positive readers aim to vindicate. The subjects of his works are ruptures, rarely followed by reconstructions, showing not absolutism defeating skepsis, but something more like its opposite—a battle for absolutes against the overwhelming force of the relative. Although Conrad is intensely aware of the existence of a world of moral and spiritual values, "every quality, every virtue, every position in which he might hope to rest in security, is at once undermined" (Douglas Hewitt, "Conrad and the 'Few Simple Notions,'" in *Conrad: A Collection of Critical Essays,* ed. Marvin Mudrick [Englewood Cliffs, N.J.: Prentice-Hall, 1966], 62).

9. Here we are in the company of, among others, Paul B. Armstrong, *The Challenge of Bewilderment* (Ithaca: Cornell University Press, 1987); William Bonney, *Thorns and Arabesques* (Baltimore: Johns Hopkins Press, 1980); J. Hillis Miller, *Poets of Reality* (Cambridge; Belknap Press of Harvard University Press, 1965); Suresh Raval, *The Art of Failure: Conrad's Fiction* (Boston: Allen & Unwin, 1986); Roy Roussel, *The Metaphysics of Darkness* (Baltimore: Johns Hopkins University Press, 1971). In these readings the awakening has no redeeming or morally sustaining effect; writing fails to achieve its disclosive end; morality lacks any legitimating basis; pessimism, solitude, and despair voice the essential wisdom of the visionary experience. Yet, by reversing the terms, we have not escaped the trap of a positive reading, for even here there exists a definitive object of the wakeful vision, bleak though it be. "The culmination of the vision," writes Miller, "is the recognition that behind 'the overwhelming realities of this strange world of plants, and water, and silence' . . . is the darkness." Such darkness is an absolute "metaphysical entity" (*Poets of Reality,* 26, 28). (Miller later moderates this categorical reading of Conrad, admitting that "from whatever angle it is approached *Jim* reveals itself to be a work which raises questions rather than answering them. . . . The overabundance of possible explanations only inveigles the reader to share in the self-sustaining motion of a process of interpretation which cannot reach an unequivocal conclusion" [*Fiction and Repetition: Seven English Novels* (Cambridge: Harvard University Press, 1982), 39.]) Ultimately, writing can "only endure endlessly its failure to bring what is real, the darkness, permanently into what is human, the light" (*Poets of Reality,* 38). Or, in Bonney's words, the dis-

junctions in Conrad's linguistic world are "loci of '*le neant*' . . . which is the ground of Conrad's phenomenal world." Those "alinguistic points of disorder" attest to an "ontic vacancy." The tension between an apparent superstructure and a hidden base amounts to a clash "between conscious simplicity and undifferentiated chaos," in which "the pursuit of an adamantine order culminates in an annihilatory revelation of its adamant absence" (*Thorns and Arabesques*, 6–7, 44, 63). Or in the words of Jones: "The only absolute in Conrad, according to the logic of the heroic journey, is the fate which Kurtz, Jim, Decoud, and Heyst all share: all destroy themselves and disappear . . . beyond the comprehensible world" (*Conrad's Heroism*, 133). And, finally, to conclude with Armstrong, whose study succeeds nevertheless in rescuing the positive nature of Conradian desiderata from his negative ontology, "If Conrad does discover a final truth, this is the ubiquity of nothingness" (*The Challenge of Bewilderment*, 12).

10. Joseph Conrad, "A Familiar Preface," *A Personal Record* (Garden City, N.Y.: Doubleday, Page, 1923), xix; "Books," *Notes on Life and Letters* (New York: Doubleday, Daran, 1937), 6; Author's Note, *Within the Tides* (Garden City, N.Y.: Doubleday, Page, 1923), viii.

11. Joseph Conrad, letter to Norman Douglas, 23 December 1909, in G. Jean-Aubry, *Joseph Conrad: Life and Letters* (Garden City, N.Y.: Doubleday, Page, 1927), 105; letter to Edmond Gosse, 23 March 1905, *The Collected Letters of Joseph Conrad*, ed. Frederick R. Karl and Laurence Davies (Cambridge: Cambridge University Press, 1983–88), 3:224.

12. "On land," as Harpham notes "values are relative and shifting and truth is obscured in shadows; at sea, by contrast, a man knows where he stands" (*On the Grotesque*, 156).

13. See Alfred Adler, *The Practice and Theory of Individual Psychology* (1918), trans. P. Radin, 2d rev. ed. (New York: Humanities Press, 1971).

14. See Otto Rank, *Will Therapy* (1929), trans. Jessie Taft (New York: W. W. Norton, 1978), 32 and passim; and *Truth and Reality* (1926), trans. Jessie Taft (New York: W. W. Norton, 1978), 13–23.

15. Joseph Conrad, "An Outpost of Progress" (hereafter *OP*), in *Tales of Unrest* (London: T. Fischer Unwin, 1898), 128.

16. See pp. 65–66 of this study.

17. For an extended discussion of work as conscious shelter in *Heart of Darkness*, see Peter J. Glassman, *Language and Being: Joseph Conrad and the Literature of Personality* (New York: Columbia University Press, 1976), 205–21; and Raval, *The Art of Failure*, 12–15. For a positive assessment of the categories of work and efficiency in Conrad (insensitive, however, to the irony with which Conrad often surrounds these terms), see Watt, *Conrad in the Nineteenth Century*, 216–53.

18. Joseph Conrad, *Nostromo: A Tale of the Seaboard* (hereafter *N*) (Garden City, N.Y.: Doubleday, Page, 1919), 556.

19. Joseph Conrad, *The Secret Agent: A Simple Tale* (hereafter *SA*), ed. Bruce Harkness and S. W. Reid (Cambridge: Cambridge University Press, 1990), 66.

20. Joseph Conrad, *The Secret Sharer* (hereafter *SS*), in *'Twixt Land and Sea* (Garden City, N.Y.: Doubleday, Page, 1926), 94.

21. On the workings of the ego ideal in Conrad, see Bruce Johnston, *Conrad's Models of Mind* (Minneapolis: University of Minnesota Press, 1971).

22. On the bad faith of all martyrs, see Friedrich Nietzsche, *On the Genealogy of Morals,* in *Basic Writings of Nietzsche,* ed. and trans. Walter Kaufmann (New York: Modern Library, 1968). On the ubiquitous "impostorship" of Conrad's characters, see Ressler, *Joseph Conrad.*

23. See Glassman, *Language and Being,* 177–83.

24. The inescapable intermediary referring me "from me to myself," as Jean-Paul Sartre writes, is the gaze or regard of the other. Two implications of this heterodetermination apply immediately to Jim: "Insofar as I am the object of values which come to qualify me . . . I am enslaved. By the same token insofar as I am the token of possibilities which are not my possibilities . . . I am *in danger*" (Sartre, "The Look," in *Being and Nothingness: An Essay on Phenomenological Ontology* (1943), trans. Hazel Barnes (New York: Citadel Press, 1971), pt. 3, chap. 1, 228–78.

25. Cf. Robert Penn Warren: "By the dream Conrad means nothing more or less than man's necessity to justify himself by the 'idea,' to idealize himself and his actions into moral significance of some order" ("Introduction," Joseph Conrad, *Nostromo: A Tale of the Seaboard* [New York: Modern Library, 1951], xxii).

26. Letter to Edward Garnett, 23/24 March 1896, Conrad, *Collected Letters,* 1:267.

27. Chapters 7 and 8 of *Lord Jim* spell out the debilitating effect on precisely Jim's will of this moment when "he felt the ground cut from under his feet." Faced with imminent death, Jim is no longer his familiar, habitual self, leading Marlow to remark that he and Jim "might have been discussing a third person" (*LJ* 51, 48).

28. For studies of the double in Conrad, see Katherine H. Burkman and J. Reid Meloy, "The Black Mirror: Joseph Conrad's *The Nigger of the 'Narcissus'* and Flannery O'Connor's 'The Artificial Nigger,'" *Midwest Quarterly: A Journal of Contemporary Thought* 28 (1987): 230–47; Guerard, *Conrad;* Barbara Johnson and Marjorie Garber, "Secret Sharing: Reading Conrad Psychoanalytically," *College English* 49 (1987): 628–40; and Romana Rutelli and Cesare Segre, *Il desiderio del diverso: Saggio sul doppio* (Napoli: Liguori, 1984).

29. This is that distinction of "seeing things as they are," which Tony Tanner observes to be the basic trait of another happy nihilist, *Lord Jim*'s

Chester ("Butterflies and Beetles—Conrad's Two Truths," *LJ* 451). On Brierly's recognition of his ostensibly inherent weakness, see John Batchelor, *Lord Jim* (London: Unwin Hyman, 1988), 89–90.

30. Nietzsche, *Genealogy*, 599.

31. On the role of words in *Heart of Darkness*, see Watt, *Conrad in the Nineteenth Century*, 224–37.

32. See Glassman, *Language and Being*, 141–83.

33. Luigi Pirandello, "La distruzione dell'uomo" ˀ(1921; "The Destruction of Man"), in *Novelle per un anno* (hereafter *NA*), ed. Mario Costanzo (Milan: Mondadori, 1985), 1:1044–45.

34. "Frankly, it is not my words that I mistrust, but your minds. I could be eloquent were I not afraid you fellows had starved your imaginations to feed your bodies. I do not mean to be offensive; it is respectable to have no illusions—and safe—and profitable—and dull" (*LJ* 138).

35. Joseph Conrad, *Under Western Eyes* (hereafter *UWE*) (Garden City, N.Y.: Doubleday, Page, 1923), 254.

36. Adorno, "Essay as Form," 159.

37. On Conradian exile as a figure for the very act of narration, see Michael Seidel, *Exile and the Narrative Imagination* (New Haven: Yale University Press, 1986), 44–70.

38. After showing why the aesthetics of realism, romanticism, naturalism, and even "sentimentalism" ultimately abandon the artist "to the stammerings of his conscience," Conrad dwells with distinct ambivalence on the aesthetic of *l'art pour l'art:* In the uneasy solitude of artistic labor, he writes, "the supreme cry of Art for Art itself loses the exciting ring of its apparent immortality. It sounds far off. It has ceased to be a cry, and is heard only as a whisper, often incomprehensible, but at times and faintly encouraging" (*NN* xv).

39. Immanuel Kant, *Critique of Judgment*, trans. J. C. Meredith (New York: Oxford University Press, 1973), "The Faculties of the Mind Which Constitute Genius," sec. 49. All additional citations are from this same section. Adorno takes this Kantian point a step further, remarking that the "truth content" of an aesthetic work is something that the work only "points to" and that must actively be pursued by philosophy: "Truth content is the objective answer or solution to the riddle posed by any particular work. By calling for a solution it points to its truth content, which in turn cannot actually be nailed down except by philosophical reflection. This alone is what legitimates aesthetics" (Theodor W. Adorno, *Aesthetic Theory*, trans. C. Lenhardt, ed. Gretel Adorno and Rolf Tiedemann [London: Routledge & Kegan Paul, 1986], 186).

40. Kant, *Critique of Judgment*, sec. 49.

41. Adorno, "Essay as Form," 12.

2. Robert Musil: The Suspension of the World

1. Robert Musil, *Die Verwirrungen des Zöglings Törless* (*GW* 6:24), trans. Eithne Wilkins and Ernst Kaiser with the title *Young Törless* (hereafter *YT*) (London: Panther Books, 1971), 33. I have often revised the Wilkins-Kaiser translation.

2. Musil began to write *Törless* one year before he enrolled in the doctoral program in philosophy under Carl Stumpf at the University of Berlin in 1903; he finished it in 1905. Wilhelm Dilthey, the philosopher of the *Geisteswissenschaften*, was the chair of Musil's department, and Georg Simmel was a regular guest lecturer. While Musil wrote his dissertation on the empiriocriticism of Ernst Mach (approved with initial resistance by Stumpf and the degree conferred in 1908), the philosophies most in vogue during the period of Musil's studies were the phenomenological return "to things themselves" of Stumpf's student Edmund Husserl and the neo-Kantian investigations of the Marburg school, focusing on the conditions for the possibility of understanding. At the same time, in Cambridge, Bertrand Russell and G. E. Moore were laying the foundations for what would turn into analytic philosophy and logical atomism. By 1913 Ludwig Wittgenstein was at work on the *Tractatus Logico-Philosophicus*. On links between *Törless* and contemporary investigations into the legitimacy of scientific method, see Jan Aler, "Als Zögling zwischen Maeterlinck und Mach: Robert Musils literarisch-philosophische Anfänge," in *Probleme des Erzählens in der Weltliteratur: Festschrift für Käte Hamburger,* ed. Fritz Martini (Stuttgart: Klett, 1971), 234–90.

3. As Renate von Heydebrand notes, the tie between epistemology and morality had been underscored for Musil not only by Mach but also Nietzsche. In both thinkers the "positivistic critique of knowledge and language . . . leads [unavoidably] to a critique of morality" (*Die Reflexionen Ulrichs in Robert Musils Roman "Der Mann ohne Eigenschaften": Ihr Zusammenhang mit dem zeitgenössischen Denken* [Münster: Aschendorff, 1966], 25).

4. Ludwig Wittgenstein, *On Certainty,* ed. G. E. M. Anscombe and G. H. von Wright (New York: Harper & Row, 1972), sec. 113. On connections between Musil and Wittgenstein, see Gerhart Baumann, *Robert Musil: Zur Erkenntnis der Dichtung* (Bern: Francke, 1965), 170–206; Jean-Pierre Cometti, *Robert Musil ou l'alternative romanesque* (Paris: Presses Universitaires de France, 1985), 223–36, and passim; Karl Corino, "Der erlöste Tantalus," *Annali* (Naples) 23:2–3 (1980); Allan Janik and Stephen Toulmin, *Wittgenstein's Vienna* (New York: Simon & Schuster, 1973), 66, 118–19; J.-C. Nyíri, "Zwei geistige Leisterne: Musil und Wittgenstein," *Literatur und Kritik* 113 (1977): 167–79; Ernst Randak, "Über die Möglichkeit," *Wort in der Zeit* 9 (1963): 25–26;

Marie-Louise Roth, *Robert Musil: Ethik und Ästhetik: Zum theoretischen Werk des Dichters* (Munich: P. List, 1972), 84, 229, 447; and Walter H. Sokel, "Kleist's Marquise of O., Kierkegaard's Abraham, and Musil's Tonka: Three Stages of the Absurd as the Touchstone of Faith," in *Festschrift für Bernhard Blume: Zaufsätze zur deutschen und europäischen Literatur,* ed. Egon Schwartz, Hannum, and Lohner (Göttingen: Vanderhöck & Ruprecht, 1967), 331.

5. Ernst Mach, *The History and Root of the Principle of Conservation of Energy* (1909), trans. Philip E. B. Jourdain (Chicago: Open Court Press, 1911), 92.

6. Ladislao Mittner, *La letteratura tedesca del Novecento e altri saggi* (Turin: Einaudi, 1960), 318. The Collateral Campaign is the focus of satire, a strategy crucial to Musil's critical, dismantling writing. On the satiric dimensions of *The Man without Qualities* and their epistemological implications, see Helmut Arntzen, *Satirischer Stil: Zur Satire Robert Musils im "Mann ohne Eigenschaften,"* 2d ed. (Bonn: Bouvier, 1970); as well as the objections to Arntzen raised by Lothar Huber in "Satire and Irony in Musil's *Der Mann ohne Eigenschaften,"* in *Musil in Focus: Papers from a Centenary Symposium,* ed. Lothar Huber and John J. White (Leeds: Institute of Germanic Studies, University of London, 1982), 99–114. For a critical discussion of *The Man without Qualities* as a whole, see Philip Payne, *Robert Musil's* The Man without Qualities: *A Critical Study* (Cambridge: Cambridge University Press, 1988).

7. Nietzsche, *Gay Science,* sec. 125. Frederick G. Peters also calls attention to Nietzsche's parable in his reading of the self-dissolution of the man without qualities as a psychological corollary of the void left by the retreat of god (*Robert Musil: Master of the Hovering Life* [New York: Columbia University Press, 1978], 37). On relations between Nietzsche and Musil, see Wilhelm Bausinger, *Studien zu einer historisch-kritischen Ausgabe von Robert Musils Roman "Der Mann ohne Eigenschaften"* (Reinbek bei Hamburg: Rowohlt, 1964); Charlotte Dresler-Brumme, *Nietzsches Philosophie in Musils Roman "Der Mann ohne Eigenschaften"* (Frankfurt am Main: Athenäum, 1987); Lynda Jeanne King, "The Relationship between Clarisse and Nietzsche in Musil's *Der Mann ohne Eigenschaften,"* *Musil-Forum* 4 (1978): 21–34; F. G. Peters, *Musil and Nietzsche* (Ph.D. diss., Cambridge University, 1974); Roberto Olmi, "La présence de Nietzsche," *L'Herne* 41 (1981): 153–66; Herbert W. Reichert, "Nietzschean Influences in *Der Mann ohne Eigenschaften,"* *German Quarterly* 39 (1966): 12–28; Ingo Seidler, "Das Nietzschebild Robert Musils," *DVjS* 39 (1965): 329–49; and Aldo Venturelli, "Die Kunst als fröhliche Wissenschaft: Zum Verhältnis Musils zu Nietzsche," *Nietzsche Studien* 9 (1980): 302–37.

8. See David S. Luft, *Robert Musil and the Crisis of European Culture 1880–1942* (Berkeley: University of California Press, 1980), 18–23.

9. Like satire, Musilian irony tends to expose the relativity and arbitrariness of a fact or phenomenon by presenting it from a disinterested or unusual perspective. On Musilian irony, see Beda Allemann, *Ironie und Dichtung* (Pfullingen, 1956), 177–220; Maurice Blanchot, *Le livre à venir* (Paris: Gallimard, 1959), 165–84; Enrico De Angelis, *Robert Musil: Biografia e profilo critico* (Turin: Piccola Biblioteca Einaudi, 1982), 175–214; Marike Finlay, *The Potential of Modern Discourse: Musil, Pierce, and Perturbation* (Bloomington: Indiana University Press, 1990), 14–18, 100–134; Dietrich Hochstätter, *Sprache des Möglichen: Stilistischer Perspektivismus in Robert Musils "Mann ohne Eigenschaften"* (Frankfurt am Main: Athenäum, 1972);Huber, "Satire and Irony"; and Payne, *Robert Musil*, 69–75.

10. The lexical resonances of Musil's passage are unmistakable. *Überzeugung, Vorurteil,* and even *Glaube* come already staggering from the blows Nietzsche had delivered them. The missing fourth is *Gewissen,* or conscience, but it is obvious why Musil failed to include it. Far from giving us a positive return, like beliefs and convictions, conscience holds us in debt; it is not a debtor but a creditor object. The findings are analogous in Freud's theory of the superego, in Heidegger's analyses of *Gewissen* and *Schuld* (*Being and Time,* secs. 54–69), and in Nietzsche's archaeology of guilt in *Genealogy of Morals.* For Nietzsche and Heidegger guilt is the very origin of debtor-objects.

11. Friedrich Nietzsche, *Human, All Too Human: A Book for Free Spirits,* trans. Marion Faber, with Stephen Lehmann (Lincoln: University of Nebraska Press, 1984), secs. 630, 18.

12. Louis Althusser, "Ideology and Ideological State Apparatuses," in *Lenin and Philosophy, and Other Essays,* trans. Ben Brewster (New York: New Left Books, 1971), 170.

13. Toward the end of 1899, inspired by figures of speech in Nietzsche's *Beyond Good and Evil* (secs. 186, 218, 229) and *The Genealogy of Morals* (1:1 and 3:4), Musil wrote sketches for a work to be entitled "Monsieur le vivisecteur." Recounting "the adventures and peregrinations of a vivisector of souls at the beginning of the twentieth century," this projected work prefigures *The Man without Qualities* (Robert Musil, *Tagebücher* [hereafter *TB*], ed. Adolf Frisé, 2 vols. [Hamburg: Rowohlt, 1983], 1:1–3, and passim). In years to come Musil continued to refer to his analyses and dismantling of cultural practices as vivisection.

14. Musil was a keen reader of the first volume of Husserl's *Logical Investigations,* transcribing and discussing its argument in his journals. On Musil's ties to Mach and Husserl, see Gerhart Baumann, "Robert Musil: Eine Vorstudie," *Germ.-Rom. Monatsschr.* 34 (1953): 292–316; Cometti, *Robert Musil,* 17–46; Hartmut Cellbrot, *Die Bewegung des Sinnes: Zur Phänomenologie Robert Musils in Hinblick auf Edmund Husserl* (Munich: Fink, 1988); Finlay, *Potential of Modern Discourse,* 26–30; Ul-

rich Karthaus, "Musil-Forschung und Musil-Deutung: Ein Literaturbericht," *DVjs* 39 (1965): 441–83; Karl Menges, "Robert Musil und Edmund Husserl: Über phänomenologische Strukturen im *Mann ohne Eigenschaften*," *Modern Austrian Literature* 9 (1976): 131–54; Claudia Monti, *Musil: La metafora della scienza* (Naples: Tullio Pironti, 1983); Gerd Müller, *Dichtung und Wissenschaft: Studien zu Robert Musils Romanen "Die Verwirrungen des Zöglings Törless" und "Der Mann ohne Eigenschaften"* (Uppsala: Almqvist & Wiksells, 1971); Walter H. Sokel, "Musil et l'existentialisme," trans. Albert Fuchs, *L'Herne* 41 (1981): 191–93; and G. H. von Wright, "Introduction," Robert Musil, *On Mach's Theories* (hereafter *MT*), trans. Kevin Mulligan (Washington, D.C.: Catholic University of America Press, 1982).

15. Quoted in Robert Musil, *Beitrag zur Beurteilung der Lehren Machs* (hereafter *B*) (Berlin: Dissertationen–Verlag Carl Arnold, 1908), 98, 81; trans. as *MT*, 67, 58, 64. The translations are mine.

16. Ernst Mach, *The Science of Mechanics: A Critical and Historical Account of Its Development* (1883), 6th ed. through 9th German ed., trans. Thomas J. McCormack (La Salle, Ill.: Open Court Press, 1960), 316.

17. Edmund Husserl, *Ideas: General Introduction to Pure Phenomenology* (1913), trans. W. R. Boyce Gibson (New York: Collier, 1962), secs. 47, 50, 47.

18. Musil's interest in Gestalt psychology (which was itself of Machian inspiration and began to develop under the influence of Carl Stumpf in the years Musil attended the University of Berlin) is well documented. Musil possessed Wolfgang Köhler's *Die physischen Gestalten in Ruhe und im stationären Zustand* (1920) and referred to it constantly. See the entries on Köhler, Kurt Lewin, Erich Maria von Hornbostel, and Max Wertheimer in *TB* (esp. 1:801, 2:583–84, 1213–15) and references in his essays (esp. *GW* 8:1085, 1141). On Musil's work as the product of a theoretical conjunction of Machian empiriocriticism and Gestalt psychology, see Monti, *Musil;* Aldo Venturelli, "Il mondo come laboratorio: Musil e la psicologia della Gestalt di Wolfgang Köhler," in *Musil nostro contemporaneo,* ed. Paolo Chiarini (Rome: Istituto Italiano Studi Germanici, 1985).

19. Robert Musil, "Ansätze zu einer neuer Ästhetik: Bemerkungen über eine Dramaturgie des Films" (1925; "Cues for a New Aesthetic: Remarks on a Dramaturgy of Film") (hereafter "Cues") *GW* 8:1146; *PS* 201). Mach admits as much in *Science of Mechanics:* Knowledge of every sort is motivated "directly or indirectly by a practical interest," in short, by the adaptation of the animal to its environment (578).

20. Robert Musil, "Das hilflose Europa oder Reise vom Hundersten ins Tausendste" (1922; "Helpless Europe, or a Digressive Journey"), *GW* 8:1081; *PS* 122.

21. Hannah Hickman proposes two more colloquial translations of *Seinesgleichen geschieht:* "History repeats itself" and "There's nothing

new under the sun" (*Robert Musil and the Culture of Vienna* [La Salle, Ill.: Open Court Press, 1984], 145).

22. Musil is obviously rejecting the distinction that Köhler draws between "a mere chance solution" and "a genuine solution," a distinction presented by Ernst Cassirer as emblematic of the difference between humans and animals, the latter presumably operating only on the basis of practical intelligence, the former on the basis of a symbolic one. The example of the dog underscores the extent to which Mach himself already acknowledges this "other," form-taking necessity in history, for it was he who first utilized the example to substantiate his claim that experimentation underlies even "instinctive" and unreflected action. The trial and error of the dog is identical in procedure to the intellectual experimentation of scientific research; both end up assuming what only appear to be "necessary" forms. See Ernst Cassirer, *An Essay on Man* (New Haven, Conn.: Yale University Press, 1965), 33; Wolfgang Köhler, *The Mentality of Apes* (New York: Harcourt Brace, & Company, 1925), 192–234 (esp. 201); and Ernst Mach, *Knowledge and Error: Sketches on the Psychology of Inquiry* (1905), trans. Thomas J. McCormack and Paul Foulkes (Dordrecht: D. Reidel, 1976).

23. See Jakob Johann von Uexküll, *Theoretical Biology* (1920), trans. A. L. MacKinnan (London: Kegan Paul, 1926); and *Umwelt und Innenwelt der Tiere* (Berlin: Springer, 1909). While the connection between Musil and Uexküll is merely incidental, it attests to Musil's tight and uneasy relation to the various mechanistic, functionalist, and behaviorist approaches to experience developed at the turn of the century (among which one might also recall Jacques Loeb's "theory of tropism" in his 1918 work, *Forced Movements, Tropisms, and Animal Conduct* [New York: Dover, 1971]).

24. Even so, the yearning for an "authentic" or "real" reality that is so characteristic of Ulrich and his contemporaries leads *The Man without Qualities* to research, with increasing ardor, the possibility of a *unio mystico* with a plenary Being underlying the mechanistic structures of history. In the wake of the debates inspired by Kaiser and Wilkin's reading of the novel in precisely this key, most scholars have agreed that Musil never succeeds in discovering a satisfactory articulation for either this intuition of plenary Being or the ethical program that it might entail. Mystical union remains only the desideratum of his essayistic quest. On the mystical goal toward which Musil and his protagonist Ulrich are working, see Dietmar Goltschnigg, *Mystische Tradition im Roman Robert Musils: Martin Bubers "Ekstatische Konfessionen" im "Mann ohne Eigenschaften"* (Heidelberg: Stiehm, 1974); Ernst Kaiser and Eithne Wilkins, *Robert Musil: Eine Einführung in das Werk* (Stuttgart: Kohlhammer, 1962); and the exchange between Cesare Cases and Walter Boehlich in *Merkur* 18 (1964): 266–74, 696–99, 897–900.

25. Cf. Oswald Spengler's cyclical account of history in terms of this

same opposition between culture and civilization. In a lengthy review Musil criticizes Spengler but remains sympathetic to the basic distinction. See Robert Musil, "Geist und Erfahrung: Anmerkungen für Leser, welche den Untergand des Abendlandes entronnen sind" (1921; "Spirit and Experience: Notes for Readers Who Have Escaped the Decline of the West"), *GW* 8: 1042–59; *PS* 134–49. For similar treatments of generative versus degenerative history in Musil's time, see Nicolas Berdyaev, *The Meaning of History* (1923), trans. George Reavey (London: Geoffrey Bles, 1936), esp. 207–24; René Guénon, *La crise du monde moderne* (Paris: Bossard, 1927); and Paul Valéry, "La crise de l'esprit" (1919), *Varieté I et II* (Paris: Gallimard, 1978), 13–51.

26. Cf. Siegfried Kracauer, "Time and History," *Zeugnisse: Theodor W. Adorno zum sechzigsten Geburtstag*, ed. Max Horkheimer (Frankfurt am Main: Europäische Verlangstalt, 1963), 50–64; "General History and the Aesthetic Approach," *Die nicht mehr schönen Künste: Grenzphänomene des Aesthetischen (Poetik und Hermeneutik* 3), ed. H. R. Jauss (Munich: Wilhelm Fink, 1968), 111–27.

27. On "volatization," see Heidegger, *Being and Time*, sec. 18; on simulation, see Jean Baudrillard, *Simulations*, trans. Paul Foss, Paul Patton, and Philip Beitchman (New York: Semiotexte, 1983).

28. On the automatism of perception, see the Russian Formalists, esp. Victor Shklovsky, "Art as Technique" (1917), in *Russian Formalist Criticism: Four Essays*, trans. Lee T. Lemon and Marion J. Reis (Lincoln: University of Nebraska Press, 1965), 3–24.

29. Husserl, *Ideas*, sec. 55.

30. On an analogous distinction between "fluid" and "static" morality, see Musil's "Skizze der Erkenntnis des Dichters" (1918; "Sketch of Scriptorial Knowledge"), *GW* 8: 1025–30; *PS* 61–65.

31. Husserl, *Ideas*, sec. 46.

32. Husserl, *Ideas*, sec. 47.

33. On Musil's constructive use of analogy, see Dorrit Cohn, "Psycho-Analogies: A Means for Rendering Consciousness," in Martini, ed., *Probleme des Erzählens*, 291–302; Dieter Kühn, *Analogie und Variation: Zur Analyze von Robert Musils Roman "Der Mann ohne Eigenschaften"* (Bonn: Bouvier, 1965); Ulrich Schelling, "Das analogische Denken bei Robert Musil," in *Robert Musil: Studien zu seinem Werk*, ed. Karl Dinklage, Elisabeth Albertson, and Karl Corino (Reinbek bei Hamburg: Rowohlt, 1970), 170–99; as well the studies by Roth, *Robert Musil*, and Monti, *Musil*.

34. Friedrich Nietzsche, *The Will to Power*, ed. Walter Kaufmann (New York: Random House, 1968), sec. 853. Cf. also his *Birth of Tragedy*, in *Basic Writings of Nietzsche*, ed. and trans. Walter Kaufmann (New York: Modern Library, 1968), "Attempt at a Self-Criticism," sec. 5.

35. This is the position taken by Georg Lukács against Musil and other modernists in "The Ideology of Modernism," *The Meaning of Con-*

temporary Realism, trans. John and Necke Mander (London: Merlin Press, 1963), 17–46.

36. Wilhelm Worringer, *Abstraction and Empathy: A Contribution to the Psychology of Style* (1907), trans. Michael Bullock (New York: International Universities Press, 1980), 15–16.

37. For a thorough study of Musil's attempt to "potentiate reality," see Roth, *Robert Musil,* 185–266.

38. See Vladimir Lenin, *Materialism and Empirio-Criticism: Critical Comments on a Reactionary Philosophy* (1909) (New York: International Publishers, 1970). Like Max Planck, Lenin took issue with what he read as Mach's advocacy of the purely subjective validity of the relations expressed by the laws of physics. Of course, Husserl had already accused Mach of a "psychologization of logic" in 1900 (*Logical Investigations,* vol. 1). It is interesting that the young Albert Einstein defended Mach against both accusations in a letter of 1913. See Alfonsina D'Elia, *Ernst Mach* (Florence: La Nuova Italia, 1971).

39. Georg Lukács, "Art and Objective Truth," *Writer and Critic and Other Essays,* ed. and trans. Arthur D. Kahn (New York: Grosset & Dunlap, 1970), 38–39. On Musil's writing as executing Lukács's dictum that irony constitutes the "objectivity of the novel," see Frank Trömmler, *Roman und Wirklichkeit: Eine Ortsbestimmung am Beispiel von Musil, Broch, Roth, Doderer und Gütersloh* (Stuttgart: Kohlhammer, 1966), 68–100.

40. Adorno, *Aesthetic Theory,* 10. In a similar vein Manfred Sera argues that the simultaneously utopian and parodic intentions of *The Man without Qualities* establish a dialectic in which narrated reality begins to border on unreality, making it the task of the novel to overcome the discrepancy between life without spirit and spirit without life. See his *Utopie und Parodie bei Musil, Broch und Thomas Mann: Der Mann ohne Eigenschaften; Die Schlafwandler; Der Zauberberg* (Bonn: Bouvier, 1969). On Musil's (pre-Adornian) critique of the Enlightenment faith in the "trinity of nature, reason, and freedom," see *GW* 8:1123; and Jacques Bouveresse's commentary in "Robert Musil ou l'anti-Spengler," *L'Herne* 41 (1981): 170. For a critical reading of Musil from the standpoint of the Frankfurt school and Freudian psychoanalysis, see Klaus Laermann, *Eigenschaftslosigkeit: Reflexionen zu Musils Roman "Der Mann ohne Eigenschaften"* (Stuttgart: Metzler, 1970).

41. Lukács, *Writer and Critic,* 47.

3. Luigi Pirandello: The Mechanical Phantasmagoria

1. On Pirandello's mature relation to *verismo,* see his essays "Soggettivismo e oggettivismo nell'arte narrativa" and "Un critico fantastico," *Saggi, poesie, scritti varii* (hereafter *SPSV*), ed. Manlio Lo Vecchio-Musti (Milan: Mondadori, 1977), 181–206, 363–87, as well as the following studies: Renato Barilli, *La barriera del naturalismo: Studi sulla narrativa*

italiana contemporanea (Milan: Mursia, 1970); A. Leone de Castris, *Storia di Pirandello* (Bari, It.: Biblioteca di Cultura Moderna, 1962); Carlo A. Madrignani, *Capuana e il naturalismo* (Bari, It.: Laterza, 1970); Piero Raffa, "La crisi del linguaggio naturalista (Pirandello)," *Avanguardia e realismo* (Milan: Rizzoli, 1967); and Carlo Salinari, *Miti e coscienza del decadentismo italiano* (Milan: Feltrinelli, 1982).

2. After the first-person narrator has engaged in a long reflection on the constructed nature of reality, he imagines himself interrupted by the reader and answers: "Do you think I have been too lofty? Then let us lower the tone. . . . What facts do you want to discuss? The fact that I was born in such and such a year, in such and such a month, on such and such a day, in the noble city of Ricchieri, in a house on such and such a street, with such and such a number, of Mr. and Mrs. Such and Such; baptized in the main church at six days old; sent to school at six years old; married at age twenty-three; one meter sixty-eight in height; redheaded, etc., etc.?" (Luigi Pirandello, *Uno, nessuno e centomila* [hereafter *Uno*], *Tutti i romanzi,* ed. Giovanni Macchia [Milan: Mondadori, 1984], 2:801). The novel has been translated by Samuel Putnam as *One, None and a Hundred Thousand* (New York: E. P. Dutton, 1933); here all cited translations are mine. In order to enable the reader to refer to this or another English edition of *Uno,* page numbers of the Italian edition will be followed by references to the chapters and sections in which they are found (here, 3:8).

3. Luigi Pirandello, *Il fu Mattia Pascal* (hereafter *FMP*), *Tutti i romanzi,* vol. 1 (Milan: Mondadori, 1984). William Weaver has translated the novel as *The Late Mattia Pascal* (hereafter *LMP*) (Hygiene, Colo.: Eridanos Press, 1987). Quotations in this paragraph are from *FMP* 580; *LMP* 256. Weaver's translations have sometimes been revised.

4. The father in *Six Characters in Search of an Author* notices the same paradox in his own life: It "is full of infinite absurdities, which, impudently, do not even have to appear believable: for they are true" (Luigi Pirandello, *Sei personaggi in cerca d'autore* [hereafter *Sei*], *Maschere nude,* ed. Manlio Lo Vecchio-Musti [Milan: Mondadori, 1985], 1:56.

5. Luigi Pirandello, *Enrico IV* (hereafter *E*), *Maschere nude,* 1:356; trans. Robert Rietty and John Wardle as *Henry IV* (hereafter *HE*), in Pirandello, *Collected Plays* (hereafter *CP*), ed. Robert Rietty (New York: Riverrun Press, 1987), 1:57. Here, too, the translations have been revised.

6. On the complex relation between truth and verisimilitude, particularly as it bears upon Pirandello's wavering between the Aristotelian option of representing philosophical universals or historical particulars, see Renato Barilli, *Pirandello: Una rivoluzione culturale* (Milan: Mursia, 1986), 191–206.

7. Immanuel Kant, *Critique of Pure Reason,* trans. Norman Kemp

Smith (New York: St. Martin's Press, 1965), "Preface to the Second Edition," 22.

8. The criterion of sincerity as a test of aesthetic success (which Pirandello shares with Conrad) is critically elaborated in Pirandello's essay "Soggettivismo e oggettivismo nell'arte narrativa" (*SPSV* 181–206). See also Anthony Caputi, *Pirandello and the Crisis of Modern Consciousness* (Urbana: University of Illinois Press, 1988), 27–30, passim.

9. Plato thus had it backwards: It is the copy that precedes the model, and even the idea of the model. To leave no doubts on this matter, Pirandello appends "empirical proof" to his "Warning on the Scruples of the Imagination." A true story reported in the *Corriere della Sera* in 1920 replicates almost exactly the plot of his *Late Mattia Pascal*. A man is found drowned in a ditch and is identified by his wife as her husband, Casati. The husband, however, is alive and in jail. The wife proceeds to marry one of the men in whose company she had identified the body and encounters no difficulty in doing so. Eventually the husband returns home. Notwithstanding his vehement demands to be declared alive, the article reports, his efforts proved in vain: "Casati now insists on his right to . . . resurrection, and as soon as this error is corrected, the presumed widow will find her second marriage annulled. Meanwhile, the odd mishap has not disturbed Casati in the least. In fact, it seems to have put him in a good humor. And, as if to seek new emotions, he decided to make a little visit to . . . his grave, and, as a tribute to his own memory, he set a fine bunch of flowers on the tomb and lighted a votive candle." At moments like these, Pirandello remarks, the imagination is delighted to prove "how incredible life can be, even in such novels that, without meaning to, she copies from art" (*FMP* 239–40; *LMP* 262).

10. See Adriano Tilgher's classic essay, included in abridged form in *Pirandello: A Collection of Critical Essays*, ed. Glauco Cambon (Englewood Cliffs, N.J.: Prentice-Hall, 1967), 19–34. After Bontempelli in Italy and Bentley in the United States, it has become habitual to attribute the life/form dichotomy in Pirandello to the strained reading of Tilgher, who admits to deriving it from Georg Simmel (cf. Eric Bentley, *The Pirandello Commentaries* [Evanston, Ill.: Northwestern University Press, 1986], 22). The truth of the matter is, however, that the dichotomy appears already in *L'umorismo* (*U* 157–68; *H* 135–45).

11. Cf. Georg Simmel, "The Conflict in Modern Culture," *The Conflict in Modern Culture and Other Essays* (1918), trans. K. Peter Etzkorn (New York: Teachers College, Columbia University, 1968), 11–26.

12. The keenness with which Pirandello feels the mutual impingement of these two categories on each other is suggested by his practical advice: The masks should be "deliberately created of a material that will not go limp with sweat, and that can nevertheless be lightly born by the

actors who will have to wear them" (*Sei* 54). Translations are mine.

13. On Pirandello's ambivalence toward the issue of immutable meaning, cf. Barilli, *Pirandello*, 191–206; and Claudio Vicentini, *L'estetica di Pirandello* (Milan: Mursia, 1970), 207–12.

14. What one might call the epiphanic reading of Pirandello, according to which some essential or authentic being is revealed by his destructurations, can be found in Barilli, *Pirandello*; Graziella Corsinovi, *Pirandello e l'espressionismo* (Genoa: Tilgher, 1979); Giacomo Debenedetti, *Il romanzo del Novecento* (1971; reprint, Milan: Garzanti, 1987), 337–39; and Monika Schmitz-Emans, "Das gespaltene Ich," *Pirandello-Studien: Akten des I. Paderborner Pirandello Symposiums* (Paderborn: Ferdinand Schöningh, 1984), 33.

15. Friedrich Nietzsche, *Twilight of the Idols*, in *The Portable Nietzsche*, ed. and trans. Walter Kaufmann (New York: Viking Press, 1968), 485–86.

16. Alongside passages in *On Humor* describing a "different reality" beyond the scope of ordinary vision, one would want to add the theosophist Anselmo Paleari's sense of the encompassing "whole" and the quasimystical ending of *Uno*. See *U* 160–61, 163–64; *H* 138, 140–41; *FMP* 487–88; *LMP* 165–66; and *Uno* 900–902; 8:4.

17. Vitiated though it be by intellectual conflations and a partisan polemic, the most concerted effort to trace a history of subjectivism, idealism, and ontological relativism in modern philosophy is Georg Lukács's *The Destruction of Reason* (1954), trans. Peter Palmer (London: Merlin Press, 1980).

18. See, for example, "Arte e coscienza oggi," "Il neo-idealismo," "Arte e scienza," and "Per le ragione estetiche della parola" (*SPSV* 891–906, 913–21, 161–79, 923–28). On Pirandello's philosophical background, see Mathius Adank, *Luigi Pirandello e i suoi rapporti col mondo tedesco* (Aurau: Druckereigenossenschaft, 1948); Gösta Andersson, *Arte e teoria: Studi sulla poetica del giovane Pirandello* (Uppsala: Almquist & Wiksell, 1966); and Franz Rauhut, *Der junge Pirandello, oder, das Werden eines existentielen Geistes* (Munich: C. H. Beck, 1964); Johannes Thomas, "Il pensiero tedesco negli anni '20," *Pirandello e la Germania*, ed. Gilda Pennica (Palermo: Palumbo, 1984), 7–32. On the similarity between Pirandello's thinking and that of Georg Simmel, see the short study by Maria Rosaria Luongo, *Il relativismo di Simmel e di Pirandello: L'opposizione della forma e della vita* (Naples: Libreria Scientifica Editrice, 1955).

19. Bentley, *Pirandello Commentaries*, 25–26; and Caputi, *Pirandello*, 24.

20. Luigi Pirandello, "Sincerità e arte," in the weekly journal *Il Marzocco* 2, no. 5 (7 March 1897): llv. The cited passage reappears in a modified version in "Illustratori, attori e traduttori" (1908; "Illustrators, Actors, and Translators"), *SPSV* 221.

21. On consciousness in Pirandello, see also *The Worm of Consciousness and Other Essays,* ed. Miriam Chiaromonte (New York: Harcourt Brace Jovanovich, 1976).

22. Luigi Pirandello, "Per le ragioni estetiche della parola" (1908; "Towards an Aesthetic Logic of the Word"), *SPSV* 927.

23. On this fruitless debate, provoked by Pirandello's attacks on Croce's *Estetica,* see Ernesto G. Caserta, "Croce, Pirandello, e il problema estetico," *Italica* 51 (1974): 20–42; Antonio Illiano, *Introduzione alla critica pirandelliana* (Verona: Fiorini, 1976), 38–45; Filippo Puglisi, *L'arte di Luigi Pirandello* (Messina: D'Anna, 1958), 5–45; and Domenico Vittorini, "Benedetto Croce and Luigi Pirandello," *High Points in the History of Italian Literature* (New York: McKay, 1958), 282–91. On the problematic that follows from Pirandello's response to Croce, see also Alberto Asor Rosa, "Pirandello saggista fra soggettivismo e oggettivismo," *Pirandello saggista* (Palermo: Palumbo, 1982), 11–21.

24. Benedetto Croce, quoted in Luigi Pirandello, "Arte e scienza" (1908; "Art and Science"), *SPSV* 171.

25. Pirandello's representation of art as ethically disinterested is inconsistent with his view that aesthetic consciousness consists of practical and emotive activity and also with his sense that expression requires studied transformation of spontaneous intuition. Nevertheless, Pirandello espouses this position against the moralistic aesthetics of his teacher Theodor Lipps. See *U* 138–39; *H* 116–17.

26. Carlo Michelstaedter, *La persuasione e la rettorica,* ed. Sergio Campailla (Milan: Adelphi, 1982).

27. Michelstaedter, *La persuasione,* 44–45.

28. See Rudolf A. Makkreel, *Dilthey: Philosopher of the Human Studies* (Princeton: Princeton University Press, 1975), 210–18.

29. On *Verstehen* in Dilthey, see H. A. Hodges, *Wilhelm Dilthey: An Introduction* (London: Routledge, 1949).

30. Wilhelm Dilthey, *Selected Writings,* ed. H. P. Rickman (Cambridge: Cambridge University Press, 1976), 183–86.

31. In the same vein, Alfred Binet, an immediate source of many of Pirandello's ideas, claims that the differentiation between an "I" and an external object is secondary to the primary operation of consciousness: "Being nothing more than an act of revelation, consciousness has neither an inside nor an outside; it does not correspond to a domain of its own [*un domaine propre*], interior to another domain" (Alfred Binet, *L'âme et le corps* [Paris: E. Flammarion, 1905], 145, 100). Cf. Barilli, *Pirandello,* 291 n. 19; on a related position in Adriano Tilgher, see p. 120 n. 11.

32. Dilthey, *Selected Writings,* 178.

33. This conception of common experience and shared beliefs as the foundation of individual consciousness has significant analogues in thinkers of Pirandello's time, especially: Emile Durkheim's concept of

the "collective conscience" (a system of shared beliefs and sentiments defining the mutual relations of members of a society); Moritz Lazarus's *Völkerpsychologie,* identifying culture as "objective mind," an idea further elaborated by Georg Simmel. According to Lazarus (a teacher of Dilthey as well as Simmel), what "the inner activity of all individuals" has in common may be called a *Volksgeist* (Lazarus and Heymann Steinhal, "Einleitende Gedanken über Völkerpsychologie," *Zeitschrift für Völkerpsychologie und Sprachwissenschaft* 1 (1860): 1–73; here 29). "Wherever several people live together it is a necessary result of their companionship that there develops an objective mental content which then becomes the content, norm and organ of their further subjective activity" (Lazarus, qtd. in K. Danziger, "Origins and Basic Principles of Wundt's *Völkerpsychologie,*" *British Journal of Social Psychology* 22 [1983]: 303–13). See Emile Durkheim, *The Division of Labor in Society* (1893), trans. W. D. Halls (New York: Free Press, 1984); David Frisby, *Georg Simmel* (London: Tavistock, 1984), 69–71; Moritz Lazarus, *Das Leben der Seele,* 3rd ed. (Berlin: Dümmler, 1883); and Georg Simmel, *The Philosophy of Money* (1900), trans. T. Bottomore and D. Frisby (London: Routledge, 1978).

34. Dilthey, *Selected Writings,* 180–81.

35. On Pascal's wandering eye, see also Gregory Lucente, *Beautiful Fables: Self-Consciousness in Italian Narrative from Manzoni to Calvino* (Baltimore: Johns Hopkins University Press, 1986), 123–27; and the study to be published in 1991 by Donatella Stocchi-Perucchio, *Pirandello and the Vagaries of Knowledge* (Saratoga, Calif.: Stanford French and Italian Studies, Anma Libri).

36. Debenedetti, *Il romanzo,* 341. On Pascal's attempt to abolish history, see 334–36.

37. On sympathy as the ethical message of Pirandello's fictions, see Bentley, *Pirandello Commentaries,* 25–35; and Massimo Bontempelli, "Pirandello o del candore," *Introduzioni e discorsi* (Milan: Bompiani, 1964), 7–31.

38. Luigi Pirandello, "Arte e coscienza d'oggi" (1893; "Today's Art and Consciousness"), *SPSV* 900–901.

39. Pirandello, "Today's Art and Consciousness," *SPSV* 898–99; "La mensogna del sentimento nell'arte" (1890; "The Lie of Feeling in Art"), *SPSV* 870.

40. Franco Zangrilli, *L'arte novellistica di Pirandello* (Ravenna: Longo Editore, 1983), 75–77.

41. Luigi Pirandello, "Quand'ero matto" (1902; "When I was Mad"), *Novelle per un anno,* ed. Mario Costanzo (Milan: Mondadori, 1987), 2:785.

42. Pirandello, *L'esclusa, Tutti i romanzi,* 1:149–50.

43. Franco Ferrucci, "Pirandello e il palcoscenico della mente," *Lettere italiane* 36 (1984): 219–25; here p. 221.

44. On Pirandello's "allegorical" aesthetic, rejecting symbolic unity, see the fascinating study by Massimo Verdicchio, "Narrativa allegorica e umoristica nel *Fu Mattia Pascal*," in *Cultura meridionale e letteratura italiana: I modelli narrativi dell'età moderna*, ed. Pompeo Giannantonio (Naples: Loffredo, 1982), 665–80.

45. On reflexivity in Pirandello, see Lucente, *Beautiful Fables*.

4. Joseph Conrad: The Ethos of Trial

1. Miller, *Poets of Reality*, 33.

2. Joseph Conrad, *The Rescue: A Romance of the Shallows* (Garden City, N.Y.: Doubleday, Page, 1923), 431–32. On some of the ambiguities attending the word existence in Conrad, see Batchelor, *Lord Jim*, 175–76.

3. Morton Dauwen Zabel, "Editor's Introduction," *The Portable Conrad*, rev. ed. (New York: Penguin, 1969), 20.

4. On the political conscience and unconscious of Conrad's work, see Fredric Jameson, "Romance and Reification: Plot Construction and Ideological Closure in Joseph Conrad," *The Political Unconscious: Narrative as a Socially Symbolic Act* (Ithaca: Cornell University Press, 1981), 206–80; Vincent Pecora, "The Sounding Empire: Conrad's *Heart of Darkness*," *Self and Form in Modern Narrative* (Baltimore: Johns Hopkins University Press, 1989), 115–75; and many of the essays included in *HD*.

5. On the "principle of hope," which bears remarkable comparison to the utopian essayism of both Conrad and Musil, see Ernst Bloch, *The Principle of Hope* (1959), 3 vols., trans. Neville Plaice, Stephen Plaice, and Paul Knight (Cambridge: MIT Press, 1986), esp. 1:45–315. Connections between Bloch and Musil have been noted by Jörg Kühne, *Das Gleichnis: Studien zur inneren Form von Robert Musils Roman "der Mann ohne Eigenschaften"* (Tübingen: Max Niemeyer, 1968), 82, 83; Annie Reniers-Servranckx, *Robert Musil: Konstanz und Entwicklung von Themen, Motiven und Strukturen in den Dichtungen* (Bonn: Bouvier Verlag Herbert Grundmann, 1972), 296; and Monti, *Musil*, 125.

6. On the anti-self, see William Butler Yeats, "Per Amica Silentia Lunae" (1917), *Mythologies* (New York: Macmillan, 1978), 317–69; "Anima Hominis" (1917), *Selected Criticism* (London: Macmillan, 1976), 165–80.

7. The narrators of both *Heart of Darkness* and *Lord Jim* are dreamers, "spinners of yarns." The same holds for Stein, the man who utters the maxim, "a man that is born falls into a dream like a man who falls into the sea" (*LJ* 130). Not only was Stein's youth as idealistic as Jim's, but even the wisdom of his maturity is spent chasing butterflies. For more on this struggle for the ideal in *Lord Jim* and the ways in which it militates against crude forms of resistance, see Tanner, "Butterflies and Beetles," *LJ* 447–62.

8. Søren Kierkegaard, *The Journals,* trans. Alexander Dru (New York: Harper & Row, 1959), 243.

9. Joseph Conrad, *Typhoon and Other Stories* (Garden City, N.Y.: Doubleday, Page, 1925), 19.

10. See Martin Heidegger, "Letter on Humanism," in *Basic Writings,* ed. David Farrell Krell (New York: Harper & Row, 1977), 231–35.

5. Robert Musil: Conscious Utopianism

1. *GW* 1:255; *MWQ* 1:303 [62]. Again it is passages like these that provide the basis for readings of Musil as "mystic." In this light, essayism would appear as an unsatisfactory strategy by which to articulate the harmonious totality of experience, and the master trope for the essay's frustrating inability to come to a conclusion would be science: "The definitive proof . . . of . . . the validity of science," Musil writes, "is never arrived at. . . , unless it is to be found in this very progress and its results, the domination of nature, technology, and commodities, this whole ingenious system of never ending with the preparations for life, in whose gestures of force [*Kraftgebärde*] there lies, at bottom, a fear of synthesis" (Robert Musil, "Das Geistliche, der Modernismus und die Metaphysik" [1912; "Spirituality, Modernism, and Metaphysics"], *GW* 8:990; *PS* 23).

2. Robert Musil, "Anmerkung zu einer Metapsychik" (1914; "Commentary on a Metapsychics"), *GW* 8:1017; *PS* 56.

3. Maurice Blanchot, *L'écriture du désastre,* trans. Ann Smock as *The Writing of the Disaster* (Lincoln: University of Nebraska Press, 1986), 46, 43.

4. According to Ulrich, these are the "two trees" into which life as it has so far been lived in the West has been divided: love and force (*Gewalt*) (*GW* 2:591–93; *MWQ* 2:358–62 [116]).

5. The idealist antecedent of this concern can be gauged by a brief glance at Schelling: Science "has one and the same problem as art," to represent the infinite in finite form. Were science "ever to have accomplished its whole task as art always has acomplished its, both would have to converge and become one" (Friedrich Wilhelm Joseph Schelling, *Deduction of a Universal Organ of Philosophy, or Main Propositions of the Philosophy of Art according to Principles of Transcendental Idealism,* in *Philosophy of German Idealism,* ed. Ernst Behler [New York: Continuum, 1987], 211). Just as for Schelling "wherever art may be, there science must first join it," so for Musil every type of consciousness stands in need of scientific rigor for its articulation (Musil, "Spirituality," *GW* 8:989–90; *PS* 22–23).

6. Heidegger, *Being and Time,* sec. 56.

7. Heidegger, *Being and Time,* sec. 60 (trans. slightly revised).

8. Cf. Heidegger on the "Situation" as constitutive of options (*Being and Time,* sec. 60).

9. Robert Musil, *Die Schwärmer* (1921), *GW* 6:311, trans. Andrea Simon as *The Enthusiasts* (New York: Performing Arts Journal Publications, 1983), 16.

10. Heidegger, *Being and Time,* secs. 54, 58.

11. Michael E. Zimmerman, *The Eclipse of the Self: The Development of Heidegger's Concept of Authenticity* (Athens: Ohio University Press, 1986), 96; Ernst Tugendhat, *Self-Consciousness and Self-Determination,* trans. Paul Stern (Cambridge: MIT Press, 1986), 206–18.

12. Blanchot, *Writing,* 22, 43. Musil is undoubtedly one of the central influences on this later thought of Blanchot, who, we remember, had in the 1950s already devoted himself to the study of Musil (in *Le livre à venir*).

13. See the similar demeanor elaborated in Hans Blumenberg, "Pensiveness," *Caliban* 6 (1989): 51–55.

14. Martin Heidegger, "Hölderlin and the Essence of Poetry," *Existence and Being,* trans. Douglas Scott (Chicago: Henry Regnery: 1949), 289.

15. On the chemical principle of Le Chatelier, with which Musil was no doubt familiar, see the short study by Loránd Jendrassik, *Das Le Chateliersche Prinzip und die Gesetze der Störung dynamischer Gleichgewichte* (Budapest: Akadémiai Kíadó, 1965). An analogous principle of dynamic equilibrium and interdependence is applied to general theory construction by Vilfredo Pareto in his baccalaureate dissertation of 1869. See Pareto, *The Transformation of Democracy,* ed. Charles H. Powers and trans. Renata Girola (New Brunswick, N.J.: Transaction Books, 1984), 3–4.

16. Heidegger, *Being and Time,* secs. 38, 31.

17. Cf. Cases's description of Musil's continuous rewriting of *The Man without Qualities:* Among his ceaseless corrections, misgivings, and rewritings of chapters, Musil "never discarded anything. . . . He considered no draft superseded or excluded by a new conception" (Cesare Cases, "Introduzione," Robert Musil, *L'uomo senza qualità,* trans. Anita Rho [Turin: Einaudi, 1970], xvi).

18. The phrase is *vorläulig definitiv;* the phrase for Heidegger's anticipatory resolve is *vorläufige Entschlossenheit (Being and Time,* sec. 62).

19. Nietzsche, *Beyond Good and Evil,* sec. 2.

20. Robert Musil, "Politisches Bekenntnis eines junger Mannes: Ein Fragment" (1913; "Political Confessions of a Young Man: A Fragment"), *GW* 8:1010; *PS* 33. Neither here nor elsewhere does the relation between Musil's historical thought and his fictional representation of the prewar years prove to be incidental. In August 1913, when *The Man without Qualities* opens, Ulrich is thirty-two years old. One can reasonably deduce that he was born on Musil's birthday, 6 November 1880.

21. All citations in this and the following two paragraphs are from Nietzsche, *Beyond Good and Evil,* secs. 209–12. A precedent for Nietzsche's *Versucher,* to which Musil occasionally alludes, is Ralph Waldo

Emerson's notion of "not yet finished men," who "walk as a prophesy of the future." See Emerson, "Culture," *Selected Writings*, ed. Brooks Atkinson (New York: Modern Library, 1968), 717–38. On Musil's debts to Emerson, see Hickman, *Robert Musil;* and Geoffrey Howes, *Robert Musil and the Legacy of Ralph Waldo Emerson* (Ph.D. thesis, University of Michigan, Ann Arbor, 1985).

22. The "characteristic thing" about Nietzsche, Musil writes at age nineteen, "is that he says: this could be this and that that. And thereupon one could built this and that. In short: he speaks of pure possibilities, pure combinations, without showing us any of them really carried out. . . . He shows us all the roads on which our brain can work, but doesn't tread any." Decades later, recognizing no doubt that his own way of thinking was much closer to Nietzsche's than he had once imagined, Musil annotates his own comments in a more revealing way: "How silly one is as a youth. Nietzsche serves only as a step for an urchin! How one sees only what one sees beneath oneself! How far thinking is from confronting the entire thought of Nietzsche" (*TB* 1 : 19).

23. Musil rejects the project of aesthetic realism in much the same spirit, considering novelistic mimesis as not a sufficiently creative end:

Depicted reality . . . is always only a pretext [*ein Vorwand*]. Once upon a time, perhaps, narration might have been simply the reactive touching-once-more of good or terrible empirical phantasms on the part of a strong but conceptually weak person, under the recollection of which his memory cringed, fascinated by expressing, repeating, discussing, and thus diffusing them. Since the beginning of the novel, however, we have come to hold to a concept of narration which has evolved further. And the development requires that the depiction of reality should finally become a means in the service of a person who is *conceptually strong*, who with its aid steals up on emotional cognitions [*Gefühlserkenntnisse*] and mental emotions [*Denkerschütterungen*]. ("Über Robert Musil's Bücher" [1913; "On Robert Musil's Books"], *GW* 8 : 997; *PS* 27)

24. It "worries me," says the narrator of Musil's story about a man who resisted the formation of a character, "that perhaps I have merely not grasped his importance at the right time and whether in the last resort he isn't some kind of pioneer or precursor" (Robert Musil, "Ein Mensch ohne Charakter," *Nachlass zu Lebzeiten* [1936; *Posthumous Papers Published in Life*], *GW* 7 : 534).

25. Being a student of experimental rather than clinical psychology, Musil was dissatisfied with the unproductive use of reason in psychoanalysis. Scientific though it may have been, or seemed to have been, psychoanalysis was incapable of doing more than reaffirming—on the basis of such imprecise concepts as instinct, fear, aggression, libido—a childlike condition of the psyche, as though that mental economy were the only one possible. It failed to break ground either in interpreting the teleology of the drives or in lending them a new means of expression. On Musil's attitudes toward psychoanalysis, see his "Der bedrohte

Ödipus," *GW* 7 : 528–30; as well as entries in his journals. For critical studies, see Karl Corino, "Ödipus oder Orest? Robert Musil und die Psychoanalyse," in *Vom Törless zum Mann ohne Eigenshaften,* ed. Uwe Bauer and Dietmar Goltschnigg (Munich: Fink, 1973); Johannes Cremerius, "Das Dilemma eines Shriftstellers vom Typus 'poeta doctus' *nach* Freud," *Psyche* 33 (1979): 733–72; Peter Henniger, "Wissenschaft und Dichtung bei Musil und Freud," *MLN* 94 (1979): 541–68; and Luft, *Robert Musil* 184ff. and n. 90. For a fascinating psychoanalytic investigation of Musil's essay, "Das Unanständige und Kranke in der Kunst," see Susan Erickson, "Essay/Body/Fiction: The Repression of an Interpretive Context in an Essay of Robert Musil," *German Quarterly* 56 (1983): 580–93.

26. "We Germans have—aside from the one great attempt [*Versuch*] of Nietzsche—no books on man; no systematizers and organizers of life" (Musil, "Commentary," *GW* 8 : 1019; *PS* 58).

27. "Der Mann ohne Eigenshaften—das ist ein Mann, der möglichst viele der besten, aber nirgends zur Synthese gelangten Zeitelemente in sich vereint—kann sich also gar nicht einen Standpunkt wählen, er kann nur versuchen, mit ihnen ordentlich fertig zu werden" (Robert Musil, letter to Adolf Frisé dated January 1931, in Musil, *Briefe 1901–1942,* ed. Adolf Frisé [Reinbek bei Hamburg: Rowohlt, 1981], 1 : 495).

28. When is a feeling really "natural" and "simple"? Ulrich asks General Stumm. "When it can be automatically expected to manifest itself in everybody when the circumstances are the same!" was his own reply. And even if one flees from this bleak regularity "into the darkest depth's of [one's] being . . . into those moist animal depths that save us from evaporating in the light of our intellect," one finds only "stimuli and reflex-tracts, the grooves of habits and skills, repetition, fixation, imposed patterns, series, monotony! *There's* uniform, barracks, regulations for you, my dear Stumm. And the civilian soul has a remarkable kinship with the military" (*GW* 2 : 378; *MWQ* 2 : 90 [85]).

29. Many of the terms used to establish this difference are adapted from Robert Rosen's *Anticipatory Systems: Philosophical, Mathematical and Methodological Foundations* (Oxford: Pergamon Press, 1985).

30. Rosen illustrates this anticipatory logic by means of an example of a man who decides to run when he sees a bear in the forest. The decision is motivated not by an observable situation so much as by an anticipation of an action that is likely to follow the situation, namely, an attack by the bear. The decision is motivated not by n but by $n + 1$ (*Anticipatory Systems,* 7).

31. Rosen, *Anticipatory Systems,* 406.

32. Nietzsche, *Will to Power,* sec. 490.

33. Nietzsche, *Gay Science,* secs. 373, 374; *Beyond Good and Evil,* sec. 62.

34. Numerous excellent analyses of Musil's literary essayism are performed by Finlay, *Potential of Modern Discourse,* 87–134. See also the

penetrating pages on Musil in Dieter Bachmann's pioneering study, *Essay und Essayismus* (Stuttgart: Kohlhammer, 1969), 157–92.

35. On some of the ways in which this hermeneutical practice is reflected in the novel's construction, see Arntzen, *Satirischer Stil;* Cometti, *Robert Musil;* Finlay, *Potential of Modern Discourse,* esp. 87–134; Werner Graf, *Erfahrungskonstruktion: Eine interpretation von Robert Musils Roman "Der Mann ohne Eigenschaften"* (Berlin: Spiess, 1981); Kühn, *Analogie und Variation;* Payne, *Robert Musil,* esp. 58–84; and Pierre V. Zima, *L'ambivalence romanesque: Proust, Kafka, Musil* (Frankfurt am Main: Peter Lang, 1988).

36. Two good examples of this pattern can be found in the mutually influencing meditations on order by Ulrich, Stumm, Fischel, and Tuzzi and the considerations of soul in Diotima, Arnheim, and Ulrich.

37. See Robert Musil, "Der Deutsche Mensch als Symptom" (1923; "The German as Symptom"), *GW* 8:1353–1400.

38. See Ulrich Karthaus, "War Musil Realist?" *Musil-Forum* 6 (1980): 115–27; and Monti, *Musil,* 195–210. Not systematic in his lexis, Musil uses the words *analogy, simile,* and *metaphor* rather synonymously. See, for example, *GW* 2:581; *MWQ* 2:346–47 (115).

39. Robert Musil, "Rede zur Rilke-Feier. In Berlin am 16. Januar 1927" ("Address at the Memorial Service for Rilke in Berlin, the 16th of January, 1927"), *GW* 8:1237; *PS* 245. "What [Rilke] succeeded in doing in the lyric domain," writes Ulrich Karthaus, "[Musil] aimed at achieving in prose" ("War Musil Realist," 121).

40. Georg Lukács, "Phänomenologische Skizze des schöpferischen und receptiven Verhaltens," *Heidelberger Philosophie der Kunst (1912– 1914): Frühe Schriften zur Ästhetik,* ed. Gyorgy Markus and Frank Benseler (Darmstadt: Hermann Luchterhand Verlag, 1974), 1:102.

41. See the last paragraph of Musil, "Cues," *GW* 8:1154; *PS* 208; and *GW* 1:156; *MWQ* 1:182 (40).

42. "When a great painting comes into being," writes Schelling, "it is as though the invisible curtain that separates the real from the ideal is raised (*Deduction,* 215). Like Adorno, Musil should be read back-to-back with the tradition of aesthetic idealism.

43. Adorno, *Aesthetic Theory,* 253, 123.

44. On this entire problem, see Adorno, *Aesthetic Theory,* 252–56.

45. "Analogy," writes F. T. Marinetti, "is but another name for that immense love which brings distant things into close relationship. Poets have always been aware of the possibilities of analogy. Their difficulty was that they kept too close to external resemblances and did not venture to take those daring leaps made possible by intuition" ("Les mots en liberté futuristes," *Poesia* [December 1919]: 42). For a theory of the audacious metaphor, see Harald Winrich, "Semantik der kühnen Metapher," *DVjs* 37 (1963): 325–44. For readings of Musil in terms of the audacious metaphor, see Monti, *Musil;* Enrico De Angelis, *Robert Musil*

(Turin: Einaudi, 1982), 175–214; Jörg Kühne, *Das Gleichnis: Studien zur inneren Form von Robert Musils Roman "Der Mann ohne Eigenschaften"* (Tübingen: Max Niemeyer, 1968).

46. For Musil irony "is not a gesture of superiority but a form of struggle" (*GW* 7:941). On the simultaneously constructive and destructive implications of irony and analogy, see *GW* 5:1939; *TB* 1:922–23; Finlay, *Potential of Modern Discourse*, 14–21; Hochstätter, *Sprache des Möglichen*, 103–13.

47. "Utopia means an experiment in which the possible transformation of an element is observed, together with the effects that it would cause in that compound phenomenon we call life" (*GW* 1:246; *MWQ* 1:292 [61]).

48. Cf., for example, Paul Ricoeur, *The Philosophy of Paul Ricoeur: An Anthology of His Work,* ed. Charles E. Reagan and David Stewart (Boston: Beacon, 1978), 97–119.

49. Lukács, *Soul and Form,* 10.

50. Adorno, "Essay as Form," 160.

51. "I am neither a philosopher nor even an essayist," writes Musil, "but a poet [*Dichter*]" (*TB* 1:665). Given that his collected works contain hardly a verse of poetry, by *Dichtung* Musil meant something more like what I conceive to be the ultimate ambition of his novel: an articulation of new possibilities of synthetic order (as opposed to a merely "micrological" diagnosis of what actually happens).

52. While Hans Georg Gadamer's understanding of the aesthetic experience as a fusion of horizons envisions the possibility of an artwork and its receptor actually *sharing* a single truth, this hypothetical union is always postulated upon a "bridging" operation, one never quite allowing for the distance between the historical subject and the interpreted text to be effaced. "Every encounter with tradition that takes place within historical consciousness," writes Gadamer, "involves an experience of tension between the text and the present. The hermeneutical task consists in not covering up this tension by attempting a naive assimilation but rather in consciously bringing it out" (Gadamer, *Truth and Method,* ed. Garrett Barder and John Cumming [New York: Seabury Press, 1975], 273; trans. slightly revised). This projected and unified truth is no more than the utopian goal, or the third possibility, of dynamic understanding. The projected union can only be engaged in through a disjunctive, essayistic bridging of the horizons in question.

53. "Das Unanständige und Kranke in der Kunst" (1911; "The Obscene and the Pathological in Art"), *GW* 8:980–81; *PS* 7. Not having yet formulated the concept of essayism in this earliest of his collected essays, Musil speaks of art in general as extending the register of the possible. Yet it is already clear how essayism will eventually be distinguished from this art in general, for this art is described as *uni*lateral, depicting persons and things "not from all sides but from one." The pre-

essayistic artist is struck neither by the question of the value of a thing nor by its extrinsic connections but simply by "one of its sides that comes suddenly to be disclosed."

54. John L. Casti, *Alternate Realities: Mathematical Models of Nature and Man* (New York: Wiley, 1989), v.

6. Luigi Pirandello: Cheating the Image

1. Cf. Wolfgang Köhler, *The Place of Value in a World of Facts* (1938; reprint, New York: Liveright, 1976): "It is the apparent independence, the objectivity and the external location of thing-percepts which make it difficult for many to admit that such things are no more than percepts, not the real and independent physical things at the same time" (104). For a conception of the image as shorthand for subjective knowledge in general, see Kenneth E. Boulding, *The Image* (Ann Arbor: University of Michigan Press, 1956).

2. Kundera, *Art of the Novel*, 128–29.

3. One of the few things, "or perhaps the only one, that I knew for certain," Pascal admits at the beginning of his autobiography, "was that my name was Mattia Pascal. And I used to take advantage of it. Whenever a friend or acquaintance revealed that he had taken such leave of his senses as to approach me for some advice or suggestion, I would shrug my shoulders, squint my eyes, and reply:

'My name is Mattia Pascal.'

'Thank you, dear. That much I know'" (*FMP* 319; *LMP* xi).

4. Pirandello thematizes this opposition most extensively in *U* 161–65; *H* 139–42.

5. Luigi Pirandello, *Lazzaro*, in *MN* 2:1218; trans. Frederick May as *Lazarus*, in *CP* 153–223. See also *SG* (662), *Shoot!* (224), where life, says Gubbio, "is not to be set before one, but felt within one and lived. . . . To set life before one as an object of study is absurd, because life, when set before one like that, inevitably loses all its real consistency and becomes an abstraction, void of meaning and value. . . . Life is not explained; it is lived."

6. Luigi Pirandello, "La carriola" (1928; "The Wheelbarrow" hereafter *C*), *Novelle per un anno II,* ed. Manlio Lo Vecchio-Musti (Milan: Mondadori, 1956), 718.

7. Borrowed from Giovanni Marchesini's *Le finzione dell'anima* (1905), the notion of the operative person as only a metaphor of spiritual possibility is expressed by Pirandello on at least three occasions; see *U* 154, *H* 132; *FMP* 583, *LMP* 259; and *SG* 641, *Shoot!* 193–94. The lawyer's argument about quotidian life as a species of death could almost have been found verbatim in the work of Pirandello's contemporary Michelstaedter. "Very few people know it," the lawyer says;

most, nearly all, struggle and wear themselves out to create, as they say, a state for themselves, to achieve a form; once they achieve it, they believe they have gained their life, and instead they begin to die. They don't know it, because they do not see themselves; because they are no longer able to detach themselves from that moribund form they have attained; they do not know themselves as dead and believe they are alive. He alone knows himself who succeeds in seeing the form he has given himself or that others have given him, fortune, chance events, the conditions into which each person is born. (*C* 133)

To know oneself—that is, to know oneself *as dead*—is, by implication, to live. Cf. Michelstaedter's *La persuasione,* a book Pirandello mentions in 1936 and probably first read in the early twenties.

8. This eminently sensible demand that life accord with its meaning lurks even in Pirandello's polemics against the theater, particularly in his concern over the inability of any dramatic image to duplicate "the idea" that informs a script: "Even though [the image] is not born spontaneously in the actor but rather suscitated in his soul by the expression of the poet, can this image ever be the same [as the idea expressed by the poet]? Can it fail to alter itself, to modify itself, as it passes from one spirit to another? It will no longer be the same. It may be an approximate image [*un'immagine approssimativa*], more or less similar; but never the same. A given character on the screen might speak the identical words of the written play, but it will never be that [play] of the poet, for the actor has recreated it in himself" (Pirandello, "Illustratori, attori e traduttori [1908; "Illustrators, Actors and Translators"], *SPSV* 216).

9. A comic figure, writes Henri Bergson, is always un-self-conscious, rendered laughable "in proportion to his ignorance of himself." Precisely where one would expect to find a "wide-awake adaptability and . . . living pliableness" in action one is confronted instead with a mind crystalized into grooves and ready-made frames, a "mechanical inelasticity" and absentmindedness. See Henri Bergson, *Laughter,* trans. Cloudesley Brereton and Fred Rothwell (New York: Macmillan, 1917), 16, 10. The more one is reduced to a thing, the greater the comic effect. As Pirandello had explained in his own treatise *On Humor,* humor, like tragedy, arises only when a comic condition is accompanied by consciousness. Pirandello usually associates this recognition of a rift between reality and its representation with the experience of looking in the mirror, an experience that, debilitating at first, offers "the only way to liberate ourselves from that false nature and false spontaneity which we have constructed day after day in the name of utilitarian need." Only that person, Barilli continues, "who has the courage to confront the awkwardness, the embarrassment, and the semiparalysis of looking at himself in the mirror will then be able, in a second moment, to achieve an effective degree of spontaneity and naturalness. For those 'straight,' capable, and spontaneous people surrounding us in everyday life are what they are only at the price of abandoning themselves to the blindness of automatism" (Barilli, *Pirandello,* 132).

10. "My friend Jevreinoff," writes Pirandello,

---

reaches the point where he says, and demonstrates in one of his books, that the entire world is a theater and that it is not only humans who recite the parts that they have assigned themselves in life, or that others have assigned them, but also all animals, and even plants, and, in short, nature as a whole.

This may be going too far. Yet, in any event there is no doubt that, before being a traditional form of literature, theater is a natural expression of life." Pirandello, "Se il film parlante abolirà il teatro" [1929; "Whether Film with Speech Will Abolish the Theater"], *SPSV* 997).

11. The "first root of our woes," Pirandello writes, "is precisely this feeling that we have of life. The tree lives and doesn't feel: for it the earth, the sun, the air, the light, the wind, the rain, are not things different from itself [*non sono cose che esso non sia*]. Man, however, is endowed at birth with this unfortunate privilege of feeling himself live, with the nice illusion in which it results: that of confusing this internal feeling of life, mutable and variable as it is, for a reality outside of himself" (*U* 163; *H* 140).

12. Invoking Sartre's distinction between thetic and nonthetic consciousness, Renato Barilli distinguishes between *coscienza* (as pure awareness) and *consapevolezza* (as awareness *of* one's awareness). See Barilli, *Pirandello,* pt. 1, chap. 4 n. 7; p. 120 n. 11.

13. Pirandello's description of this process whereby life is translated into a feeling of life and then into a logical articulation of the feeling may be found in *U* 161–63; *H* 138–40. And yet a close analysis of his texts reveals that this *sentimento della vita* producing a world of images is more than mere feeling. As in Pareto's usage, these *sentimenti* are already ideological in nature: "subconscious beliefs that serve as standards of evaluation" (Charles H. Powers, "Introduction," Vilfredo Pareto, *The Transformation of Democracy* [1921], trans. Renata Girola [New Brunswick, N.J.: Transaction Books, 1984], 83); see also 10, 63–72; Pareto, *Sociological Writings,* ed. S. E. Finer, trans. Derick Mirfin (London: Pall Mall Press, 1966), 222–30.

14. "Will, like reflection, certainly plays a part in the conceiving and, more importantly, in the execution of the work; the former holds the idea fixed in the spirit, the latter is the mirror in which it [the idea] gazes at itself" (Luigi Pirandello, "Scienza e critica estetica" [1900; "Aesthetic Criticism and Science"], an essay not included in *SPSV* but published in Andersson, *Arte e teoria,* 225–29; here p. 229). Cf. also "Towards an Aesthetic Logic of the Word": "Now, I ask, if linguistic expression is a form of sensations, [or] pure intuition [or] consciousness, and thus only a theoretical activity, how can such a linguistic expression turn into *creation?* Creation occurs through the will [*La creazione è della volontà*]. Until will intervenes, we cannot have creation but only consciousness" (*SPSV* 926).

15. "The reflection I have in mind . . . does not involve an opposition of consciousness towards spontaneity; it is a type of projection of

one and the same imaginative activity: it is generated by the image [*fantasma*], like the shadow by a body; it has all the traits of spontaneous 'ingenuity' or inbredness [*natività*]; it lies in the very germ of creation" (*U* 142; *H* 120).

16. For readings of this *oltre* as an "epiphanization" of a character's authentic being, see Barilli, *Pirandello*, 283–89; Corsinovi, *Pirandello*, 157–64; Debenedetti, *Il romanzo*, 463–71; and Zangrilli, *L'arte novellistica*, 83.

17. Luigi Pirandello, *L'uomo dal fiore in bocca* (hereafter *UF*), MN 1:505; trans. Gigi Gatti and Terry Doyle as *The Man with the Flower in his Mouth* (hereafter *MF*), *CP* 73.

18. Luigi Pirandello, "La distruzione dell'uomo" (hereafter *DU*), *NA*, 1:1046.

19. As Fabio Girelli-Carasi has put it in conversation, Moscarda represents the first instance of selfhood as reader-response.

20. The father-son relation is treated, psychoanalytically and literarily, in Jean-Michel Gardair, *Pirandello: Fantasmes et logique du double* (Paris: Larousse, 1972); Elio Gioanola, *Pirandello: La follia* (Genoa: Il Melangolo, 1983), 227–54; Stocchi-Perucchio, *Vagaries of Knowledge*.

21. Giovanni Croci, "Introduzione," Luigi Pirandello, *Uno, nessuno e centomila* (Milan: Mondadori, 1987), xxix. And yet even Moscarda's ascetic retirement involves an ironic caricature of (and symbolic atonement for) the destiny from which Moscarda already suffers, analogous to the outcome of "The Wheelbarrow": Moscarda relinquishes all of his personal appurtenances to live on alms as meekly received as the forms of his previous life, including standardized food and uniforms. Every aspect of this dispossessed lifestyle is "annexed" to a person who possesses nothing, as Moscarda comes to inhabit "a hospice for the homeless with an annexed frugal kitchen open all year round, for the recuperation not solely of the ill but also of all the poor who might need it; and also an annexed cloakroom for both sexes and every age, of a fixed number of outfits per year. . . . I myself would take a room there, sleeping with no special distinction, like every other pauper, on a cot, eating like all the others soup in a wooden bowl, and wearing the community robe destined to a person of my age and sex" (*Uno* 899; 8:3).

22. Luigi Pirandello, *Il giuoco delle parti* (hereafter *GP*) 1:513–80.

23. Gala speaks of this process of emptying as abstracting from life, or extracting the "concept" from every situation, like the pulp from the shell of an egg that has been thrown at you: "[You have to] immediately seize it and empty it, draw the concept out of it, and then you can even play with it. . . . If you're not ready to seize it, you will let yourself be struck or will let it drop. In either case, it will spew forth in front or on top of you. If you are ready, you can grab it, prick a hole in it, and drink it" (*GP* 532).

24. It is in the light of this radical epistemology (and not merely the

haze of subjective relativism) that the ending of *Così è (se vi pare)* (1918; *Right You Are* [*If You Think You Are*]) should be read. The play involves the efforts of a petit bourgeois community to determine which of their new neighbors is mad, Mr. Ponza or his mother-in-law. Mr. Ponza will not allow his mother-in-law to see his wife for, so he says, this wife is not really the mother-in-law's daughter, but a second wife of his. The first has been killed, and the mother-in-law does not have the courage to recognize it. To spare her feelings Mr. Ponza pretends that his second wife is indeed the first one and simply keeps the mother-in-law at a safe enough distance from the wife not to recognize the difference in identity. In turn, the mother-in-law claims that it is her son-in-law who is mad and who, out of deep psychological fear of loss, has forced himself to believe that his wife is not his first and only wife (her daughter) but a second one. How will the people decide who is right? Obviously, by summoning this wife and asking her who she really is. Invoked to say which of two mutually exclusive persons she is, Mrs. Ponza makes an unequivocal assertion of duplicity: "yes, I am the daughter of Mrs. Frola . . . and [also] the second wife of Mr. Ponza." The case is undecidable, even for her. Mrs. Ponza both is and is not the person she is said to be, both characters and neither; "and as for myself I am no one! No one!" (Pirandello, *Così è (se vi pare) MN* 2:1077). On relations between Pirandello and poststructuralist research, see Jennifer Stone, *Pirandello's Naked Prompt: The Structure of Repetition in Modernism* (Ravenna: Longo Editore, 1989). For an incisive reading of some of the epistemological paradoxes of *Right You Are (If You Think You Are),* see Albert Ascoli, "Mirror and Veil: *Così è (se vi pare)* and the Drama of Interpretation," *Stanford Italian Review* 7 (1987): 29–46.

25. On the mirror experience in Pirandello, see Ascoli, "Mirror and Veil," 36–37; Gian-Paolo Biasin, "Moscarda's Mirror," in *Literary Diseases: Theme and Metaphor in the Italian Novel* (Austin: University of Texas Press, 1975), 100–126; Lucente, *Beautiful Fables,* 137–39; Stocchi-Perucchio, *Vagaries of Knowledge.*

26. It is true that Pirandello, particularly when allowing himself to fall under the sway of Séailles, sometimes speaks of "the simultaneous and synthetic combinations spontaneously created by art." And yet the eulogy of *Hamlet* in this same essay is the more revealing admission, to the effect that even aesthetic organization resists comprehensive, synthetic intuition:

Why, after so much research and so much reflection, have we still not succeeded in attaining a clear and precise idea of Shakespeare's *Hamlet.* . . ? Precisely because the protagonist and the characters of that terrible drama all live a life of their own [*di propria vita*], each for himself, and overwhelm each other in the poet's soul, variously disconnected and reconstituted into many other souls, in battle with each other and coexisting in the mind of the poet, who cannot succeed in tying them together, in subjecting them to a conception of his own, to a supreme principle" (Luigi Pirandello, "Aesthetic Criticism and Science" in Andersson, *Arte e teoria*, 227, 228]).

If Séailles imagined "contiguity" and "similarity" to be the two principles enabling the organization of images into an aesthetic whole (168), Pirandello presents the prime movers as contrast and strife. Indeed, Pirandello criticizes Séailles's notion of aesthetic organization based on contiguity and similarity in *U* 141; *H* 119, and he parodies it in his account of the spontaneous association of images which occurs in the ordinary experience of solitude (*Uno* 747–48; 1:3). For critical readings of this aesthetics of contrast, as Pirandello presents it in *On Humor*, see Umberto Eco, "Pirandello *Ridens*," *The Limits of Interpretation* (Bloomington: Indiana University Press, 1990), 163–73; Jorn Moestrup, *The Structural Patterns of Pirandello's Work* (Odense: Odense University Press, 1972), 61–66; and Olga Ragusa, "Nota su *L'umorismo* di Luigi Pirandello," *Italianistica: Rivista di letteratura italiana* 17 (1988): 139–44.

27. Franz Brentano, *Sensory and Noetic Consciousness: Psychology from an Empirical Standpoint III* (1929), ed. Oscar Kraus and Linda L. McAlister, trans. Margarete Schättle and Linda L. McAlister (London: Routledge, 1981), 31.

28. William James, "The Self" (1892) *The Philosophy of William James*, ed. Horace M. Kallen (New York: Modern Library), 135, 133.

29. Caught through to the end in the second moment of metaphoricity, Moscarda made himself "utterly remote from everything that could have any sort of meaning or value for others [that is, from all linguistic conventions], . . . absolutely alienated from myself and from everything belonging to me, but also with the horror of remaining still *somebody* in any way, in the possession of something." Ironically, Moscarda's real hope was that his undefinition of self would constitute a "path that led to becoming one for everyone" (*Uno* 899; 8:3). "Far from being the beginning of rational self-reflection," Lucente remarks, "this new life represents . . . its end, in what now amounts to a continual flight from the sort of dualistic *self*-consciousness with which the narrative began" (*Beautiful Fables*, 151). On the failure of Moscarda's attempts to transcend subjectivity, see Robert S. Dombroski, *Le totalità dell'artificio; Ideologia e forma nel romanzo di Pirandello* (Padova: Liviani, 1978), 119–56.

30. Denis Ferraris, "Essai d'analyse du roman de L. Pirandello, *Il fu Mattia Pascal*," in *Lectures pirandelliennes* (Vincennes, Fr.: F. Paillart, 1978), 50.

31. On the theme of creative, therapeutic repetition in Pirandello, see Stone, *Pirandello's Naked Prompt*. On the disjunction between the subject and the object of narration in *Uno* (which makes it less of an autobiography than *Mattia Pascal*), see Lucente, *Beautiful Fables*, 152–55.

32. The concept of the pivot alludes to a connotation of the word *role* not immediately visible in its etymon (the Latin *rotulus,* or the scroll on which the actor's part was written), for a *rotulus* can also mean a roll from one position to another.

33. "If what we desire is not a relatively faithful translation but the *original* truly on stage, we end up with commedia dell'arte: an embryonic scheme, and the actor's free creation. It will always be trivial, just as it [the commedia dell'arte] was, for it is improvisational work, in which the rejection of obvious and common details, the ideal simplification and concentration characteristic of every superior work of art cannot take place" (Pirandello, "Illustrators," *SPSV,* 224). Like all seemingly spontaneous behavior, improvisation ends up producing the most stringent rules of the games, as anyone knows who is familiar with how many "reliable props [*sostegni sicuri*] [an actor] needs to be able to take a step to the right instead of to the left." The author-actors of the commedia dell'arte become "each a *type,* with an entirely predetermined stage-life; up to the point of that convention by which one stages a diversified and complex performance with ten of them, ten of these types, neither more nor less, to the complete satisfaction of the audience; which by now is familiar with those conventions, the rules of the game" (Luigi Pirandello, "Introduzione al teatro italiano," qtd. in Vicentini, *L'estetica,* 232).

Conclusion

1. Jean-François Lyotard, "Philosophy and Painting in the Age of Their Experimentation: Contribution to an Idea of Postmodernity," *The Lyotard Reader,* ed. Andrew Benjamin (Oxford: Basil Blackwell, 1989), 190–91.

2. On this philosophical definition of modernism, traceable at least as far back as the Renaissance humanists, see Gianni Vattimo, "The Structure of Artistic Revolutions," *The End of Modernity: Nihilism and Hermeneutics in Postmodern Culture,* trans. Jon Snyder (Baltimore: Johns Hopkins University Press, 1989), 90–109.

3. On the theoretically retrograde nature of some of these aesthetic techniques, see the polemic against Lukács in Theodor W. Adorno, "Reconciliation under Duress," *Aesthetics and Politics,* ed. Ronald Taylor (London: Verso, 1988), 151–75.

4. Gaetano Negri, *Segni dei tempi,* 4th ed. (Milan: Hoepli, 1904), 19.

5. Robert Musil, quoted in Marie-Louise Roth, "Dans le 'carnaval de l'Histoire,'" *L'Herne* 41 (1981): 21, 23.

6. Roth, "Dans le 'carnaval,'" 23.

7. The phrase "Cartesian anxiety" is borrowed from Richard J. Bernstein, *Beyond Objectivism and Relativism: Science, Hermeneutics, and Praxis* (Philadelphia: University of Pennsylvania Press, 1985), 16–20.

8. Ulrich Schultz-Buschhaus, "L'umorismo: L'anti-retorica e l'anti-

sintesi di un secondo realismo," *Pirandello saggista* (Palermo: Palumbo, 1982), 82, 85.

9. Adorno, *Aesthetic Theory,* 81.

10. Theodor W. Adorno, *Minima Moralia: Reflections from Damaged Life,* trans. E. F. N. Jephcott (London: Verso, 1985), 154, 50.

11. Heidegger, *Nietzsche,* 4:56, 55.

12. Ernst Bloch, *A Philosophy of the Future,* trans. John Cumming (New York: Herder & Herder, An Azimuth Book, 1970), 99.

13. Theodor W. Adorno, *Zur Metakritik der Erkenntistheorie: Studien über Husserl und die phänomenologischen Antinomien* (Stuttgart: Kolhammer, 1956), 47.

Index

inherent to history, 6, 136; philosophical, 7, 102–4, 107, 108–9
Idealization, 7, 69–72, 84, 92–93,
96, 159, 248 n. 17
Identity, 40, 41, 98, 211–12;
attempt to transcend, 38, 98–99,
113–14, 212–13; as metaphorical
activity, 213–15. *See also* Soul;
Spirit; Subjectivity
Ideology, 45, 61–69. *See also* belief;
Consciousness; Idea; Idealization
Illiano, Antonio, 249 n. 23
Image, 189, 233 n. 6; as phenomenal likeness, 37, 41, 119,
189–94, 195, 202, 205, 213, 258
n. 1; transcendence of, 205, 212;
transformation of, 191, 204, 207,
209. See also *Seinesgleichen*
Imagination, 15, 79, 133, 169, 183,
185, 199
Improvisation, 214, 264 n. 33
Irony: in Conrad, 10, 35; in Musil,
10, 241 n. 9, 245 n. 39, 257 n. 46

James, William, "The Self," quoted,
212
Jameson, Fredric, 251 n. 4
Janik, Allan, 239 n. 4
Jendrassik, Loránd, 253 n. 15
Johnson, Barbara, 237 n. 28
Johnston, Bruce, 237 n. 21
Jones, Michael P., 23, 233 n. 3,
236 n. 9
Joyce, James, 218

Kaiser, Ernst, 243 n. 24
Kant, Immanuel: aesthetics, 51–53,
238 nn. 39, 40; epistemology, 67,
77, 90, 170
Karl, Frederick, 234 n. 8
Karthaus, Ulrich, 241 n. 14, 256
nn. 38, 39
Kierkegaard, Søren, 205, 251 n. 8
King, Lynda Jeanne, 240 n. 7
Klages, Ludwig, 151
Köhler, Wolfgang, 242 n. 18, 243
n. 22, 258 n. 1
Kracauer, Siegfried, 244 n. 26

Kühn, Dieter, 244 n. 33, 256 n. 35
Kühne, Jörg, 251 n. 5, 257 n. 45
Kundera, Milan, 190, 233 n. 22,
258 n. 2

Laermann, Klaus, 245 n. 40
Lanternosophy, 90–91, 100,
104, 114
Law of contradiction. *See*
Contradiction
Lawrence, D. H., 1, 218
Lazarus, Moritz, 250 n. 33
Lebensphilosophie. See Philosophy
Le Chatelier principle, 156, 253 n. 15
Lenin, Vladimir, 84, 245 n. 38
Lewin, Kurt, 242 n. 18
Life: as death, 99, 192–94, 258
n. 7; feeling of, 90–91, 195, 200,
203, 260 nn. 11, 13. *See also*
Living vs. seeing oneself live
Lipps, Theodor, 110, 249 n. 25
Living: hypothetically, 161, 165,
167, 174; vs. seeing oneself live,
191–95, 258 nn. 4, 7
Loeb, Jacques, 243 n. 23
Logic: essayistic, 16, 159, 169, 170,
175–76, 182–83, 185, 186–88,
205–8, 210, 218–21; mechanical, 10, 88, 89, 92, 101–2,
158–59, 193–94, 196, 206, 212
Love, 177–78, 225, 252 n. 4
Lucente, Gregory, 250 n. 35, 251
n. 45, 262 n. 25, 263 nn. 29, 31
Luft, David S., 240 n. 8, 255 n. 25
Lukács, Georg: aesthetic theory,
17, 87, 118, 119, 231 n. 4, 245
n. 39, 256 n. 40, 264 n. 3; on
essay, 3, 14–15, 16, 185, 233
n. 16, 244 n. 35; on idealization,
9, 13, 84, 103, 244 n. 35, 248
n. 17, 256 n. 40
Lyotard, Jean-François, 217,
264 n. 1

McCarthy, John A., 231 n. 4
Mach, Ernst, 9; and epistemology,
56, 59, 84, 171, 239 nn. 2, 3, 242
n. 19, 245 n. 38; on experience,

Mach, Ernst (*continued*)
58, 69–71, 243 n. 22; *The Science
of Mechanics*, quoted, 242 n. 16
Madness, 93, 58, 194, 197, 207,
222; of Henry IV, 189, 193–94
Madrignani, Carlo A., 246 n. 1
Makkreel, Rudolf A., 249 n. 28
Mann, Thomas, 218
Marchesini, Giovanni, 258 n. 7
Marinetti, F. T., 256 n. 45
Mechanical phantasmagoria, 87,
94, 100, 101–2, 114, 133, 151
Meloy, J. Reid, 237 n. 28
Menges, Karl, 241 n. 14
Messianism, 225. *See also* Not-
yetness
Metaphor: as constituting reality,
81–86, 180, 183–88, 193; self-
hood as, 211, 258 n. 7, 263 n. 29;
as semantic bridging, 181, 196,
198, 211
Metaphysical feeling, 219, 221
Metaphysics: art as, 82; logic of,
150, 158–59; of realization and
nonrealization, 4–6, 8–9
Michelstaedter, Carlo, 109, 249
nn. 26, 27, 258 n. 7
Miller, J. Hillis, 123, 235 n. 9,
251 n. 1
Mittner, Ladislao, 240 n. 6
Modernism, 7, 218, 244 n. 35;
and postmodernism, 217, 223,
264 n. 2
Moestrup, Jorn, 263 n. 26
Montaigne, Michel, 2, 217
Monti, Claudia, 242 nn. 14, 18, 244
n. 33, 251 n. 5, 256 nn. 38, 45
Moore, G. E., 239 n. 2
Morality, 1, 138–39, 224; as con-
vention, 78, 79, 161; of the next
step, 154, 172, 174
Moser, Thomas, 233 n. 7, 234 n. 8
Müller, Gerd, 242 n. 14
Musil, Robert, 1–2, 253 n. 20;
philosophical formation of, 239
n. 2, 240 n. 7, 241 n. 14, 242 n. 18.
Works: "Anmerkung zu einer
Metapsychik" ["Commentary on
a Metapsychics"], 149, 252 n. 2,

255 n. 26; "Anzätze zu einer
neuer Ästhetik" ["Cues for a
New Aesthetic"], 149, 242 n. 19,
256 n. 41; *Beitrag zur Beurteilung
der Lehren Machs* [*On Mach's
Theories*], 69–71, 227, 228, 242
nn. 14, 15; *Briefe* [*Letters*], 255
n. 27; "Der Deutsche Mensch als
Symptom" ["The German as
Symptom"], 256 n. 37; "Franz
Blei," 170, 233 n. 15; "Das
Geistliche, der Modernismus und
die Metaphysik" ["Spirituality,
Modernism, and Metaphysics"],
162, 252 nn. 1, 5; "Geist und
Erfahrung" ["Spirit and Experi-
ence"], 244 n. 25; *Gesammelte
Werke* [*Collected Works*], 227; "Das
Hilflose Europa" ["Helpless
Europe"] 242 n. 20; *Leben, Werk,
Wirkung* [*Life, Work, Influence*],
228, 231 n. 2; *Der Mann ohne
Eigenschaften* [*The Man without
Qualities*], 1, 7, 11, 12, 44, 59,
60–69, 72–84, 133, 144, 148–
50, 154–58, 164–70, 173–74,
175–76, 177–85, 186–88, 225,
228, 231 n. 1; "Ein Mensch ohne
Charakter" ["A Man without
Character"], 254 n. 24; "Mon-
sieur le vivisecteur," 241 n. 13;
Nachlass zu Lebzeiten [*Posthumous
Papers Published in Life*], 85, 254
n. 24; "Politisches Bekenntnis"
["Political Confessions"], 253
n. 20; *Precision and Soul*, 228, 232
n. 8; "Rede zur Rilke-Feier"
["Address at the Memorial Service for Rilke"], 256 n. 39; *Die
Schwärmer* [*The Enthusiasts*],
152–53, 252 n. 9; "Skizze
der Erkenntnis des Dichters"
["Sketch of Scriptorial Knowl-
edge"], 233 n. 19, 244 n. 30;
Tagebücher [*Journals*], 171–73,
229, 241 n. 13, 242 n. 18; "Über
Robert Musils Bücher" ["On
Robert Musil's Books"], 232 n. 8;
"Das Unanständige und Kranke

Index   273

Pirandello, Luigi (*continued*)
["Illustrators, Actors, and Translators"], 248 n. 20, 259 n. 8, 264 n. 33; "Introduzione al teatro italiano" ["Introduction to Italian Drama"], 264 n. 33; *Lazzaro* [*Lazarus*], 258 n. 5; *Maschere nude* [*Naked Masks*], 98, 228, 246 n. 4; "La mensogna del sentimento nell'arte" ["The Lie of Feeling in Art"], 116, 250 n. 39; "Il neo-idealismo" ["Neo-idealism"], 248 n. 18; *Novelle per un anno* [*Stories for a year*], 228, 238 n. 33, 250 n. 41; *Quaderni di Serafino Gubbio, operatore* [*Shoot!*], 8, 196–97, 228, 232 n. 9, 258 n. 5; "Quand'ero matto" ["When I Was Mad"], 116, 250 n. 41; "Per le ragioni estetiche della parola" ["Towards an Aesthetic Logic of the Word"], 105, 248 n. 18, 249 n. 22, 260 n. 14; *Saggi, poesie, scritti varii* [*Essays, Poetry, Sundry Writings*], 229, 245 n. 1; "Scienza e critica estetica" ["Aesthetic Criticism and Science"], 260 n. 14, 263 n. 26; "Se il film parlante abolirà il teatro" ["Whether Film with Speech Will Abolish the Theater"], 260 n. 10; *Sei personaggi in cerca di autore* [*Six Characters in Search of an Author*], 94–96, 103–4, 118, 228, 246 n. 4, 247 n. 12; "Sincerità e arte" ["Sincerity and Art"], 103, 104, 248 n. 20; "Soggettivismo e oggettivismo" ["Subjectivity and Objectivity"], 245 n. 1, 247 n. 8; *L'umorismo* [*On Humor*], 11, 16, 93, 98, 112, 205–9, 228, 229, 232 n. 11, 247 n. 10, 248 n. 16; *Uno, nessuno e centomila* [*One, None, and a Hundred Thousand*], 2, 87, 93, 190, 192, 202–3, 212–13, 229, 246 n. 2, 248 n. 16, 261 n. 21, 263 n. 29; *L'uomo dal fiore in bocca* [*The Man with a*

Flower in His Mouth], 198–200, 228, 229, 261 n. 17
Planck, Max, 245 n. 38
Positivism, 218; critique of, 220
Possibilitarianism, 7, 165–66, 174, 176, 187, 202–3
Possibility, 7, 79–80, 131; and actuality, 7, 13, 86, 156, 165–66; and existence, 6–7
Postmodernism, 217, 223, 264 n. 2
Potentiality. *See* Possibility
Pound, Ezra, 218
Powers, Charles H., 260 n. 13
Pragmatism, 219, 222
Precision, 15, 168–69; and soul, 169, 174
Principle of hope, 129, 251 n. 5. *See also* Idealism
Project, 156, 174
Psychology, Musil and, 254 n. 25
Puglisi, Filippo, 249 n. 23

Raffa, Piero, 246 n. 1
Ragusa, Olga, 263 n. 26
Randak, Ernst, 239 n. 4
Rank, Otto, 29, 236 n. 14
Rauhut, Franz, 248 n. 18
Raval, Suresh, 235 n. 9, 236 n. 17
Readiness, 136, 139–42
Reality: as actuality, 8, 69, 135; as figurative process, 68–77, 81–86, 92–93, 101–2; sense of, 143; undefinition of, 56, 100–102
Reality principle, 6, 9, 12–13, 82, 129
Realization of world, 103–4, 107–8, 118–20, 134
Reflection: Croce and Pirandello on, 16, 195–96, 205, 209, 260 nn. 14, 15; and death, 211; and essayism, 206, 209–10
Reichert, Herbert W., 240 n. 7
Relativism, 115; ontological, 89, 102, 108, 248 n. 17, 261 n. 24
Reniers-Servranckx, Annie, 251 n. 5
Representation: aesthetic (*see* Aesthetics; Order; Truth); of experience, 69–72, 76–77, 92–94,